会计学专业新系列教材·企业会计准则

PROFESSIONAL ENGLISH FOR ACCOUNTING AND AUDITING

会计审计专业英语【第4版】

编著 贺欣 温倩 罗殿英

机械工业出版社
CHINA MACHINE PRESS

图书在版编目（CIP）数据

会计审计专业英语 / 贺欣，温倩，罗殿英编著 . —4 版 . —北京：机械工业出版社，2019.5
（2023.10 重印）
（会计学专业新企业会计准则系列教材）

ISBN 978-7-111-62574-2

I. 会… Ⅱ. ①贺… ②温… ③罗… Ⅲ. ①会计学－英语－高等学校－教材 ②审计学－
英语－高等学校－教材 Ⅳ. ① F230 ② F239.0

中国版本图书馆 CIP 数据核字（2019）第 072841 号

本书与当前国际会计协调发展的趋势相适应，突出国际会计审计准则的最新进展。全书共分为
5 个部分，分别介绍了会计的基本概念和基本程序，国际会计准则下财务会计的基本处理方法，国
际上常用的成本与管理会计方法，国际会计的内容和国际会计的协调发展，以及最新的国际审计准
则下的审计基本框架。本书内容全面，使会计审计工作人员和财经专业的学生既能了解国际会计审
计的最新发展，又能熟练掌握会计审计英语。每章开头和结尾分别附有小案例和知识扩展，以引导
学生深入思考。

本书适用于会计类相关专业的本科高年级学生、研究生及 MBA 学生。对于商务英语相关专业
的学生而言，本书也是一本很好的参考教材。

出版发行：机械工业出版社（北京市西城区百万庄大街 22 号　邮政编码：100037）
责任编辑：宋　燕　　　　　　　　　　　　　　责任校对：李秋荣
印　　刷：北京捷迅佳彩印刷有限公司　　　　　版　　次：2023 年 10 月第 4 版第 8 次印刷
开　　本：185mm×260mm　1/16　　　　　　　印　　张：17.5
书　　号：ISBN 978-7-111-62574-2　　　　　　定　　价：45.00 元

客服电话：(010) 88361066　68326294

自改革开放以来，我国逐渐融入世界经济，特别是建立社会主义市场经济以来，我国在国际贸易、外商投资、对外投资以及国际融资等领域，均取得了飞速发展，我国企业管理、会计及审计理论与实务的国际化也在逐步深入。2006年我国会计准则和审计准则体系颁布实施以来，我国的会计审计准则与国际会计审计准则已基本实现趋同。

时至今日，我国仍存在一个与自身经济发展不匹配的问题——缺乏大量的会计、审计国际化人才。我国有超过1 200万名会计人员，由于历史原因，他们大部分的外语应用能力较差，尤其表现在专业外语和运用外语沟通方面。因此，会计审计国际化人才的培养是我国高校当前及未来的重要任务，当然，成为会计审计国际化人才应是会计人员在职学习的重要任务。

本书包括会计原理、财务会计、成本与管理会计、国际会计、审计等内容，内容较为全面，并且以国际会计审计准则为基础，反映了国际会计审计准则的最新发展，这与目前国内大多数引进的原版教材和编写的会计审计英语教材有所区别——它们主要以美国的准则为基础。

本书的三位作者均是会计学博士、会计学副教授，具有多年的双语教学经验，还有在英语国家学习研究的经历，她们以其专业眼光和丰富的教学经验编写了本书。这是一本实用性较强、适用面较广的教材，既可以作为在校学生的会计基础教材，也可以作为在职会计审计人员及其他经济管理人员的在职学习用书。

希望本书的出版能对我国会计审计人员的专业外语学习和专业学习有所帮助，并能推动会计审计英语教材的研究和编写。

罗飞

中南财经政法大学会计学院教授

教育部工商管理类学科专业教学指导委员会委员

国家级精品课程"高级财务会计"主持人

2006 年，我国会计准则与国际会计准则实现趋同；2010 年，中国审计准则与国际审计准则实现了持续全面趋同。我国会计审计准则的国际趋同是我国经济全球化的需要，是社会主义市场经济体制逐步建立健全的需要，也体现了我国作为一个负责任的大国的担当。党的二十大报告提出"两个相结合"，这意味着会计审计实务工作需要与企业实际相结合，与中国特色社会主义市场经济的实际情况相结合，才能有助于实现中华民族伟大复兴。为了使会计审计工作人员和财经专业的学生了解会计审计的国际规则，熟练掌握会计审计英语，为了我国企业适应我国经济和企业发展国际化的需要，我们编写了本书。

本书的主要内容是基于作者国外学习和国内教学经验的积累而完成的，并参考了部分国外经典教材的内容。

本书分为 5 个部分：第一部分是会计原理，介绍会计的基本概念和基本程序；第二部分是财务会计，介绍国际会计准则下企业经济业务的基本会计处理方法；第三部分是成本与管理会计，介绍常用的成本计算方法和管理会计基本知识；第四部分是国际会计，包括国际会计的内容及国际会计的协调发展；第五部分是审计，介绍现行国际审计准则下的审计理论与基本规范。

本书的特点是：

1. 与当前我国会计审计准则国际趋同的趋势相适应，适应国际会计审计准则的最新发展变化。

2. 内容全面，包含财务会计、成本管理会计、国际会计和审计，通过学习本书，学生能够对会计及审计有一个全面系统的了解。

3. 每章开头有一个小案例，引导学生对本章内容进行思考，每章末都附有知识扩展，作为对该章基本内容的延伸，启发学生进一步获取相关知识。

4. 章末的练习题覆盖了各章的知识要点，供各位读者和老师选择使用，帮助读者和学生熟练掌握教学内容及基本的实务处理。

本次改版修改了之前版本中存在的一些错误，并依据国际会计审计准则的最新变化修改了部分内容及课后练习，以帮助读者更好地掌握国内外会计、审计及管理会计的最新知识。本书习题答案请扫描下方二维码获取。

第 1～4 章及第 8～10 章由罗殿英编写，第 5～7 章及第 14～16 章由温倩编写，第 11～13 章及第 17～19 章由贺欣编写。

书中难免存在遗漏和错误，欢迎各位读者批评指正。

目录

Part 2　Financial Accounting 财务会计

Part 3   Cost and Management Accounting 成本与管理会计

Chapter 16　Special Accounting Treatments in Multinational Corporations

Part 5　Audit 审计

Chapter 17　Audit Framework 审计框架 ·················· 212

Chapter 18　Collecting Audit Evidence 收集审计证据 ·················· 223

Accounting Principle
会计原理

01

Accounting and Its Environment
会计与环境

◎ 小案例 Mini Case

Matthew & Co. makes navigation equipment and wishes to diversify into the production of hang gliders. The business is based in Shanghai but the owners may be willing to move. The owners have little knowledge about the market for hang gliders but feel that there is money to be made in that field. Identify(1) the accounting information that would be relevant; (2) any other information that would be relevant.

正文 Text

Accounting has been called "the language of business" and most people interact on a daily basis in some way with business enterprises.

1. 1　Nature and Content of Accounting

1. 1. 1　Business Environment

Most organizations engage in some forms of economic activity. Some of them exist as not-for-profits. These groups may provide services or goods to others but seek to do so without the underlying goal of generating profits. Most of organizations are businesses. They attempt to earn a return over the cost of providing services or goods that satisfy the needs or wants of others. Businesses are typically categorized into three broad groups: Service, manufacturing, and merchandising companies. Businesses operate in many different legal forms according to different jurisdictions. Generally there are three legal forms of businesses: Sole proprietorships, partnerships, and corporations. Nearly all organizations use accounting to generate information about their economic activities. This book focuses on business organizations.

1. 1. 2　The Nature and Role of Accounting

First and foremost, accounting is a service activity. "Its function is to provide quantitative information, primarily financial in nature, about economic entities that is intended to be useful in making economic decisions—in making reasoned choices among alternative courses of action."[1] Thus, accounting is a means to assist a wide variety of parties in making economic decisions. Sound decisions, based on reliable information, are essential for the efficient distribution and use of the scarce economic resources. Accounting, therefore, plays an important role in our economic and social system.

1. 1. 3　Users and Accounting Information

In general, the users (decision makers) of accounting information are divided into two major categories: Internal and external.

The major internal users are management and directors of the business enterprise. Internal users need information to assist in planning and controlling enterprise operations and managing enterprise resources. The accounting system must provide timely information needed to control day-to-day operations and to make major planning decisions, such as: Do we make this product or another one? Do we build a new production plant or expand existing facilities? **Managerial accounting** (sometimes referred to as **management accounting**) is concerned primarily with financial reporting for internal users.

External users include both individuals who have or intend to have a direct economic interest in a business and those who have an indirect interest because they advise or represent those individuals with a direct interest. These users include present and potential investors and creditors, suppliers[2], customers, financial analysts and advisors, regulatory authorities, the public, etc. Investors use accounting information to make decision to buy, hold, or sell ownership shares of a company. Creditors, such as suppliers and bankers, use accounting information to evaluate the risk of granting credit or lending money. **Financial accounting** emphasizes these users' needs.

1. 1. 4　Fields of Accounting

1. Financial Accounting

Financial accounting is the preparation and presentation of financial reports for users who

---

1　AICPA. Statement of the Accounting Principles Board No. 4, "Basic Concepts and Accounting Principles Underlying Financial Statements of Business Enterprises", New York: American Institute of Certified Public Accountants, 1970, par. 40.

2　Suppliers can be also considered creditors when they provide services or materials on account.

are not involved in the day-to-day operations of an organization. The information is distributed primarily through general purpose financial statements which suit the decision-making needs of a range of users. However, many companies issue their financial statements only after an **audit** by independent CPAs. Audit is a thorough check of an organization's accounting systems and records; it is performed to add credibility to the financial statements prepared by an organization's own accountants. The objective of audit is to decide whether the statements reflects the company's financial position and the operating results agree with generally accepted accounting principles (GAAP).

2. Managerial Accounting

Managerial accounting involves several activities providing information to managers. **Cost accounting** is a process of accumulating the information managers need about operating costs and is useful for evaluating each manager's performance. Cost accounting may involve accounting for the costs of products, services, or specific activities. **Budgeting** is the process of developing formal plans for an organization's future activities. After the budget has been adopted, it provides a basis for evaluating actual performance.

1. 1. 5　The Accounting Process

Accounting process is "identifying, measuring, recording, and communicating economic information to permit informed judgments and decisions by users of information."[1] The first component of the process is identifying information relevant to business decision making. Only business transactions will be recognized by the accounting system. A business transaction is an event which affects the financial position of an entity and can be reliably measured and recorded. Events such as an increase in interest rates which will not immediately affect an entity's financial position will not be categorized as business transaction.

The second component is the measuring of information, which refers to the analysis of business transactions and classifying of business transactions. This component identifies how transactions will affect an entity's position, groups together similar items such as expenses and income, and determining the monetary aspect of the transactions.

The third component is recording. The company records the economic events in order to provide a history of its financial activities. Recording consists of keeping a systematic, chronological diary of events. In recording, the company also classifies and summarizes economic events.

The final component is the communicating of relevant information through accounting reports. The most common of these reports are called financial statements, such as income statement and

---

1　AAA. A Statement of Basic Accounting Theory(Evanston) , Illinois: American Accounting Association, 1966, p. 1.

balance sheet[1] ,for decision-making purposes for the various users.

1. 2 Objectives of Financial Reporting

The overall objective of financial reporting is to provide financial information useful to external users in making economic decisions. To provide different reports for different users,or to make available all of the information that users would need to assemble their own custom-designed reports, would be expensive. IASB concluded that(1)the **primary user group** should be the existing and potential investors,lenders and other creditors of a reporting entity;(2)a **general purpose financial report** is the most efficient and effective way to meet the information needs of a variety of users.

The objective of general purpose financial reporting is to provide financial information about the reporting entity that is useful to existing and potential investors, lenders and other creditors in making decisions relating to providing resources to the entity. Those decisions involve decisions about:

(a)*buying, selling or holding equity and debt instruments*;

(b)*providing or settling loans and other forms of credit*; *or*

(c)*exercising rights to vote on, or otherwise influence, management's actions that affect the use of the entity's economic resources.*[2]

The general purpose financial reports do not and cannot provide all of the information that the external users need. Those users need to consider pertinent information from other sources,for example,general economic conditions and expectations,political events and political climate,and industry and company outlooks.

1. 2. 1 Decisions by Primary Users and Information Needs

Decisions by investors about buying,selling or holding equity and debt instruments depend on the returns that they expect from those instruments,for example dividends,principal and interest payments or market price increases. Similarly,decisions by creditors about providing or settling loans and other forms of credit depend on the principal and interest payments. Investors and creditors may also make their decisions about exercising rights to vote on, or otherwise influence, management's actions that affect the use of the entity's economic resources. Investors' and creditors' expectations about returns depend on their assessment of the amount,timing and uncertainty of(the prospects for)future net cash inflows to the entity.

1　The name"balance sheet"(资产负债表)was changed to"statement of financial position"(财务状况表),"income statement"(利润表)to"statement of profit or loss"(损益表) in IAS1. But the names is still used in practice. Sometimes, statement of profit or loss is also called statement of operations, statement of earnings, etc.

2　IASB, 2018, The Conceptual Framework for Financial Reporting, par 1. 2.

To assess an entity's prospects for future net cash inflows, investors and creditors need for information about the resources of the entity, claims against the entity, and how efficiently and effectively the entity's management and governing board have discharged their responsibilities to use the entity's resources.

1.2.2 Financial Information Provided-Financial Position

General purpose financial reports provide information about the **financial position** of a **reporting entity**, which is information about the entity's economic resources and the claims against the reporting entity.

The financial position of an entity is affected by the economic resources it controls, its financial structure, its liquidity and solvency, and its capacity to adapt to changes in the environment in which it operates. Information about the economic resources controlled by the entity and its capacity in the past to modify these resources is useful in predicting the ability of the entity to generate cash and cash equivalents in the future. Information about financial structure is useful in predicting future borrowing needs and how future profits and cash flows will be distributed among those with an interest in the entity; it is also useful in predicting how successful the entity is likely to be in raising further finance. Information about liquidity and solvency is useful in predicting the ability of the entity to meet its financial commitments as they fall due. Information about financial position is primarily provided in a balance sheet, or a statement of financial position.

1.2.3 Financial Information Provided-Changes in Economic Resources and Claims

Financial reports also provide information about the effects of transactions and other events that change a reporting entity's economic resources and claims. The changes result from that entity's **financial performance** and from other events or transactions such as issuing debt or equity instruments.

1. Performance

Information about a reporting entity's financial performance helps users to understand the return that the entity has produced on its economic resources. Information about the variability and components of that return is also important, especially in assessing the uncertainty of future cash flows.

Information about the return the entity has produced provides an indication of how well management has discharged its responsibilities to make efficient and effective use of the reporting entity's resources.

Information about a reporting entity's past financial performance and how its management discharged its responsibilities is usually helpful in predicting the entity's future returns on its economic resources.

2. Others

A reporting entity's economic resources and claims may also change for reasons other than financial performance, such as issuing additional ownership shares. Information about this type of change is necessary to give users a complete understanding of why the reporting entity's economic resources and claims changed and the implications of those changes for its future financial performance.

1. 2. 4 Financial Information Provided-Efficiency of the Entity's Economic Resources

Information about how efficiently and effectively the reporting entity's management has discharged its responsibilities to use the entity's economic resources helps users to assess management's stewardship of those resources.

Management and governing board are accountable for planning and controlling the operations of the entity to those who provide resources. Examples of such responsibilities include protecting the entity's resources from unfavourable effects of economic factors such as price and technological changes and ensuring that the entity complies with applicable laws, regulations and contractual provisions. In a broad sense, because of the influence entities exert on community at both microeconomic and macroeconomic levels, they are accountable to the public. Information about management's discharge of its responsibilities is also useful for decisions by existing investors, lenders and other creditors who have the right to vote on or otherwise influence management's actions. For example, users may decide whether to hold or sell their investment in the entity or whether to reappoint or replace the management.

1. 3 Underlying Assumptions

Traditionally, there are four underlying assumptions: Economic entity, going concern, unit of measurement and accounting period. However IASB emphasizes only one underlying assumption in the Conceptual Framework for Financial Reporting: Going concern.

1. Economic Entity

The business enterprise is viewed as a specific economic entity separate and distinct from its owners and any other business unit. For example, China National Petroleum Corporation (CNPC) owns about 81. 49% equity of PetroChina Company Limited[1]. Nevertheless, PetroChina

---

1 PetroChina Company Limited, 2018 interim report, 2018-08-31.

Company Limited accounts for its operations as a separate entity and prepares its own financial statements.

2. Going Concern

The going-concern assumption reflects accountants' belief that a business will continue to operate "long enough to use its longest-lived asset", unless there is evidence to the contrary. Thus, a company reports its long-term assets, such as property, plant and equipment, based on their cost rather than the liquidation values.

3. Unit of Measurement

The unit of measurement assumption mandates that the business use a common unit of measurement in accounting for their transactions. This assumption allows financial data to be quantified, summarized, and reported in a uniform, timely, and consistent manner. Traditionally, the unit of measurement is assumed to be a stable monetary unit. Because of this assumption, changes in the purchasing power of money unit resulting from inflation have been ignored. However, many foreign countries with historically high inflation routinely require inflation-adjusted financial statements.

4. Accounting Period

The profitability of a business cannot be truly assessed until it ceases operations. However, decision makers demand financial information about business entities on a timely basis. The accounting period assumption allows accountants to prepare meaningful financial reports for ongoing business by dividing their lives into reporting intervals of equal length. List companies regulated by China Securities Regulatory Commission must issue financial statements on a quarterly, a semiannually and an annual basis.

1. 4　Accounting Basis

1. 4. 1　Accrual Basis

Accounting recognizes the effects of transactions and other events when they occur rather than only when cash or its equivalent is received or paid, and reports these effects in the financial statements of the periods to which they relate. This is known as the accrual basis of accounting. The accrual basis recognizes that a company's financial position and performance can change without any cash changing hands, although it usually occurs with a right to receive cash or an obligation to pay cash in the future. Accrual accounting recognizes these changes when they occur.

1. 4. 2　Cash Basis

An alternative to the accrual basis of accounting is the cash basis of accounting, which recognizes changes in financial position and performance only when cash is received or paid. The cash basis is not consistent with IASB framework.

► 核心词汇 Core Words and Expressions

accounting period　会计期间,又称为会计分期

accounting process　会计程序

accounting　会计,会计学

accrual basis　权责发生制,又称为应计制基础

annual report　年度报告

audit　审计

auditing　审计,审计学

balance sheet　资产负债表

budgeting　预算

cash and cash equivalents　现金及现金等价物

cash basis　现金收付制,又称为坝金基础

cash flow statement　现金流量表

certified public accountant(CPA)　注册会计师

corporation　公司

cost accounting　成本会计

economic entity　经济实体

financial accounting　财务会计

financial position　财务状况

forecast　预测

general purpose financial reports　通用目的财务报告,为外部信息使用者提供满足他们共同需求的财务信息

generally accepted accounting principles(GAAP)　一般公认会计原则

going concern　持续经营

income statement　利润表

internal auditing　内部审计

International Accounting Standard Board(IASB)　国际会计准则理事会

managerial(or management)accounting　管理会计

(monetary)unit of measurement　货币计量

not-for-profits　非营利组织

partnership　合伙

performance　业绩

sole proprietorship　独资(企业)

the conceptual framework for financial reporting　财务报告的概念框架

► 知识扩展 More Knowledge

会计

会计（accounting）的定义有很多种,并随着经济环境的变化而有所不同。常见的定义有信息系统、管理活动、管理工具、服务活动等。本书采用了会计是一项服务活动的观点,这一定义强调会计在市场经济环境中的地位和作用,突出会计理论框架的起点——会计目标,并且被各国会计准则制定机构（包括国际会计准则理事会）采纳。

一般公认会计原则

一般公认会计原则（GAAP）是指被会计职业界采纳的用于指导报告企业经济活动的原则,包含一般原则（broad principles）和特定原则（specific principles）。一般原则来自长期采纳的会计实务,特定原则主要由规则制定者建立和发布。会计准则是 GAAP 的主要组成部分。

会计信息的局限性

虽然会计信息为内外部使用者提供了大量对决策有用的信息,但是使用者仍然需要其他方面的

信息。例如，潜在投资者除了研究公司的财务报告外，还需要其他来源的信息，如该公司的市场份额、上市时间、公司未来发展战略、行业信息等。会计信息的局限性还表现在：（1）一般只提供财务信息，即那些可以用货币量化的信息；（2）披露时间滞后，会计年度结束到年度报告对外公布一般需要 2~4 个月；（3）财务信息主要基于历史信息，而使用者的决策主要面向未来；（4）会计信息制作过程有很多主观判断因素，如固定资产使用年限、残值等，并且存在会计政策选择问题，如存货发出的计价可以采用先进先出法或者加权平均法。

▶ 问答题 Questions

1. Accounting has been defined as a service activity. Who is served by accounting and how are they benefited?

2. What are the major objectives of financial reporting as specified by the IASB?

3. Briefly describe the four traditional assumptions that influence the conceptual framework.

4. Identify and describe the underlying assumptions specified by the IASB.

5. Alan Rod has recently completed his first year of studying accounting. His instructor for next semester has indicated that the primary focus will be the area of financial accounting.

  (a) Differentiate between financial accounting and managerial accounting.

  (b) One part of financial accounting involves the preparation of financial statements. What are the financial statements most frequently provided?

  (c) What is the difference between financial statements and financial reporting?

Accounting Concepts and Principles
会计概念与原则

◎ 小案例 Mini Case

China Securities Regulatory Commission（CSRC）requires the listed companies disclose their annual reports within four months after the end date of each accounting period. Mark Yu, a student major in accounting, argued, "Nowadays, timeliness is a vital characteristic of information. Information provided four months later is useless because the situations have changed greatly." Do you agree or not? Why?

正文 Text

Accountants are continually faced with new situations, technological advances, and business innovations that present new accounting and reporting problems. Accounting concepts and principles are the theoretical foundation keeping accounting practice in pace with the changing business environment. This chapter introduces the *Conceptual Framework for Financial Reporting* established by IASB.

2.1 Qualitative Characteristics of Useful Accounting Information

The overriding objective of financial reporting is to provide useful information. This is a very complex objective because of many alternatives. To assist in choosing among alternatives, IASB identifies two fundamental qualitative characteristics of useful information: Relevance and faithful representation.

2.1.1 Relevance

Relevant financial information is **capable of making a difference** in the decisions made by users.[1] If some users choose not to take advantage of it or are already aware of it from other sources, the information may still be capable of making a difference in a decision. To be capable of making a difference in decisions, financial information should has predictive value, confirmatory value or both.

1. Predictive Value and Confirmatory Value

Information helps users predict the ultimate outcome of past, present, and future events. That is, it has **predictive value**. "Financial information has predictive value if it can be used as an input to processes employed by users to predict future outcomes."[2] For example, a user may use an entity's revenue data in the last three years to predict the revenues in the future. So, financial information need not be a prediction or forecast to have predictive value.

Information also helps users confirm or change prior expectations; it has **confirmatory value**. "Financial information has confirmatory value if it provides feedback about (confirms or changes) previous evaluations."[3]

The predictive value of financial information is interrelated with its confirmatory value. Information that has predictive value often also has confirmatory value. For example, revenue information for the current year, which can be used as the basis for predicting revenues in future years, can also be compared with revenue predictions for the current year that were made in past years. The results of those comparisons can help a user to correct and improve the processes that were used to make those previous predictions.

2. Materiality

Information is **material** if omitting it or misstating it could influence decisions that users make on the basis of financial information about a specific reporting entity. In other words, **materiality** concerns an item's impact on a company's overall financial operations. It is an entity-specific aspect of relevance based on the nature or magnitude, or both, of the items to which the information relates in the context of an individual entity's financial report. The point involved here is of relative size and importance. If the amount involved is significant when compared with the other revenues and expenses, assets and liabilities, or net income of the company, sound and acceptable standards should be followed in reporting it.

2. 1. 2 Faithful Representation

"To be useful, financial information must not only represent relevant phenomena, but it

---

1　IASB, 2018, The Conceptual Framework for Financial Reporting, par 2. 6.

2　Ibid. , par 2. 8.

3　Ibid. , par 2. 9.

must also faithfully represent the phenomena that it purports to represent. "[1] Financial reports represent economic phenomena in words and numbers. **Faithful representation** means that the numbers and descriptions match what really existed or happened. If a company reports sales of $12 million when it had sales of $9.9 million, then it fails to faithfully represent the proper sales amount.

IASB further stated that "To be a perfectly faithful representation, a depiction would have three characteristics. It would be **complete**, **neutral** and **free from error**. Of course, perfection is seldom, if ever, achievable. "[2]

1. Complete

An omission can cause information to be false or misleading. A **complete** depiction includes all information necessary for a user to understand the phenomenon being presented, including all necessary descriptions and explanations. For example, a complete depiction of a group of assets would include, at a minimum, a description of the nature of the assets in the group, a numerical depiction of all of the assets in the group, and a description of what the numerical depiction represents (for example, original cost, adjusted cost or fair value). For some items, a complete depiction may also entail explanations of significant facts about the quality and nature of the items, factors and circumstances that might affect their quality and nature, and the process used to determine the numerical depiction.

2. Neutral

Neutrality means without bias in the selection or presentation of financial information. The information is not designed in a way that intentionally leads the users of that information to make an economic decision that the preparer of the information would like them to make. A neutral depiction is not slanted, weighted, emphasized, de-emphasized or otherwise manipulated to increase the probability that financial information will be received favorably or unfavorably by users.

3. Free from Error

Free from error means there are no errors or omissions in the description of the phenomenon, and the process used to produce the reported information has been selected and applied with no errors in the process. [3] In this context, free from error does not mean perfectly accurate in all respects. For example, an estimate of an unobservable price or value cannot be determined to be accurate or inaccurate. However, a representation of that estimate can be faithful if the amount is described clearly and accurately as being an estimate, the nature and limitations of the estimating

---

1 Ibid. , par 2.12.

2 Ibid. , par 2.13.

3 Ibid. , par 2.18.

process are explained, and no errors have been made in selecting and applying an appropriate process for developing the estimate.

2.1.3　Enhancing Qualitative Characteristics

IASB distinguished between the fundamental qualitative characteristics that are the most critical and the enhancing qualitative characteristics that are less critical but still highly desirable. The enhancing qualitative characteristics enhance the usefulness of information that is relevant and faithfully represented. They are **comparability**, **verifiability**, **timeliness** and **understandability**. The enhancing qualitative characteristics may also help determine which of two ways should be used to depict a phenomenon if both are considered equally relevant and faithfully represented.

1. Comparability

Information about a reporting entity is more useful if it can be compared with similar information about other entities and with similar information about the same entity for another period or another date. **Comparability** is the qualitative characteristic that enables users to identify and understand similarities in, and differences among, items. [1] An important implication of comparability is that users be informed of the accounting policies employed in the preparation of the financial statements, any changes in those policies and the effects of such changes.

Although related to comparability, consistency is not the same. **Consistency** refers to the use of the same methods for the same items, either from period to period within a reporting entity or in a single period across entities. Consistency helps to achieve the goal-comparability.

2. Verifiability

Verifiability means that different knowledgeable and independent observers could reach consensus, although not necessarily complete agreement, that a particular depiction is a faithful representation. Verification can be direct or indirect. Direct verification means verifying an amount or other representation through direct observation, for example, by counting cash. Indirect verification means checking the inputs to a model, formula or other technique and recalculating the outputs using the same methodology. An example is verifying the carrying amount of inventory by checking the inputs (quantities and costs) and recalculating the ending inventory using the same cost flow assumption (for example, using the average-cost method).

3. Timeliness

Timeliness means having information available to decision-makers in time to be capable of in-

---

1　Ibid. , par 2.25.

fluencing their decisions. To provide information on a timely basis it may often be necessary to report before all aspects of a transaction or other events are known. Generally, the older the information is the less useful it is. However, some information may continue to be timely long after the end of a reporting period because, for example, some users may need to identify and assess trends.

4. Understandability

Understandability means that the information provided in financial statements is readily understandable by users. The ability of users to understand financial information depends on two parts: the users' own capabilities and the way in which the information is displayed. Thus, it is not necessary that financial statements be understandable to "everyone", but they should be understandable to a broad range of users. Users of financial information are assumed to have a reasonable knowledge of business, economic activities, and accounting, and a willingness to study the information with reasonable diligence.

To be understandable, classifying, characterising and presenting information clearly and concisely is needed.

2.1.4 The Cost Constraint on Useful Financial Reporting

Cost is a pervasive constraint on the information that can be provided by financial reporting. The benefits derived from information should exceed the cost of providing it. The evaluation of benefits and costs is, however, substantially a judgmental process. Furthermore, the costs do not necessarily fall on those users who enjoy the benefits. For these reasons, it is difficult to apply a cost test in any particular case.

2.2 Elements of the Financial Statements

The elements comprise the building blocks upon which the financial statements are constructed. IASB defines five elements. The elements directly related to the measurement of financial position are assets, liabilities and equity. And those directly related to the measurement of performance are income and expenses.

2.2.1 Financial Position

Assets, liabilities and equity are elements directly related to the measurement of financial position in balance sheet.

1. Assets

An **asset** is a present economic resource controlled by the entity as a result of past events. An economic resource is a right that has the potential to produce economic benefits. [1]

The definition of asset identifies three essential characteristics:

First, rights. The entity has a right that has the potential to produce economic benefits. Rights may take many forms, such as rights to receive cash, rights to receive goods or services, rights over physical objects (property, plant and equipment or inventories), etc.

Second, potential to produce economic benefits. For example, an economic resource could produce economic benefits for an entity by entitling or enabling it to: Receive contractual cash flows; exchange economic resources with another party on favourable terms; receive cash or other economic resources by selling the economic resource; or extinguish liabilities by transferring the economic resource; etc. For that the potential to exist, it does not need to be certain, or even likely, that the right will produce economic benefits.

Third, control. The entity must have control over the future economic benefits such that it is able to enjoy the benefits and deny or regulate the access of others to the benefits. The future economic benefits from that resource must flow to the entity either directly or indirectly rather than to another party.

2. Liabilities

A **liability** is a present obligation of the entity to transfer an economic resource as a result of past events. [2] The definition of liability also identifies three essential characteristics:

First, obligation. An obligation is a duty or responsibility that an entity has no practical ability to avoid. Obligations are normally established by contract, legislation or similar means and are legally enforceable by the party (or parties) to whom they are owed.

Second, transfer of an economic resource. The obligation must have the potential to require the entity to transfer an economic resource to another party (or parties). Such as obligations to pay cash, obligations to deliver goods or provide services, obligations to exchange economic resources with another party on unfavourable terms, etc. It does not need to be certain, or even likely, that the entity will be required to transfer an economic resource—the transfer may, for example, be required only if a specified uncertain future event occurs.

Third, present obligation as a result of past events. A present obligation exists as a result of past events only if: (a) the entity has already obtained economic benefits (such as goods or services) or taken an action; and (b) as a consequence, the entity will or may have to transfer an economic resource that it would not otherwise have had to transfer.

3. Equity

Equity is the residual interest in the assets of the entity after deducting all its liabilities. [3] De-

---

1 Ibid. , par 4. 3-4. 4.

2 Ibid. , par 4. 26.

3 Ibid. , par 4. 63.

fining equity as a residual is based on the view that equity cannot be defined independently of the assets and liabilities. Equity ranks after liabilities as a claim to the assets of an entity. Also, equity bears the results of operations and the consequences of other events affecting the entity.

2.2.2 Performance

Performance is the proficiency of a reporting entity in acquiring resources economically and using those resources efficiently in achieving specified objectives.

1. Concepts of Performance

Economists have generally adopted a wealth maintenance concept of performance. Under this concept, performance is the amount that can be consumed during a period and still leave the entity with the same amount of wealth (or capital) at the end of the period as existing at the beginning. Wealth is determined with reference to the current market values of the net assets at the beginning and end of the period. Therefore, this definition of performance would fully incorporate market value changes.

On the other hand, accountants have generally defined performance by reference to specific events that gives rise to recognizable elements of income and expenses during an accounting period. This approach to measuring performance is called transaction approach, sometimes referred to as matching method. Under this approach, performance, referred to as profit in income statement, is measured as the difference between resource inflows (income) and outflows (expenses) over a period of time.

2. Income

Income is increases in assets, or decreases in liabilities, that result in increases in equity, other than those relating to contributions from holders of equity claims. [1]

Income may result from the receipts or enhancements of various kinds of assets; examples include cash, receivables and goods and services received in exchange for goods and services supplied. Income may also result from the settlement of liabilities. For example, an entity may provide goods and services to a lender in settlement of an obligation to repay an outstanding loan.

Income encompasses both revenue and gains. **Revenue** arises in the course of the ordinary activities of an entity and is referred to by a variety of different names including sales, fees, interest, dividends, royalties and rent. Whereas **gains** represent other items that meet the definition of income and may, or may not, arise in the course of the ordinary activities of an entity. Gains include, for example, those arising on the disposal of non-current assets. The definition of income also includes unrealized gains; for example, those arising on the revaluation of marketable securi-

---

1 Ibid., par 4.68.

ties and those resulting from increases in the carrying amount of long-term assets. When gains are recognized in the statement of profit or loss, they are usually displayed separately because knowledge of them is useful for the purpose of making economic decisions. Gains are often reported net of related expenses.

3. Expenses

Expenses are decreases in assets, or increases in liabilities, that result in decreases in equity, other than those relating to distributions to holders of equity claims. [1]

Expenses encompass **losses** as well as those expenses that arise in the course of the ordinary activities of the entity. Expenses include, for example, cost of sales, wages and depreciation. Losses represent other items that meet the definition of expenses and may, or may not, arise in the course of the ordinary activities of the entity. Losses represent decreases in economic benefits and as such they are no different in nature from other expenses. Hence, they are not regarded as a separate element in IASB's *Framework*.

Losses include those resulting from disasters such as fire and flood, as well as those arising on the disposal of non-current assets. Expenses also includes unrealized losses, for example, those arising from the effects of increases in the rate of exchange for a foreign currency in respect of the borrowings of an entity in that currency. Losses are usually displayed separately because knowledge of them is useful for the purpose of making economic decisions. Losses are often reported net of related income.

2. 3　Recognition and Measurement Principles

The definitions of the elements of financial statements identify their essential characteristics, whereas the recognition criteria specify the conditions under which an item which satisfies the definition of an element should be included in financial statements. Measurement is closely related to recognition. How much an element appears in financial statements relies on which measurement basis is used.

2. 3. 1　Recognition of the Elements of Financial Statements

Recognition is the process of capturing for inclusion in the statement of financial position or the statement (s) of financial performance an item that meets the definition of one of the elements of financial statements—an asset, a liability, equity, income or expenses. [2]

Two recognition criteria set out by IASB are: (a) the item meets the definition of an element-

---

1　Ibid. , par 4. 69.

2　Ibid. , par 5. 1.

asset, liability or equity, income or expense; and (b) the recognition of that item provides information useful to the users of financial statements.

Recognition of a particular asset or liability is appropriate if it provides not only relevant information, but also a faithful representation of that asset or liability and of any resulting income, expenses or changes in equity. It may be a combination of factors and not any single factor that determines whether an item should be recognized or not.

For example, a receivable owed to an entity is recognized as an asset. The recognition provides relevant information. For a large population of receivables, some degree of non-payment is normally considered; hence an expense representing the expected reduction in economic benefits is recognized. It is also a faithful representation.

To be recognized in financial statements, an item should possesses a cost or value that can be measured. In many cases, cost or value must be estimated; the use of reasonable estimates is an essential part of the preparation of financial statements and does not undermine the usefulness of the information if the estimates are clearly and accurately described and explained. Faithful representation of a recognized asset, liability, equity, income or expenses involves not only recognition of that item, but also its measurement as well as presentation and disclosure of information about it.

2.3.2　Measurement of the Elements of Financial Statements

Measurement is the process of determining the monetary amounts at which the elements are to be recognized and carried in the financial statements. IASB describes two categories of measurement bases: Historical cost and current value. Current value bases include three ones: Fair value, value in use for assets and fulfilment value for liabilities, and current cost.

1. Historical cost

The **historical cost of an asset** when it is acquired or created is the value of the costs incurred in acquiring or creating the asset, comprising the consideration paid to acquire or create the asset plus transaction costs. [1] For example, the historical cost of inventory purchased would be the total price plus freight. The historical cost is updated over time to depict: (a) the consumption from depreciation or amortisation; (b) payments received that extinguish part or all of the asset (such as accounts receivables); (c) the effect of impairment; and (d) accrual of interest to reflect any financing component of the asset (such as interest accrued on bonds investments); etc.

The historical cost of a liability when it is incurred or taken on is the value of the consideration received to incur or take on the liability minus transaction costs. For example, the historical cost of bonds payable is the price received minus commission fees. The historical cost is updated

---

1　Ibid. , par 6.5.

over time to depict: (a) payment of part or all of the liability; and (b) accrual of interest to reflect any financing component of the liability; etc.

2. Fair value

Fair value is the price that would be received to sell an asset, or paid to transfer a liability, in an orderly transaction between market participants at the measurement date. [1]

The fair value is measured using the same assumptions that market participants would use when pricing the asset or liability if those market participants act in their economic best interest. In some cases, fair value can be determined directly by observing prices in an active market. For example, the market price of a certain company's shares is the best estimate of fair value of investment in those shares. In other cases, it is determined indirectly using measurement techniques, for example, cash-flow-based measurement techniques.

Note that fair value does not reflect the transaction costs because fair value is not derived from the price of the transaction or other event that gave rise to the asset or liability.

3. Value in use and fulfilment value

Value in use for an asset is the present value of the cash flows, or other economic benefits, that an entity expects to derive from the use of an asset and from its ultimate disposal. **Fulfilment value for a liability** is the present value of the cash, or other economic resources, that an entity expects to be obliged to transfer as it fulfils a liability. [2]

Different from fair value, value in use and fulfilment value reflect entity-specific assumptions rather than assumptions by market participants. In practice, there may sometimes be little difference between the assumptions that market participants would use and those that an entity itself uses.

Value in use and fulfilment value are based on future cash flows, so they do not include transaction costs incurred on acquiring an asset or taking on a liability. However, they include the present value of any transaction costs an entity expects to incur on the ultimate disposal of the asset or on fulfilling the liability.

4. Current cost

The current cost of an asset is the cost of an equivalent asset at the measurement date, comprising the consideration that would be paid at the measurement date plus the transaction costs that would be incurred at that date. **The current cost of a liability** is the consideration that would be received for an equivalent liability at the measurement date minus the transaction costs that would be incurred at that date. [3]

1　Ibid. , par 6. 12.

2　Ibid. , par 6. 17.

3　Ibid. , par 6. 21.

Current cost, like historical cost, is an entry value: It reflects prices in the market in which the entity would acquire the asset or would incur the liability. Hence, it is different from fair value, value in use and fulfilment value, which are exit values.

Unlike historical cost, current cost reflects conditions at the measurement date. In some cases, current cost cannot be determined directly by observing prices in an active market and must be determined indirectly by other means. For example, if prices are available only for a new fixed asset, the current cost of a used fixed asset might need to be estimated by adjusting the current price of the new one to reflect the current age and condition of the old one held by the entity.

In financial statements different measurement bases are employed to different degrees and in varying combinations. Historical cost is the measurement basis most commonly adopted by entities in preparing their financial statements. However, other measurement bases are also frequently combined with historical cost. For example, an impaired asset is usually carried at the value in use (which is lower than historical cost); marketable securities may be carried at their fair values; and long-term liabilities may be carried at their fulfilment values.

▶ 核心词汇 Core Words and Expressions

assets　资产

comparability　可比性

completeness　完整性

confirmatory value　确证价值

consideration　对价

consistency　一致性

cost constraint　成本约束

current cost　现行成本

current value　现行价值

enhancing qualitative characteristics　增强的质量
　特征

equity　权益

expense　费用

fair value　公允价值

faithful representation　如实反映

free from error　免于差错

fulfilment value　清偿价值

fundamental qualitative characteristics　基本质量
　特征

gain　利得

historical cost　历史成本

income　收益

income tax　所得税

inventory　存货

liabilities　负债

loss　损失

materiality　重要性

measurement basis　计量基础

measurement date　计量日

neutrality　中立性

predictive value　预测价值

present value　现值

qualitative characteristics　质量特征

receivable　应收款项

relevance　相关性

reliability　可靠性

revenue　收入

substance over form　实质重于形式

timeliness　及时性

transaction cost　交易成本，交易费用

understandability 可理解性   verifiability 可验证性

value in use 在用价值，使用价值

▶ 知识扩展 More Knowledge

国际财务报告准则第 13 号——公允价值计量（IFRS 13）

关于公允价值的争议一直不断。公允价值计量可靠吗？公允价值信息有用吗？符合成本效益原则吗？与其他计量属性之间是什么关系？2011 年 5 月，国际会计准则委员会发布第 13 号准则——公允价值计量。该准则没有回答上述问题，但是为多个具体准则中已经出现的公允价值计量提供了统一的指导框架和披露要求。以下简要介绍该准则的主要内容。

公允价值的定义

IFRS 13 将公允价值定义为"市场参与者之间在计量日进行的有序交易中出售一项资产所收到的价格或转移一项负债所支付的价格"。这有时被称为"脱手价"。

主要（或最有利）市场

IFRS 13 指出，公允价值是在主要市场（即该资产或负债拥有最大交易量及交易水平的市场）中向市场参与者出售资产（或转移负债）所使用的价格。如果不存在主要市场，则应使用在最有利市场（即主体可获得最有利价格的市场）中的价格。在不存在相反证据的情况下，假设主体通常进行交易的市场为其主要市场或最有利市场。交易成本不应纳入公允价值计量。

公允价值的确定估值技术

当交易可直接从市场观察时，公允价值的确定可能相对较为简单；但当交易无法直接从市场观察时，应使用估值技术。IFRS 13 阐述了主体可用于确定公允价值的 3 项估值技术。

- 市场法：主体采用涉及相同或可比（即类似）资产、负债或一组资产和负债的市场交易所使用的价格。
- 收益法：主体将未来现金流量金额转换成单一的折现后的金额。
- 成本法：主体确定一个反映当前取代资产的服务能力所需金额（即当前重置成本）的价值。

IFRS 13 要求主体选择能够以最大限度地使用相关可观察变量的估值技术，即尽量采用非主观变量来增强公允价值的可靠性。

我国企业会计准则（2006）的概念框架

2006 年 2 月，我国会计准则体系发布。在发布的基本准则中，建立了与 IASB 概念框架类似的概念体系。基本准则第一章第四条，"财务会计报告的目标是向财务会计报告使用者提供与企业财务状况、经营成果和现金流量等有关的会计信息，反映企业管理层受托责任履行情况，有助于财务会计报告使用者做出经济决策"。第五条至第九条，分别反映了会计主体、持续经营、会计分期、货币计量、权责发生制 4 个基本假设和会计基础。准则第二章是会计信息质量要求，包括如实反映、相关性、明晰性（可理解性）、可比性、实质重于形式、重要性、谨慎性、及时性。在我国的概念框架中，没有对信息质量划分层次。基本准则第三章至第八章规定了 6 个会计要素及其确认标准，这 6 个要素是：资产、负债、所有者权益、收入、费用和利润。第九章会计计量，规定可采用的计量属性包括历史成本、重置成本、可变现净值、现值和公允价值。第十章财务会计报告规定会计报表至

少应当包括资产负债表、利润表、现金流量表等报表。

▶ 问答题 Questions

1. One characteristic of useful accounting information is understandability. Understandable to whom?

2. Distinguish between the qualities of relevance and faithful presentation.

3. Does faithful presentation imply absolute accuracy? Explain.

4. Define comparability.

5. Why is it so difficult to measure the cost and the benefit of accounting information?

6. For each item below, indicate to which category of elements of financial statements it belongs.

   (a) Retained earnings   (b) Sales   (c) Additional paid-in capital   (d) Inventory

   (e) Depreciation   (f) Dividends   (g) Gain on sale of investment   (h) Interest payable

   (i) Loss on sale of equipment   (j) Issuance of common stock

7. What three elements are contained in a balance sheet?

8. What are the two measurement methods of performance that may be used to determine income? How do they differ?

9. Identify the criteria that an item must meet to qualify for recognition.

10. Identify and describe four different measurement bases.

Financial Statements

财务报表

◎ 小案例 Mini Case

Assume that you just inherited one million yuan. You are advised that investments in equity securities give the highest rate of return. You find annual reports of several companies recommended by the analysts. What useful information would you expect to find in the statements of financial position, the statements of comprehensive income, statements of changes in equity, and the statements of cash flows?

正文 Text

Financial statements are a structured representation of the financial position and financial performance of an entity. A complete set of financial statements comprises (IAS 1, par. 10):

(a) a statement of financial position as at the end of the period;

(b) a statement of profit or loss and other comprehensive income for the period;

(c) a statement of changes in equity for the period;

(d) a statement of cash flows for the period;

(e) notes, comprising a summary of significant accounting policies and other explanatory information; comparative information in respect of the preceding period; and

(f) a statement of financial position as at the beginning of the preceding period when an entity applies an accounting policy retrospectively or makes a retrospective restatement of items in its financial statements, or when it reclassifies items in its financial statements.

3.1 Statement of Financial Position

The statement of financial position, used to be called the balance sheet, is a listing of an organization's assets, liabilities and equity as of a certain point of time, known as the reporting date.

3. 1. 1　Classification of Assets and Liabilities

Items presented in the statement of financial position are generally classified as current (or short-term) items and non-current (or long-term) items. How long is "current"? **Current** means "one year or less than the normal course of the entity's operating cycle. " The operating cycle is the time between the acquisition of materials for processing and their realization in cash or cash equivalents. Accordingly, assets expected to be used and liabilities expected to be paid or otherwise satisfied within short-term are current items.

Current assets include cash, receivables, short-term investments, inventories and prepaid expenses.

Non-current assets, also called fixed assets, generally include those assets which were acquired with the intention of retaining them for the purpose of generating income over a number of years. Non-current assets include investments, property, plant and equipment, intangible assets, and other non-current assets.

Current liabilities are obligations the liquidation of which is reasonably expected to require the use of current assets, or the creation of other current obligations. Common current liabilities are obligations arising from the acquisition of goods and services entering the operating cycle, such as accounts payable, short-term notes payable, wages payable, taxes payable. Collections of money in advance for the future delivery of goods or performance or services are accrued current liabilities. The current maturity of long-term liabilities is also classified as current liabilities.

Non-current liabilities include obligations not requiring the use of current funds for their retirement, such as long-term borrowings, bonds, mortgages.

3. 1. 2　Classification of Equity

In a corporation, the net assets are referred to as stockholders' equity. In presenting the statement of financial position, a distinction is made between the equity originating from the stockholders' investments, referred to as share capitals (or contributed capitals), and the equity originating from earnings, referred to as retained earnings.

In case of a sole proprietorship, the owners' equity is reported by means of a single capital account. In case of a partnership, capital accounts are established for each partner.

3. 1. 3　Format of Statement of Financial Position

The format of statement of financial position is not presently specified by IAS1. In general, the two types of formats are the report form and the account form. In the report form the statement of financial position continues line by line from the top to bottom as Table 3-1:

Table 3-1

Assets	$ x x x
Liabilities	$ x x x
Stockholders' equity	x x x
Total liabilities and stockholders' equity	$ x x x

In the account form the statement of financial position appears in a balancing concept with assets on the left and liabilities and equity amounts on the right as Table 3-2:

Table 3-2

Assets	$ x x x	Liabilities	$ x x x
		Stockholders' equity	x x x
Total assets	$ x x x	Total liabilities and stockholders' equity	$ x x x

3.1.4 Illustrative Statement of Financial Position

IASB gives an illustrative statement of financial position as the following with the assets of longer useful lives listed first. The statement of financial position of Apple Inc in appendix of this chapter, illustrates current items listed first.

Table 3-3 XYZ Group-Statement of financial position as at 31 December 20×7

(in thousands of currency units)

	31 Dec 20×7	31 Dec 20×6
ASSETS		
Non-current assets		
Property, plant and equipment	350 700	360 020
Goodwill（商誉）	80 800	91 200
Other intangible assets	227 470	227 470
Investments in associates（联营企业的投资）	100 150	110 770
Investments in equity instruments（其他权益投资）	142 500	156 000
	901 620	945 460
Current assets		
Inventories	135 230	132 500
Trade receivables	91 600	110 800
Other current assets	25 650	12 540
Cash and cash equivalents（现金及现金等价物）	312 400	322 900
	564 880	578 740
Total assets	1 466 500	1 524 200

(continued)

	31 Dec 20 ×7	31 Dec 20 ×6
EQUITY AND LIABILITIES		
Equity attributable to owners of the parent		
Share capital	650 000	600 000
Retained earnings	243 500	161 700
Other components of equity	10 200	21 200
	903 700	782 900
Non-controlling interests（非控制股东权益）	70 050	48 600
Total equity	973 750	831 500
Non-current liabilities		
Long-term borrowings	120 000	160 000
Deferred tax（递延所得税负债）	28 800	26 040
Long-term provisions	28 850	52 240
Total non-current liabilities	177 650	238 280
Current liabilities		
Trade and other payables	115 100	187 620
Short-term borrowings	150 000	200 000
Current portion of long-term borrowings	10 000	20 000
Current tax payable	35 000	42 000
Short-term provisions	5 000	4 800
Total current liabilities	315 100	454 420
Total liabilities	492 750	692 700
Total equity and liabilities	1 466 500	1 524 200

3.2　Statement of Comprehensive Income

IASB requires an entity to present a single statement of comprehensive income, or two statements: a statement displaying components of profit or loss (separate statement of profit or loss) and a second statement beginning with profit or loss and displaying components of other comprehensive income (statement of comprehensive income).

3.2.1　An Illustrative Statement of Comprehensive Income

The following statement illustrates the presentation of comprehensive income in one statement and the classification of expenses within profit by function.

Table 3-4 XYZ Group-Statement of comprehensive income for the year ended
31 December 20 ×7

(in thousands of currency units)

	20 ×7	20 ×6
Revenue	390 000	355 000
Cost of sales	(245 000)	(230 000)
Gross profit	145 000	125 000
Other income	20 667	11 300
Distribution costs	(9 000)	(8 700)
Administrative expenses	(20 000)	(21 000)
Other expenses	(2 100)	(1 200)
Finance costs	(8 000)	(7 500)
Share of profit of associates	35 100	30 100
Profit before tax	161 667	128 000
Income tax expense	(40 417)	(32 000)
Profit for the year from continuing operations	121 250	96 000
Loss for the year from discontinued operations	—	(30 500)
PROFIT FOR THE YEAR	121 250	65 500
Other comprehensive income:		
Exchange differences on translating foreign operations (境外经营折算差额)	5 334	10 667
Investments in equity instruments	(24 000)	26 667
Cash flow hedges (现金流量套期)	(667)	(4 000)
Gains on property revaluation	933	3 367
Actuarial gains (losses) on defined benefit pension plans	(667)	1 333
Share of other comprehensive income of associates	400	(700)
Income tax relating to components of other comprehensive income	4 667	(9 334)
Other comprehensive income for the year, net of tax	(14 000)	28 000
TOTAL COMPREHENSIVE INCOME FOR THE YEAR	107 250	93 500

3.2.2 Classification of Expenses

IAS1 requires that "an entity shall present an analysis of expenses using a classification based on either the nature of expenses or their function within the entity, whichever provides information that is reliable and more relevant." (IAS 1, par. 99)

An example of a classification using the nature of expense method is as Table 3-5:

Table 3-5

Revenue		×
Other income		×
Changes in inventories of finished goods and work in progress	×	
Raw materials and consumables used	×	
Employee benefits expense	×	
Depreciation and amortization expense	×	
Other expenses	×	
Total expenses		(×)
Profit before tax		×

An example of a classification using the function of expense method is as Table 3-6:

Table　3-6

Revenue	×
Cost of sales	(×)
Gross profit	×
Other income	×
Distribution costs	(×)
Administrative expenses	(×)
Other expenses	(×)
Profit before tax	×

3. 2. 3　Format of Statement of Comprehensive Income

Traditionally, profit or loss has been presented in either a single-step form or a multiple-step form. With the single-step form, all revenues and gains are placed first on the income statement, followed by all expenses and losses. The difference between total revenues and gains and total expenses and losses represents net income. With the multiple-step form, the statement of comprehensive income is divided into separate sections, and subtotals are reported that reflect different levels of profitability. The statement of comprehensive income of Apple Inc, in appendix, illustrates a multiple-step format.

3. 3　Statement of Changes in Equity

3. 3. 1　Information to Be Presented in the Statement of Changes in Equity

IAS 1 identifies the major information an entity shall present on the face of the statement of changes in equity as follows:

(a) total comprehensive income for the period, showing separately the total amounts attributable to owners of the parent and to non-controlling interests;

(b) for each component of equity, the effects of retrospective application or retrospective restatement recognized in accordance; and

(c) for each component of equity, a reconciliation between the carrying amount at the beginning and the end of the period, separately disclosing changes resulting from:

(i) profit or loss;

(ii) other comprehensive income; and

(iii) transactions with owners in their capacity as owners, showing separately contributions by and distributions to owners and changes in ownership interests in subsidiaries that do not result in a loss of control.

Other items an entity shall present, either on the face of the statement of changes in equity or in the notes, are as follows:

(a) an analysis of other comprehensive income by item for each component of equity; and

(b) the amount of dividends recognized as distributions to owners during the period, and the related amount of dividends per share.

3.3.2　Illustrative Statement of Changes in Equity

Table 3-7　XYZ Group-Statement of changes in equity for the year ended
31 December 20×7

(in thousands of currency units)

	Share capital	Retained earnings	Translation of foreign operations	Investments in equity instruments	Cash flow hedges	Revaluation surplus	Total	Noncontrolling interests	Total equity
Balance at 1 January 20×6	600 000	118 100	(4 000)	1 600	2 000	—	717 700	29 800	747 500
Changes in accounting policy	—	400	—	—	—	—	400	100	500
Restated balance	600 000	118 500	(4 000)	1 600	2 000	—	718 100	29 900	748 000
Changes in equity for 20×6									
Dividends	—	(10 000)	—	—	—	—	(10 000)	—	(10 000)
Total comprehensive income for the year	—	53 200	6 400	16 000	(2 400)	1 600	74 800	18 700	93 500
Balance at 31 December 20×6	600 000	161 700	2 400	17 600	(400)	1 600	782 900	48 600	831 500
Changes in equity for 20×7									
Issue of share capital	50 000	—	—	—	—	—	50 000	—	50 000
Dividends	—	(15 000)	—	—	—	—	(15 000)	—	(15 000)
Total comprehensive income for the year	—	96 600	3 200	(14 400)	(400)	800	85 800	21 450	107 250
Transfer to retained earnings	—	200	—	—	—	(200)	—	—	—
Balance at 31 December 20×7	650 000	243 500	5 600	3 200	(800)	2 200	903 700	70 050	973 750

3. 4   Statement of Cash Flows

The statement of cash flows reveals how an entity generated and spent cash during a given accounting period. The accounting period covered by a statement of cash flows is the same period as that covered by the statement of comprehensive income. When decision makers review a company's statement of cash flows, the question foremost in their minds is " How do the company's cash flows from its profit-oriented activities compare to its net income?" Successful companies should, over the long run, generate the majority of their cash from their operating activities.

The statement of cash flows begins with a summary of the cash inflows and outflows from three major types of activities engaged in by entities: operating, investing, and financing. The final section of the statement reconciles an entity's cash balance at the beginning of a period to its cash balance at the end of that period. The ending cash balance is also found on the statement of financial position along with the other assets.

3. 4. 1   Cash and Cash Equivalents

The statement of cash flows, under international standards, includes transactions in cash equivalents as well as cash. Cash includes cash on hand and demand deposits with banks or other financial institutions. Cash equivalents are short-term highly liquid investments that are (1) readily convertible to known amounts of cash, and (2) so near to their maturity (original maturity of three months or less) that they present insignificant risk of changes in value. Original maturity in this case is determined from the date an investment is acquired by the reporting entity. For example, both a three-month treasury bill and a three-year treasury note purchased three months prior to maturity qualify as cash equivalents. However, if the treasury note were purchased three years ago, it would not qualify as cash equivalent during the last three months prior to its maturity.

3. 4. 2   Three Categories of Cash Flows

The statement of cash flows prepared in accordance with IAS 7 requires classification into these three categories:

The primary **investing activities** are the purchase and sale of land, buildings, equipment, and other assets not generally held for resale. In addition, investing activities include the purchase and sale of financial instruments not intended for trading purposes, as well as the making and collecting of loans.

Financing activities include transactions and events whereby cash is obtained from or repaid to owners (equity financing) and creditors (debt financing). Examples of financing activities are cash proceeds from issuing stock or bonds, payments to reacquire stock or to retire bonds and the payment of dividends.

Operating activities include all transactions that are not investing and financing activities. Operating activities are principal revenue-producing activities of an entity and include delivering or producing goods for sale and providing services.

3.4.3　Direct and Indirect Method

The operating activities section of the statement of cash flows can be presented under the direct or the indirect method.

The direct method shows the items that affected cash flows and the magnitude of those cash flows. Cash received from, and cash paid to, specific sources are presented. An example of cash flows from operating activities—a classification using the direct method is as Table 3-8:

Table　3-8

Cash flows from operating activities		
Cash receipts from customers		$ 30 150
Cash paid to suppliers and employees	$ 27 600	
Interest paid	270	
Income taxes paid	900	(28 770)
Net cash from operating activities		$ 1 380

The indirect method focuses on the differences between net operating results and cash flows. It begins with net income, which can be obtained directly from the statement of comprehensive income. Revenue and expense items not affecting cash are added or deducted to arrive at net cash provided by operating activities. For example, depreciation and amortization would be added back because these expenses reduce net income without affecting cash. Changes in the components of most current asset and current liability accounts are analyzed to determine the cash flows from operating activities. The statement of cash flows of Apple Inc, in appendix, illustrates an indirect method.

▶ **核心词汇** Core Words and Expressions

account form　账户式

accounts payable　应付账款

accrued liability　应计负债

administrative expense　管理费用

amortization　摊销

available-for-sale security　可供出售证券（投资）

bond　债券	multiple-step form　多步式
borrowing　借款	non-current asset（fixed asset）　非流动资产
comprehensive income　综合收益，又译为全面收益	notes　附注
	notes payable　应付票据
cost of sales　销售成本	operating activities　经营活动
current asset　流动资产	operating cycle　营业周期
current item　流动性项目	partnership　合伙
current liability　流动负债	prepaid expense　预付费用
(capital) reserve　（资本）公积	sole proprietorship　独资
depreciation　折旧	property, plant and equipment　直译为不动产、工厂与设备，即固定资产
direct method　直接法	
distribution cost　销售费用	raw material　原材料
finance cost　财务费用	receivable　应收款项
financing activities　筹资活动	report form　报告式
finished good　产成品	reporting date　报告日
foreign currency translation adjustment　外币折算差额	retained earnings　留存收益
	share capital　股本
goodwill　商誉	single-step form　单步式
indirect method　间接法	taxes payable　应交税金
intangible asset　无形资产	treasury bill　一年以内的短期国债
inventory　存货	treasury note　五年以内的中期国债
investing activities　投资活动	wages payable　应付工资
investment　投资	work in progress　在产品

▶ 知识扩展 More Knowledge

苹果公司 2017 年的报表

以下报表摘录自苹果公司（Apple Inc.）披露的 2017 年年度报告，限于篇幅略去了所有者权益变动表。附注是财务报表的必要部分，是理解财务报表所必需的，限于篇幅，此处也略去。

Apple Inc.

Consolidated Statements of Operations

（$ in millions）

	2017	2016	2015
Net sales	229 234	215 639	233 715
Cost of sales	141 048	131 376	140 089
Gross margin	88 186	84 263	93 626

	2017	2016	2015
			(continued)
Operating expenses:			
Research and development	11 581	10 045	8 067
Selling, general and administrative	15 261	14 194	14 329
Total operating expenses	26 842	24 239	22 396
Operating income	61 344	60 024	71 230
Other income/(expense), net	2 745	1 348	1 285
Income before provision for income taxes	64 089	61 372	72 515
Provision for income taxes	15 738	15 685	19 121
Net income	48 351	45 687	53 394

Apple Inc.

Consolidated Statements of Comprehensive Income

($ in millions)

	2017	2016	2015
Net income	48 351	45 687	53 394
Other comprehensive income/(loss):			
Change in foreign currency translation, net of tax effects of $ (77), $ 8 and $ 201, respectively	224	75	(411)
Change in unrealized gains/losses on derivative instruments:			
Change in fair value of derivatives, net of tax benefit/(expense) of $ (478), $ (7) and $ (441), respectively	1 315	7	2 905
Adjustment for net (gains)/losses realized and included in net income, net of tax expense/(benefit) of $ 475, $ 131 and $ 630, respectively	(1 477)	(741)	(3 497)
Total change in unrealized gains/losses on derivative instruments, net of tax	(162)	(734)	(592)
Change in unrealized gains/losses on marketable securities:			
Change in fair value of marketable securities, net of tax benefit/(expense) of $ 425, $ (863) and $ 264, respectively	(782)	1 582	(483)
Adjustment for net (gains)/losses realized and included in net income, net of tax expense/(benefit) of $ 35, $ (31) and $ (32), respectively	(64)	56	59
Total change in unrealized gains/losses on marketable securities, net of tax	(846)	1 638	(424)
Total other comprehensive income/(loss)	(784)	979	(1 427)
Total comprehensive income	47 567	46 666	51 967

Apple Inc.

Consolidated Statements of Financial Position

($ in millions)

	2017	2016
Assets:		
Current assets:		
Cash and cash equivalents	20 289	20 484
Short-term marketable securities	53 892	46 671
Accounts receivable, less allowances of $ 58 and $ 53, respectively	17 874	15 754
Inventories	4 855	2 132
Vendor non-trade receivables	17 799	13 545
Other current assets	13 936	8 283
Total current assets	**128 645**	**106 869**
Long-term marketable securities	194 714	170 430
Property, plant and equipment, net	33 783	27 010
Goodwill	5 717	5 414
Acquired intangible assets, net	2 298	3 206
Other non-current assets	10 162	8 757
Total assets	**375 319**	**321 686**
Liabilities and Shareholders' equity:		
Current liabilities:		
Accounts payable	49 049	37 294
Accrued expenses	25 744	22 027
Deferred revenue	7 548	8 080
Commercial paper	11 977	8 105
Current portion of long-term debt	6 496	3 500
Total current liabilities	**100 814**	**79 006**
Deferred revenue, non-current	2 836	2 930
Long-term debt	97 207	75 427
Other non-current liabilities	40 415	36 074
Total liabilities	**241 272**	**193 437**
Commitments and contingencies		
Shareholders' equity:		
Common stock and additional paid-in capital, $ 0.00 001 par value: 12 600 000 shares authorized; 5 126 201 and 5 336 166 shares issued and outstanding, respectively	35 867	31 251
Retained earnings	98 330	96 364
Accumulated other comprehensive income/(loss)	(150)	634
Total shareholders' equity	**134 047**	**128 249**
Total liabilities and shareholders' equity	**375 319**	**321 686**

Apple Inc.

Consolidated Statements of Cash Flows

($ in millions)

	2017	2016	2015
Cash and cash equivalents, beginning of the year	**20 484**	**21 120**	**13 844**
Operating activities:			
Net income	48 351	45 687	53 394
Adjustments to reconcile net income to cash generated by operating activities:			
Depreciation and amortization	10 157	10 505	11 257
Share-based compensation expense	4 840	4 210	3 586
Deferred income tax expense	5 966	4 938	1 382
Other	(166)	486	385
Changes in operating assets and liabilities:			
Accounts receivable, net	(2 093)	527	417
Inventories	(2 723)	217	(238)
Vendor non-trade receivables	(4 254)	(51)	(3 735)
Other current and non-current assets	(5 318)	1 055	(283)
Accounts payable	9 618	1 837	5 001
Deferred revenue	(626)	(1 554)	1 042
Other current and non-current liabilities	(154)	(2 033)	9 058
Cash generated by operating activities	**63 598**	**65 824**	**81 266**
Investing activities:			
Purchases of marketable securities	(159 486)	(142 428)	(166 402)
Proceeds from maturities of marketable securities	31 775	21 258	14 538
Proceeds from sales of marketable securities	94 564	90 536	107 447
Payments made in connection with business acquisitions, net	(329)	(297)	(343)
Payments for acquisition of property, plant and equipment	(12 451)	(12 734)	(11 247)
Payments for acquisition of intangible assets	(344)	(814)	(241)
Payments for strategic investments, net	(395)	(1 388)	—
Other	220	(110)	(26)
Cash used in investing activities	**(46 446)**	**(45 977)**	**(56 274)**
Financing activities:			
Proceeds from issuance of common stock	555	495	543
Excess tax benefits from equity awards	627	407	749
Payments for taxes related to net share settlement of equity awards	(1 874)	(1 570)	(1 499)
Payments for dividends and dividend equivalents	(12 769)	(12 150)	(11 561)
Repurchases of common stock	(32 900)	(29 722)	(35 253)
Proceeds from issuance of term debt, net	28 662	24 954	27 114
Repayments of term debt	(3 500)	(2 500)	—
Change in commercial paper, net	3 852	(397)	2 191
Cash used in financing activities	**(17 347)**	**(20 483)**	**(17 716)**
Increase/(Decrease) in cash and cash equivalents	(195)	(636)	7 276
Cash and cash equivalents, end of the year	**20 289**	**20 484**	**21 120**
Supplemental cash flow disclosure:			
Cash paid for income taxes, net	11 591	10 444	13 252
Cash paid for interest	2 092	1 316	514

资料来源: Apple Inc. 官方网站。http://investor.apple.com/investor-relations/financial-information/default.aspx.

▶ 问答题 Questions

1. How does separating current assets from property, plant, and equipment in the statement of financial position help analysts?

2. Should available-for-sale securities always be reported as a current asset? Explain.

3. What is the objective of statement of changes in equity?

4. What is the purpose of statement of cash flows? How does it differ from a statement of financial position and statement of comprehensive income?

5. The net income for the year for Won Long, Inc. is ＄750 000, but the statement of cash flows reports that the cash provided by operating activities is ＄640 000. What might account for the difference?

6. Net income for the year for Jenkins, Inc. was ＄750 000, but the statement of cash flows reports that cash provided by operating activities was ＄860 000. What might account for the difference?

7. Differentiate between operating activities, investing activities, and financing activities.

▶ 练习题 Exercises

Exercise 1

Presented below are the captions of Faulk Company's statement of financial position .

(a) Current assets.

(b) Investments.

(c) Property, plant, and equipment.

(d) Intangible assets.

(e) Other assets.

(f) Current liabilities.

(g) Non-current liabilities.

(h) Capital stock.

(i) Additional paid-in capital.

(j) Retained earnings.

Instructions

Indicate by letter where each of the following items would be classified.

1. Preferred stock.

2. Goodwill.

3. Wages payable.

4. Trade accounts payable.

5. Buildings.

6. Trading securities.

7. Current portion of long-term debt.

8. Premium on bonds payable.

9. Allowance for doubtful accounts.

10. Accounts receivable.

11. Cash surrender value of life insurance.

12. Notes payable (due next year) .

13. Office supplies.

14. Common stock.

15. Land.

16. Bond sinking fund.

17. Merchandise inventory.

18. Prepaid insurance.

19. Bonds payable.

20. Taxes payable.

Exercise 2

Assume that Denis Saved Inc. has the following accounts at the end of the current year.

1. Common Stock.

2. Discount on Bonds Payable.

3. Treasury Stock (at cost) .

4. Note Payable, short-term.

5. Raw Materials.

6. Preferred Stock Investments—Long-term.

7. Unearned Rent Revenue.

8. Work in Process.

9. Copyrights.

10. Buildings.

11. Notes Receivable (short-term) .

12. Cash.

13. Accrued Salaries Payable.

14. Accumulated Depreciation—Buildings.

15. Cash Restricted for Plant Expansion.

16. Land Held for Future Plant Site.

17. Allowance for Doubtful Accounts—Accounts Receivable.

18. Retained Earnings.

19. Premium on Common Stock.

20. Unearned Subscriptions Revenue.

21. Receivables—Officers (due in one year) .

22. Finished Goods.

23. Accounts Receivable.

24. Bonds Payable (due in 4 years) .

Instructions

Prepare a classified statement of financial position in good form. (No monetary amounts are necessary.)

Exercise 3

Turner Corporation had net sales of $2 400 000 and interest revenue of $31 000 during 20 ×5. Expenses for 20 ×5 were: cost of goods sold $1 250 000; administrative expenses $212 000; selling expenses $280 000; interest expense $45 000. Turner's tax rate is 30%. The corporation had 100 000 shares of common stock authorized and 70 000 shares issued and outstanding during 20 ×5.

Instructions

Prepare a single-step statement of comprehensive income and a multiple-step statement of comprehensive income for the year ended December 31, 20 ×5.

Exercise 4

The major classifications of activities reported in the statement of cash flows are operating, investing, and financing.

The transactions are as follows.

(a) Issuance of capital stock.

(b) Purchase of land and building.

(c) Redemption of bonds.

(d) Sale of equipment.

(e) Depreciation of machinery.

(f) Amortization of patent.

(g) Issuance of bonds for plant assets.

(h) Payment of cash dividends.

(i) Exchange of furniture for office equipment.

(j) Purchase of treasury stock.

(k) Loss on sale of equipment.

(l) Increase in accounts receivable during the year.

(m) Decrease in accounts payable during the year.

Instructions

Classify each of the transactions listed above as:

1. Operating activity—add to net income.

2. Operating activity—deduct from net income.

3. Investing activity.

4. Financing activity.

5. Reported as significant noncash activity.

Exercise 5

Ges Company reported 20 × 5 net income of $ 151 000. During 20 × 5, accounts receivable increased by $ 13 000 and accounts payable increased by $ 9 500. Depreciation expense was $ 39 000.

Instructions

Prepare the cash flows from operating activities section of the statement of cash flows.

Exercise 6

York Perez Corporation engaged in the following cash transactions during 20 × 5.

Sale of land and building	$ 181 000
Purchase of treasury stock	40 000
Purchase of land	37 000
Payment of cash dividend	85 000
Purchase of equipment	53 000
Issuance of common stock	147 000
Retirement of bonds	100 000

Instructions

(1) Compute the net cash provided (used) by investing activities.

(2) Compute the net cash used (provided) by financing activities.

The Accounting Cycle
会计循环

◎ 小案例 Mini Case

John Han, a professor, stated that in the computer world one computer database of business events is enough for all reporting purposes, such as accounting, marketing, and production. Accountants can prepare financial reports upon the information directly abstracted from database. It is no longer necessary to record business events in sequential order as it has been traditionally done in accounting journals. What advantages and disadvantages do you think this proposal has?

正文 Text

The accounting information system must capture the relevant data about the entity's transactions, categorize them, and store them in such a way that one can retrieve the information and prepare the financial statements of the entity. This process is called the accounting cycle, or the accounting process. This chapter focuses on manual, rather than computer-based, accounting cycle, because the computer does not change the fundamental nature of how transaction data are collected, processed, and assimilated into a set of financial statements.

4.1 Accounting Equation and Double-Entry Bookkeeping

4.1.1 Accounting Equation

The accounting equation states that assets equal liabilities plus equity (Assets = Liabilities + Equity). This equation will always hold as long as no error has been made. This equation is the basis of double-entry bookkeeping system, and the basis of the statement of financial position.

For example, consider the transactions for Linda Future, Inc. given in Table 4-1. The owners invest cash of $10 000 to start the company. Thus the company has an asset of $10 000, and equity of the same amount. Assets equal liabilities plus equity.

Table 4-1　Transactions and Accounting Equation

	Assets	=	Liabilities	+	Equity
Start the company	$10 000	=	$0	+	$10 000
Purchase equipment	5 000	=	5 000		
	$15 000	=	$5 000	+	$10 000
Issue common stock	20 000	=	—	+	20 000
	$35 000	=	$5 000	+	$30 000
Pay for supplies	1 000				
	(1 000)		—		—
	$35 000	=	$5 000	+	$30 000
Pay for debts	(3 000)	=	(3 000)		
	$32 000	=	$2 000	+	$30 000

The company purchases equipment of $5 000 on credit. The transaction increases equipment by $5 000, and increases liabilities by $5 000. Total assets are now $15 000, total liabilities are $5 000, and equity remains $10 000. The accounting equation remains valid.

The second transaction is issuing common stock for $20 000. The cash and common stock increase by $20 000. Again, the accounting equation holds.

The third transaction is paying $1 000 for supplies. The transaction increases supplies by $1 000, and decreases cash by $1 000. It doesn't change total assets, total liabilities, or equity.

The forth transaction is paying $3 000 of its debts. The cash and debts decrease by $3 000. Again, the accounting equation holds.

4.1.2　Double-Entry Bookkeeping

Preparation of financial statements requires that information about an organization's economic events be captured and recorded in a rational and systematic manner. The origins of modern accounting, the double-entry bookkeeping system, can be traced to a mathematic book written in 1494 by Luca Pacioli living in what is now Italy. The fundamental rule of double-entry bookkeeping is that debits must equal credits.

Debits and Credits

Debits and credits are accounting terms with specialized meanings. Essentially, the term debit and credit means left and right respectively. A T-account is used to illustrate the use of debits and credits. A T-account is not really part of any formal accounting system; it is a device used for illustrative or analytical purposes, whose name is derived from its shape. Following is a T-account for cash.

Cash	
Debit	Credit

When debit is used as a noun, it refers to an amount entered on the left-hand side of an accounting record, such as a T-account. Debit can also be used as a verb, meaning to enter a given amount on the left-hand side of an accounting record. The term credit is similar with the term debit whereas it refers to the right-hand side. The debit/credit rules can be correlated with the accounting equation. Assets appear on the left-hand side of the accounting equation. To increase an asset, it must be debited, with the appropriate amount being entered on the left-hand side of the account. Liabilities and equity appear on the right-hand side of the accounting equation. An increase in one of these accounts means that the appropriate amount is credited or entered on the right-hand side of the account.

As an entity begins its operations, two additional account types are used: revenues, and expenses. Revenues cause equity to increase and because increases in equity are shown as credits, revenues also increase with credits. Alternatively, expenses cause equity to decrease, and decreases in equity are shown as debits. The more expenses an entity has, the smaller equity becomes. Thus, expenses increase with debits. The expanded accounting equation is as following:

$$Assets = Liabilities + Equity + (Revenues - Expenses)$$

The normal balance of each account is on the side where increases are recorded. Thus, assets and expenses normally have debit balances; liabilities, equity, and revenues typically have credit balances. Table 4-2 summarizes the debit/credit relationships of accounts.

Table 4-2   Debit and Credit Relationships of Accounts

	Assets	Liabilities	Equity	Revenues	Expenses
Increases	Debits	Credits	Credits	Credits	Debits
Decreases	Credits	Debits	Debits	Debits	Credits
Normal balance	Debits	Credits	Credits	Credits	Debits

A few accounts, which are designed to show offsets to other related accounts, are referred to as contra-accounts and have opposite balances. For example, contra-assets such as accumulated depreciation and allowance for doubtful accounts have credit balances. Contra-revenues include sales discount and sales returns and allowances which have debit balances.

4.2 Accounting Cycle

Accounting reports should be prepared on a periodic basis. So while one accounting cycle ends at the close of an operating period, another cycle begins for the next period. There are four steps to the accounting cycle.

a. Collect, examine and process transactions.

- prepare journal entries for the transactions;
- post journal entries to the general ledger;
- prepare a trial balance.

b. Adjust account balances as necessary.

- record adjustments in the general journal;
- post adjustments to the general ledger;
- prepare an adjusted trial balance.

c. Prepare financial statements.

- statement of comprehensive income;
- statement of changes in equity;
- statement of financial position;
- statement of cash flows.

d. Close temporary accounts.

- record closing entries in the general journal;
- post closing entries to the general ledger;
- prepare a post-closing trial balance.

4.2.1 Collect, Examine and Process Transactions

1. Prepare Journal Entries for the Transactions

To gather the information needed to prepare a general journal entry, business transactions must be analyzed to determine the accounts affected and the amounts of those effects. The format of a general journal is as Table 4-3:

Table 4-3

| General Journal | | | | |
Date	Descriptions	PR	Debit	Credit

The first column records the date of the transaction. The second column gives the names of accounts that are affected by the transaction; debits are entered before the credits, followed by a brief description of the transaction. The third column is called posting reference(PR) column. Debits and credits make up the fourth and fifth columns where the amount entered.

Illustration

Let's suppose that company Mars starts its business. The following transactions take place in its first month, June of the year. These transactions are recorded in general journal as shown in Table 4-4.

Table 4-4   Mars General Journal

General Journal					
Date		Descriptions	PR	Debit($)	Credit($)
June	1	Cash	101	30 000	
		Common Stock	301		30 000
		Issuing common stock			
	1	Furniture	150	24 000	
		Cash	101		6 000
		Accounts Payable	201		18 000
		Purchase of furniture with cash down payment			
	3	Prepaid Rent	126	12 000	
		Cash	101		12 000
		Paid one-year rent for office space			
	5	Purchases	502	18 000	
		Accounts Payable	201		18 000
		Purchase of inventory on credit			
	9	Accounts Payable	201	8 000	
		Cash	101		8 000
		Paid an account payable			
	15	Cash	101	15 000	
		Sales	501		15 000
		Cash sales			
	18	Wages Expense	505	800	
		Cash	101		800
		Paid wages for two weeks			
	20	Accounts Receivable	102	10 000	
		Sales	501		10 000
		Sales on credit			
	28	Cash	101	7 000	
		Accounts Receivable	102		7 000
		Received payment on accounts receivable			
June	30	Utility Expense	510	300	
		Cash	101		300
		Paid utility bill for June			
	30	Dividends	401	400	
		Cash	101		400
		Declared and paid cash dividend			

June 1. Mars issues 3 000 shares of $10 par value common stock. Checks totaling $30 000 are received from stockholders.

June 1. Mars purchases furniture costing $24 000, paying $6 000 in cash and the balance is due in six months. The furniture is expected to have a four-year useful life with no salvage value.

June 3. Mars pays $12 000 for one year's rent of office space.

June 5. Mars purchases $18 000 of inventory on credit.

June 9. Mars pays off $8 000 of the debt incurred on June 5.

June 15. Cash sales are made for $15 000.

June 18. Mars pays two-week wages of $800 to employees.

June 20. Credit sales are made for $10 000.

June 28. Customers pay $7 000 of accounts receivable originating from June 20.

June 30. Mars receives and pays the $300 electricity bill for June.

June 30. Mars declares and pays a cash dividend of $400.

2. Post Journal Entries to the General Ledger

After a transaction has been journalized, the information is then posted to accounts in the general ledger. Each account in the ledger has three monetary columns: one for debits; one for credits; and one for the account balance. Journal entry data may be posted daily, weekly, or even monthly in a manual accounting system. In computer-based accounting systems, transaction data are typically posted to general ledger accounts simultaneously with the journalizing process. Table 4-5 shows the general ledgers for the above transactions for Mars.

Table 4-5   Mars General Ledger

Cash					Account No. 101	
Date		Explanation	PR	Debit($)	Credit($)	Balance($)
June	1	Issued common stock	GJ1	30 000		30 000
	1	Made furniture down payment	GJ1		6 000	24 000
	3	Paid one-year rent	GJ1		12 000	12 000

Cash					Account No. 101	
Date		Explanation	PR	Debit($)	Credit($)	Balance($)
June	9	Paid account payable	GJ1		8 000	4 000
	15	Sales	GJ1	15 000		19 000
	18	Paid wages	GJ1		800	18 200
	28	Accounts receivable	GJ1	7 000		25 200
	30	Utility expense	GJ1		300	24 900
	30	Dividend	GJ1		400	24 500

Accounts Receivable					Account No. 102	
Date		Explanation	PR	Debit($)	Credit($)	Balance($)
June	20	Credit sales	GJ1	10 000		10 000
	28	Collections	GJ1		7 000	3 000

(continued)

Prepaid Rent						Account No. 126
Date		Explanation	PR	Debit($)	Credit($)	Balance($)
June	3	Payment	GJ1	12 000		12 000

Furniture						Account No. 150
Date		Explanation	PR	Debit($)	Credit($)	Balance($)
June	1	Purchase	GJ1	24 000		24 000

Accounts Payable						Account No. 201
Date		Explanation	PR	Debit($)	Credit($)	Balance($)
June	1	Bought furniture	GJ1		18 000	18 000
	5	Purchase of inventory	GJ1		18 000	36 000
	9	Payment	GJ1	8 000		28 000

Common Stock						Account No. 301
Date		Explanation	PR	Debit($)	Credit($)	Balance($)
June	1	Issued common stock	GJ1		30 000	30 000

Dividend						Account No. 401
Date		Explanation	PR	Debit($)	Credit($)	Balance($)
June	1	Cash dividend	GJ1	400		400

Sales						Account No. 501
Date		Explanation	PR	Debit($)	Credit($)	Balance($)
June	15	Sales	GJ1		15 000	15 000
	20	Credit sales	GJ1		10 000	25 000

Purchases						Account No. 502
Date		Explanation	PR	Debit($)	Credit($)	Balance($)
June	5	Purchase on account	GJ1	18 000		18 000

Wages Expense						Account No. 505
Date		Explanation	PR	Debit($)	Credit($)	Balance($)
June	18	Wages for two weeks	GJ1	800		800

Utility Expense						Account No. 510
Date		Explanation	PR	Debit($)	Credit($)	Balance($)
June	30	June electricity	GJ1	300		300

3. Prepare a Trial Balance

The trial balance is a listing of all the accounts and their balances to ensure that total debits equal total credits. Obviously, if total debits do not equal total credits, an error has occurred, and the accountant has to track down the error and correct it. On the other hand, even if a trial balance has equal debits and credits, there may be errors in the accounting records. For example, the debits and credits of a journal entry were posted to incorrect accounts. Table 4-6 is the trial balance for Mars.

Table 4-6 Mars Trial Balance

(June 30, 20 ×1)

Account	Debit($)	Credit($)
Cash	$ 24 500	
Accounts receivable	3 000	
Prepaid rent	12 000	
Furniture	24 000	
Accounts payable		$ 28 000
Common stock		30 000
Dividend	400	
Sales		25 000
Purchases	18 000	
Wages expense	800	
Utility expense	300	—
Totals	$ 83 000	$ 83 000

4. 2. 2 Adjust Account Balances as Necessary

The accrual accounting requires that the economic impact of a transaction is recorded whether or not the transaction involves cash. Therefore, a special category of journal entries is needed at the end of an accounting period, adjusting entries.

1. Record Adjustments in the General Journal

There are two main types of year-end adjustments: (1) valuation adjustments; (2) accruals and deferrals adjustments.

Valuation adjustments   Depreciation is one of the most common items included in this group. **Depreciation** is the systematic allocation of the cost of an asset over the different periods benefited by the use of the asset. The benefit received from the non-current asset will extend more than one year. Therefore, the cost of the non-current asset ought to be charged to those accounting periods. Assume Mars uses the straight-line method of depreciation. The yearly portion of the depreciation is computed by the straight-line formula:

$$Depreciation = (Cost - Salvage\ Value)/Life$$

The cost is the amount paid for the asset. The salvage value is the estimated amount of proceeds that will be collected upon disposal of the asset. The life is the number of years that the firm expects to utilize the asset. The depreciation expense for the furniture is computed as $ 24 000 divided by 48 months or $ 500 per month. The adjusting entry in general journal for Mars is as Table 4-7.

Accruals and deferrals adjustments   A deferred item is one for which the cash has been paid or received, but the expense or revenue has not yet been recognized. An accrual item is one for which the cash has not yet been paid or received, but the expense or revenue has already been recognized.

Table 4-7

General Journal					
Date		Descriptions	PR	Debit	Credit
June	30	Depreciation Expense	508	500	
		Accumulated Depreciation	151		500
		Record one month depreciation			
⋮	⋮	⋮	⋮	⋮	⋮

A **deferred expense** is an asset that represents a prepayment of an expense item. For example, when Mars prepaid its $ 12 000 one-year rent on 3 June, the company debited an asset account, prepaid rent, and credited cash. Over the rent period, the economic benefit provided by the asset will be gradually used up. As a result, by the end of the accounting period, the decrease in the asset should be recognized as an expense so that the company's assets are not overstated and expenses are not understated. The adjusting entry in general journal for Mars is as Table 4-8:

Table 4-8

General Journal					
Date		Descriptions	PR	Debit	Credit
June	30	Rent Expense	506	1 000	
		Prepaid Rent	126		1 000
		Expired one month's rent			
⋮	⋮	⋮	⋮	⋮	⋮

A **deferred revenue** is a liability that represents an amount received by a business for a service or product that will be provided or delivered in the future. Suppose a training company receives $ 1 200 from customers for one-year training program starting on August 1. At August 31 there should be $ 100 on the statement of profit or loss as revenue, and $ 1 100 on the statement of financial position as unearned revenue(liability).

If the original entry is recorded as

Cash $ 1 200

　　Unearned Revenue $ 1 200[1]

Then the adjusting entry is

Unearned Revenue $ 1 100

　　Training Revenue $ 100

An **accrued asset** is a receivable one resulting from revenue that has been earned but has not yet been received. An account receivable is the most common accrued asset. Another one is interest that has not yet been received on an amount loaned to others. For example, if a company issues a one-year $ 10 000 note on July 1 for 6% interest, then it journalizes the entry as

---

1 这种形式的分录是对日记账分录的简化。

Notes Receivable	$ 10 000
Cash	$ 10 000

At July 31 , the firm earns interest because it has provided services to the borrower the use of the money. Interest is computed with the simple interest formula:

$$Interest = Principal \times rate \times time$$

Interest earned equals $ 10 000 \times 6\% \times 1/12$ or $ 50. The adjusting entry is

Interest Receivable	$ 50
Interest Revenue	$ 50

An **accrued liability** is a liability for an expense that has been incurred but has not yet been paid. For example, the employees of Mars have earned another ten days' wages $ 600 , but not been paid , by the ending of June. The adjusting entry for Mars is as Table 4-9.

Table　4-9

General Journal					
Date		Descriptions	PR	Debit	Credit
June	30	Wages Expense	505	600	
		Wages Payable	205		600
		Record wages for ten days			
⋮	⋮	⋮	⋮	⋮	⋮

At the end of each year , Mars will be required to pay a corporate income tax on any earned profits. On June 30 , Mars did not know how much would be earned for the year , therefore , it could not determine an exact amount of income tax that would need to be paid. However , a business must estimate its income tax expense each accounting period to match the expenses with the revenues earned. After reviewing the tax rate schedule , Mars recorded a $ 700 accrued liability as an estimate of the corporate income tax that would eventually be paid on the profit earned during June. The adjusting entry for Mars is as Table 4-10.

Table　4-10

General Journal					
Date		Descriptions	PR	Debit	Credit
June	30	Income Tax Expense	520	700	
		Income Tax Payable	208		700
		Recording estimated income taxes			
⋮	⋮	⋮	⋮	⋮	⋮

2. Post Adjustments to the General Ledger

The adjusting journal entries are posted to the general ledger. Then the balances in some accounts have been added. Table 4-11 shows the posting of adjusting entries of Mars.

Table 4-11 Posting Adjusting Entries to General Ledger

Depreciation Expense				Account No. 508		
Date		Explanation	PR	Debit	Credit	Balance
June	30	Adjustment	GJ1	500		500

Accumulated Depreciation				Account No. 151		
Date		Explanation	PR	Debit	Credit	Balance
June	30	Adjustment	GJ1		500	500

Prepaid Rent				Account No. 126		
Date		Explanation	PR	Debit	Credit	Balance
June	3	Payment	GJ1	12 000		12 000
	30	Adjustment	GJ1		1 000	11 000

Rent Expense				Account No. 506		
Date		Explanation	PR	Debit	Credit	Balance
June	30	Adjustment	GJ1	1 000		1 000

Wage Expenses				Account No. 505		
Date		Explanation	PR	Debit	Credit	Balance
June	18	Wages for two weeks	GJ1	800		800
	30	Adjustment	GJ1	600		1 400

Wages Payable				Account No. 205		
Date		Explanation	PR	Debit	Credit	Balance
June	30	Adjustment	GJ1		600	600

Income Tax Expense				Account No. 520		
Date		Explanation	PR	Debit	Credit	Balance
June	30	Adjustment	GJ1	700		700

Income Tax Payable				Account No. 208		
Date		Explanation	PR	Debit	Credit	Balance
June	30	Adjustment	GJ1		700	700

3. Prepare an Adjusted Trial Balance

Table 4-12 presents the adjusted trial balance for Mars.

Table 4-12 Mars Adjusted Trial Balance

(June 30, 20 × 1)

Account	Debit($)	Credit($)
Cash	24 500	
Accounts receivable	3 000	
Prepaid rent	11 000	
Furniture	24 000	
Accumulated depreciation		500
Accounts payable		28 000
Wages payable		600
Income tax payable		700

(continued)

Account	Debit($)	Credit($)
Common stock		30 000
Dividend	400	
Sales		25 000
Purchase	18 000	
Wage expense	1 400	
Utility expense	300	
Rent Expense	1 000	
Depreciation expense	500	
Income tax expense	700	—
Totals	84 800	84 800

4. 2. 3　Prepare Financial Statements

When preparing financial statements Mars needs to count its inventory at hand. Assume Mars determines that the ending inventory is $3 500. With this information and the account balances in the adjusted trial balance, Mars's financial statements are developed. The statement of profit or loss, the statement of changes in equity, and the statement of financial position for Mars are given in Table 4-13.

Table 4-13　Mars Financial Statements

Statement of Profit or Loss		
(For the Month Ended June 30, 20×1)		
Sales		$25 000
Cost of goods sold:		
Beginning inventory	$ 0	
Purchase	18 000	
Less: Ending inventory	(3 500)	(14 500)
Gross profit		$10 500
Expenses:		
Wage expense	$1 400	
Utility expense	300	
Rent Expense	1 000	
Depreciation expense	500	(3 200)
Income before taxes		$7 300
Income tax expense		(700)
Net income		$6 600

	Common Stock	Retained Earnings	Total
Balance, June 1, 20×1	$0	$0	$0
Sales of common stock	30 000		30 000
Net income		6 600	6 600
Dividend		(400)	(400)
Balance, June 30, 20×1	$30 000	$6 200	$36 200

(continued)

Statement of Financial Position

(June 30, 20 × 1)

Assets

Current assets		
Cash		$ 24 500
Accounts receivable		3 000
Inventory		3 500
Prepaid rent		11 000
Total current assets		$ 42 000
Property, plant and equipment		
Furniture	$ 24 000	
Less: Accumulated depreciation	(500)	
Property, plant and equipment		23 500
Total assets		$ 65 500

Liabilities and owner's equity

Current liabilities		
Accounts payable		$ 28 000
Wages payable		600
Income tax payable		700
Total current liabilities		$ 29 300
Owner's equity		
Common stock (3 000 shares; $ 10 par value)	$ 30 000	
Retained earnings	6 200	36 200
Total liabilities and owner's equity		$ 65 500

4.2.4 Close Temporary Accounts

The accounts of an entity are divided into two categories: permanent accounts and temporary accounts. Balance sheet accounts are called permanent accounts because their period-ending balances are carried forward to the next accounting period. Alternately, revenue, expense, and dividend accounts are referred to as temporary accounts because they begin each new accounting period with zero balance. These temporary accounts all affect the balance of one permanent account: Retained Earnings.

Closing entries are designed to transfer the amounts stored in the temporary accounts to Retained Earnings. An Income Summary account, also a temporary account, is used to channel the balances of all temporary accounts into the Retained Earnings account through closing entries.

There are four closing entries that entities make at the end of an accounting period:

1. transfer credit balances of income statement accounts to the Income Summary account;

2. transfer debit balances of income statement accounts to the Income Summary account;

3. transfer the balance of Income Summary account to the Retained Earnings account;

4. transfer the balance of the Dividends account to the Retained Earnings account.

Normally the closing process only takes place at the end of the entity's fiscal year but for illustrative purposes, it is assumed that Mars closes its books at the end of each month.

Table 4-14 presents the closing entries for Mars at June 30, 20×1.

Table 4-14　Mars General Journal-Closing Entries

General Journal					
Date		Descriptions	PR	Debit	Credit
June	30	Sales	501	25 000	
		Income Summary	550		25 000
		To close the revenue account			
	30	Income Summary	550	18 400	
		Inventory①	105	3 500	
		Purchases	502		18 000
		Wages Expense	505		1 400
		Rent Expense	506		1 000
		Depreciation Expense	508		500
		Utility Expense	510		300
		Income Tax Expense	520		700
		To close the expense account			
	30	Income Summary	550	6 600	
		Retained Earnings	305		6 600
		To close Income Summary and trans-			
		fer net income to Retained Earnings			
	30	Retained Earnings	305	400	
		Dividends	401		400
		To close the dividends account			

①销货成本＝期初存货＋本期购进－期末存货,所以期末存货在分录中与其他费用方向相反。参见第 2 部分第 5 章有关存货的处理。此外,部分教科书把期末存货的处理作为调整事项,本书作结账分录处理。

The closing entries then are posted to general ledgers. After the closing entries are recorded and posted, Mars produces the post-closing trial balance. This is left as an exercise for the reader, and you should obtain total debits and credits equaling $66 000.

▶ 核心词汇 Core Words and Expressions

account　账户

accounting equation　会计等式、会计平衡式

accrual　应计

accrued asset　应计资产

accrued liability　应计负债

accumulated depreciation　累计折旧

adjusted trial balance　调整后的试算平衡表

adjusting entry　调整分录

allowance for doubtful accounts　坏账准备

cash dividend　现金股利

closing entry　结账分录

common stock　普通股

contra account　抵减账户

credit　贷项;信贷

debit 借项；借方；记入借方的款项

deferral 递延

deferred expense 待摊费用

deferred revenue 递延收入

depreciation 折旧

dividend 股利

double-entry bookkeeping system 复式记账

entry 分录

Income Summary account 本年利润账户

journal 日记账

ledger 分类账

par value 面值

permanent account 永久性账户

post 过账

post-closing trial balance 结账后试算平衡表

sales discount 销售折扣

sales returns and allowances 销售退回与折让

salvage value 残值

temporary account 暂时性账户

trial balance 试算平衡表

T-account T型账户

unearned revenue 预收收入

valuation adjustments 计价调整

▶ 知识扩展 More Knowledge

本章涉及的账户列表（Chart of accounts）

101 Cash 现金

102 Accounts Receivable 应收账款

105 Inventory 存货

126 Prepaid Rent 预付租金

150 Furniture 家具（固定资产）

151 Accumulated Depreciation 累计折旧

201 Accounts Payable 应付账款

205 Wages Payable 应付工资

208 Income Tax Payable 应交所得税

301 Common Stock 普通股股本

305 Retained Earnings 留存收益

401 Dividends 分配股利

501 Sales 销售收入

502 Purchases 采购

505 Wages Expense 工资费用

506 Rent Expense 租金费用

508 Depreciation Expense 折旧费用

510 Utility Expense 公用事业费用

520 Income Tax Expense 所得税费用

550 Income Summary 损益汇总（本年利润）

会计账簿的分类

会计账簿按用途可以分为以下3种。

1. 序时账簿

序时账簿又称日记账，是按照经济业务发生或完成时间的先后顺序逐日逐笔进行登记的账簿。在我国，大多数单位一般只设现金日记账和银行存款日记账。

2. 分类账簿

分类账簿是对全部经济业务事项按照会计要素的具体类别而设置的分类账户进行登记的账簿。分类账簿按照反映的经济业务详细程度不同：按照总分类账户分类登记经济业务事项的是总分类账簿，简称总账；按照明细分类账户分类登记经济业务事项的是明细分类账簿，简称明细账。

3. 备查账簿

备查账簿简称备查簿，是对某些在序时账簿和分类账簿等主要账簿中都不予登记或登记不够详细的经济业务事项进行补充登记时使用的账簿。

我国常用的账务处理程序

我国常用的账务处理程序主要有：记账凭证账务处理程序、汇总记账凭证账务处理程序、科目汇总表账务处理程序等。

1. 记账凭证账务处理程序

记账凭证账务处理程序是指对发生的经济业务事项，都要根据原始凭证或汇总原始凭证编制记账凭证，然后直接根据记账凭证逐笔登记总分类账的一种账务处理程序。它是基本的账务处理程序，其一般程序是：

（1）根据原始凭证编制汇总原始凭证；（2）根据原始凭证或汇总原始凭证，编制记账凭证；（3）根据收款凭证、付款凭证逐笔登记现金日记账和银行存款日记账；（4）根据原始凭证、汇总原始凭证和记账凭证，登记各种明细分类账；（5）根据记账凭证逐笔登记总分类账；（6）期末，现金日记账、银行存款日记账和明细分类账的余额同有关总分类账的余额核对相符；（7）期末，根据总分类账和明细分类账的记录，编制会计报表。

记账凭证账务处理程序简单明了，易于理解，总分类账可以较详细地反映经济业务的发生情况。其缺点是：登记总分类账的工作量较大。该财务处理程序适用于规模较小、经济业务量较少的单位。

2. 汇总记账凭证账务处理程序

汇总记账凭证账务处理程序是根据原始凭证或汇总原始凭证编制记账凭证，定期根据记账凭证分类编制汇总收款凭证、汇总付款凭证和汇总转账凭证，再根据汇总记账凭证登记总分类账的一种账务处理程序。其一般程序是：（1）根据原始凭证编制汇总原始凭证；（2）根据原始凭证或汇总原始凭证，编制记账凭证；（3）根据收款凭证、付款凭证逐笔登记现金日记账和银行存款日记账；（4）根据原始凭证、汇总原始凭证和记账凭证，登记各种明细分类账；（5）根据各种记账凭证编制有关汇总记账凭证；（6）根据各种汇总记账凭证登记总分类账；（7）期末，现金日记账、银行存款日记账和明细分类账的余额同有关总分类账的余额核对相符；（8）期末，根据总分类账和明细分类账的记录，编制会计报表。

汇总记账凭证账务处理程序减轻了登记总分类账的工作量，便于了解账户之间的对应关系。其缺点是：按每一贷方科目编制汇总转账凭证，不利于会计核算的日常分工，当转账凭证较多时，编制汇总转账凭证的工作量较大。该财务处理程序适用于规模较大、经济业务较多的单位。

3. 科目汇总表账务处理程序

科目汇总表账务处理程序又称记账凭证汇总表账务处理程序，它是根据记账凭证定期编制科目汇总表，再根据科目汇总表登记总分类账的一种账务处理程序。其一般程序是：（1）根据原始凭证编制汇总原始凭证；（2）根据原始凭证或汇总原始凭证编制记账凭证；（3）根据收款凭证、付款凭证逐笔登记现金日记账和银行存款日记账；（4）根据原始凭证、汇总原始凭证和记账凭证登记各种明细分类账；（5）根据各种记账凭证编制科目汇总表；（6）根据科目汇总表登记总分类账；（7）期末，现金日记账、银行存款日记账和明细分类账的余额同有关总分类账的余额核对相符；（8）期末，根据总分类账和明细分类账的记录，编制会计报表。

科目汇总表账务处理程序减轻了登记总分类账的工作量，并可做到试算平衡，简明易懂，方便易学。其缺点是：科目汇总表不能反映账户对应关系，不便于查对账目。它适用于经济业务较多的单位。

▶ 问答题 Questions

1. Under double-entry accounting, what are the debit/credit relationships of accounts?

2. Give an example of a transaction that results in:

   (a) A decrease in an asset and a decrease in a liability.

   (b) A decrease in one asset and an increase in another asset.

   (c) A decrease in one liability and an increase in another liability.

3. Name the accounts debited and credited for each of the following transactions.

   (a) Billing a customer for work done.

   (b) Receipt of cash from customer on account.

   (c) Purchase of office supplies on account.

   (d) Purchase of 10 gallons of gasoline for the delivery truck.

4. What are adjusting entries and why are they necessary?

5. Employees are paid every Saturday for the preceding work week. If a statement of financial position is prepared on Thursday, December 31, what does the amount of wages earned during the first four days of the week represent? Explain.

6. Give three common examples of contra accounts. Explain why contra accounts are used.

7. What are closing entries and why are they necessary?

▶ 练习题 Exercises

Exercise 1

Lydia Service Shop had the following transactions during the first month of business.

Aug. 2 Invested $12 000 cash and $2 500 of equipment in the business.

7 Purchased supplies on account for $400. (Debit asset account.)

12 Performed services for clients, for which $1 300 was collected in cash and $670 was billed to the clients.

15　Paid August rent ＄600.

19　Counted supplies and determined that only ＄270 of the supplies purchased on August 7 are still on hand.

Instructions

Journalize the transactions.

Exercise 2

On July 1, 20×5, Blair Co. pays ＄18 000 to Bush Insurance Co. for a 3-year insurance contract. Both companies have fiscal years ending December 31.

Instructions

1. For Blair Co. journalize the entry on July 1 and the adjusting entry on December 31.

2. Journalize the entry on July 1 and the adjusting entry on December 31 for Bush Insurance Co. Bush uses the accounts Unearned Insurance Revenue and Insurance Revenue.

Exercise 3

Greens Co. uses the following account titles: Service Revenue, Accounts Receivable, Interest Expense, Interest Payable, Salaries Expense, Salaries Payable, Allowance for Doubtful Accounts, and Bad Debt Expense.

Instructions

Prepare the following adjusting entries at December 31 for Greens.

(a) Interest on notes payable of ＄400 is accrued.

(b) Fees earned but unbilled total ＄1 400.

(c) Salaries earned by employees of ＄700 have not been recorded.

(d) Bad debt expense for year is ＄900.

Exercise 4

Sparkie has year-end account balances of Sales ＄828 900; Interest Revenue ＄13 500; Cost of Goods Sold ＄556 200; Operating Expenses ＄189 000; Income Tax Expense ＄35 100; and Dividends ＄18 900.

Instructions

Prepare the year-end closing entries.

Exercise 5

The journal entries below are subtracted from Mar's book.

1	Cash	400	
	Accounts Receivable		400
2	Accounts Payable	100	
	Inventory		100
3	Cash	7 000	
	Loan Payable		7 000

4	Cash	200	
	Accounts Receivable	700	
	Sales		900
	Cost of Goods Sold	600	
	Inventory		600
5	Prepaid Insurance	200	
	Cash		200
6	Wages payable	130	
	Wages Expense	75	
	Cash		205

Instructions

For each of the journal entries above, write a description of the underlying event.

Financial Accounting
财务会计

02

Current Assets

流动资产

◎ 小案例 Mini Case

Olin Company currently makes only cash sales. Given the number of potential customers who have requested to buy on credit, Olin is considering allowing credit sales. What factors should Olin consider in making the decision whether to allow credit sales? Many companies are changing to the LIFO inventory method to save taxes in the current years while most countries around the world do not allow use of the LIFO method. Should Olin make a change to LIFO? What factors should be considered?

正文 Text

In most countries, non-current and current assets are presented as separate headings in the statement of financial position. An asset should be classified as a current asset when it:

- is expected to be realized in or is held for sale or consumption in the normal course of the enterprise's operating cycle; or
- is held primarily for trading purposes or for the short-term and expected to be realized within 12 months of the reporting date; or
- is cash or cash equivalent asset which is not restricted in its use.

The main items of current assets are cash, current receivables and inventories.

5. 1 Cash and Current Receivables

5. 1. 1 Composition of Cash

Cash is the most liquid of current assets and consists of those items that serve as a medium of exchange and provide a basis for accounting measurement. Cash comprises cash on hand and demand deposits. That is coin and currency on hand and unrestricted funds available on deposit in a bank. Petty cash funds are also items commonly reported as cash. Some items like postage stamps, postdated checks, IOUs should not be reported as cash. A credit balance in the cash account resulting from the issuance of checks in excess of the amount on deposit is known as a cash overdraft and should be reported as a current liability.

In addition, many companies report investments in very short-term and interest-earning securities as cash equivalents. Cash equivalents are short-term, highly liquid investments that are readily convertible to known amounts of cash and which are subject to an insignificant risk of changes in value. They are not held for investment or other long-term purposes, but rather to meet short-term cash commitments. An investment's maturity date should normally be three months from its acquisition date. Therefore, equity investments (i. e. shares in other companies) are not cash equivalents. An exception would be where redeemable preference shares were acquired with a very close redemption date.

5. 1. 2　Control of Cash

Because cash is the most liquid asset, it is particularly susceptible to theft or fraud unless properly safeguarded. In general, systems of cash control deny access to the accounting records to those who handle cash. This reduces the possibility of improper entries to conceal the misuse of cash receipts and cash payments. Cash payments should never be made out of cash receipts. Payments should be made by check with the exception for small ones from petty cash fund.

In recording the establishment of petty cash fund, petty cash is debited and cash is credited. The cash is then turned over to some person who is solely responsible for payments made out of the fund. Whenever the amount of cash in the fund runs low and also at the end of each accounting period, the fund is replenished by writing a check equal to the payments made. In recording replenishment, expenses and other proper accounts are debited for payments from petty cash and cash is credited. When the fund fails to balance, an adjustment is usually made to "Cash Short and Over" account. Unless theft is involved, this will usually involve only a nominal amount arising from errors in making changes.

5. 1. 3　Bank Reconciliation

A bank reconciliation is a comparison of a bank statement (sent monthly, weekly or even daily by the bank) with the cash book (the record of how much a company believes that it has in the bank). Differences between the balance on the bank statement and the balance in the cash book will be errors or timing differences and they should be identified and satisfactorily explained.

Several common types of differences arise in the following situations:

- Deposit in transit. A deposit made near the end of the month and recorded on the cash book is not received by the bank in time to be reflected on the bank statement.
- Outstanding checks. Checks written near the end of the month have reduced the cash balance in the cash book but have not cleared by the bank as of the bank statement date.
- Bank service charges or bank interest. The bank might deduct charges for interest on an overdraft or for its services and note the amount on the bank statement.
- Deposits made directly by the bank. A bank often acts as a collection agency for its customers on items such as notes receivable.

In preparing a bank reconciliation it is good practice to begin with the balance shown by the bank statement and end with the balance shown by the cash book. It is this corrected cash book balance that will appear in the statement of financial position as "cash at bank".

5.1.4　Classifications of Receivables

In classifying receivables, an important distinction is made between trade and other receivables. Trade receivables, generally the most significant category of receivables, result from the normal operating activities of a company, that is, credit sales of goods or services to customers. Trade receivables may be evidenced by a formal written promise to pay and classified as notes receivables. Other or nontrade receivables are due from anyone else owing money to the company. They arise from a variety of transactions, such as dividends and interest receivables and deposits to guarantee contract performance.

Another way of classifying receivables relates to the current versus non-current nature of receivables. For classification purposes, all trade receivables are considered current receivables while other receivables require separate analysis to determine whether they can be collected within one year or an operating cycle, whichever is longer.

5.1.5　Valuation of Trade Receivables: Accounting for Bad Debts

A bad debt is a debt which is not expected to be paid. Customers who buy goods on credit might fail to pay for them perhaps out of dishonesty or because they have gone bankrupt and cannot pay. Because of the risks involved in selling goods on credit, it might be accepted that a certain percentage of outstanding debts at any time are unlikely to be collected. An allowance for doubtful accounts is just the estimate of the percentage of debts which are not expected to be paid.

The value of trade receivables in the statement of financial position must be shown after deducting the allowance for doubtful accounts. This is because the net realizable value of all the receivables of the company is estimated to be less than their sales value. Such an allowance for doubtful accounts is an example of the prudence concept.

When an allowance is first made, the amount of this initial allowance is charged as an expense in the income statement for the period in which the allowance is created. When an allowance already exists but is subsequently increased in size, the amount of the increase in allowance is charged as an expense in the related income statement. However, when an allowance is subsequently reduced in size, the amount of the decrease in allowance is recorded as an item of income in the income statement for the period in which the reduction in allowance is made.

The estimate for bad debts may be based on sales for the period or the amount of trade receivables outstanding at the end of the period. When a sales basis is used, the amount of bad debts in past years relative to total sales (or net credit sales) provides a percentage of estimated bad debts. For example, if 2% of sales are considered doubtful in terms of collection and sales for the period are $100 000, the charge for bad debts expense would be 2% of the current period's sales, i. e. $2 000. In practice companies may base their estimates on a percentage of total trade receivables outstanding. This method emphasizes the relation between the trade receivables and the allowance for doubtful accounts balances. For example, if total trade receivables are $50 000 and it is estimated that 3% of those accounts will be uncollectible, then the allowance account should have a balance of $1 500. The most commonly used method for establishing an allowance based on outstanding receivables involves aging receivables. Individual accounts are analyzed to determine those not yet due and those past due. Past-due accounts are classified in terms of the length of the period past due. A series of estimated loss percentages can be developed and applied to the different receivables classifications. The aging method brings the allowance account to the required balance just with the previous method based on a percentage of total receivables outstanding.

5. 2　Inventory

5. 2. 1　Classifications of Inventory

Inventories are assets that are held for sale in the ordinary course of business in the process of production for such sale, or in the form of materials or supplies to be consumed in the production process or in the rendering of services. Inventories can include any of the following:

- Goods purchased and held for resale, e. g. goods held for sale by a retailer, or land and buildings held for resale by a real estate concern.
- Finished goods produced.
- Work in progress being produced.
- Materials and supplies awaiting use in the production process (raw materials).

A service company generally doesn't have a physical inventory that is material. However, it often has an inventory of services that it has provided but not yet billed. For example, a company that provides consulting services will pay its employees each period but may only bill its services when certain contract stages are reached. The company has an inventory of "unbilled services provided".

5.2.2　Inventory Systems

A company may account for inventory quantities and costs using the perpetual system or the periodic system.

Under perpetual system, a continuous record of physical quantities in inventory is maintained. It records the purchase, production and use of each item of inventory in detailed subsidiary records, although often only in units without including costs. It should take a physical count at least once a year to confirm the balance in the inventory account. Differences between physical count and inventory account balance resulting from errors in recording, waste and theft etc. should be adjusted whether to increase cost of sales or to recognize a loss.

Under periodic system, it takes physical counts periodically without a continuous record of physical quantities or costs of inventory held. It is at the physical count that physical quantities on hand, quantities used or sold during the period will be determined. In the periodic system a company typically does not record the costs of acquisitions of inventory in an inventory account but in a temporary account, Purchases, while the opening inventory cost remains in inventory account.

5.2.3　Measurement of Inventories

Inventories should be measured at the lower of cost and net realizable value. There are three issues in the measurement of inventories.

The **cost of inventory** includes costs directly or indirectly incurred in bringing an item to its present condition and location. The cost of purchased inventory should include purchase price (net of trade discounts, rebates and other similar amounts) plus any other cost directly attributable to acquisition, such as import duties and other taxes, transport, handling, insurance and similar costs. When a company manufactures inventory, costs of inventory consist of two main parts, costs directly related to the units of production, e.g. direct materials, direct labor and fixed and variable production overheads that are incurred in converting materials into finished goods, allocated on a systematic basis. Fixed production overheads are those indirect costs of production that remain relatively constant regardless of the volume of production, e.g. machinery depreciation, cost of factory management and administration. Variable production overheads are those indirect costs of production that vary directly or nearly directly with the volume of production, e. g. indirect materials and labor (overtime premium). Any other costs should only be recognized if they are incurred in bringing the inventories to their present condition and location. Under IAS 2, some types of cost would not be included in the cost of inventories. Instead they should be recognized as an expense in the period they are incurred, for example, abnormal amounts of wasted materials, labor or other production costs, storage costs (except costs which are necessary in the production process before a further production stage), administrative overheads not incurred in bringing inventories to their present condition and location and selling costs.

There are two techniques mentioned by IAS 2 to measure inventory cost and both of which may be used for convenience.

- Standard costs are set up to take account of normal production values involving amount of raw materials used, labor time etc. They are reviewed and revised on a regular basis.

- Retail method is often used in retail industry where there is a large turnover of inventory items, which have similar profit margins. The only practical method of inventory valuation may be to take the total selling price of inventories and deduct an overall average profit margin, thus reducing the value to an approximation of cost. The percentage will take account of reduced price lines with different percentage for different department.

For financial statement purposes, a company must attach costs to inventory items. The cost of opening inventory is the beginning balance in inventory account. Such cost plus the cost of purchases or production (discussed earlier) is allocated between cost of sales (or issues of materials) and closing inventory by means of a **cost flow assumption**. The major cost flow assumptions currently used are specific identification; first-in, first-out (FIFO); average cost and last-in, first-out (LIFO). Different cost flow assumptions will provide different profit figures. When preparing financial statements, FIFO or average cost is normally expected to use. IAS 2 does not permit the use of LIFO. However, all of the four should be known for differences between them.

- Specific identification. Specific costs should be attributed to individual items of inventory when they are segregated for a specific project, but not where inventories consist of a large number of interchangeable (i. e. identical or very similar) items. In the latter circumstances, one of two approaches (i. e. FIFO or average cost) may be taken.

- FIFO assumes that materials are issued out of inventory in the order in which they were delivered into inventory, i. e. issues are priced at the cost of the earliest delivery remaining in inventory.

- Average cost. As purchase prices change with each new batch, the average price of inventories is constantly changing. A weighted average price for all units in inventory is calculated. Issues are priced at this average cost and the balance of inventory remaining would have the same unit valuation. A new weighted average price is calculated whenever a new delivery of materials into store is received. Therefore, a recalculation can be made after each purchase (moving or cumulative weighted average) or alternatively only at the end of the period.

- LIFO assumes that materials are issued out of inventory in the reverse order to which they are delivered, i. e. most recent deliveries are issued before earlier ones and are priced accordingly.

As a general rule assets should not be carried at amounts greater than those expected to be realized from their sale or use. In the case of inventories this amount could fall below cost when items are damaged or become obsolete, or where the costs to completion have increased in order to make the sale. IAS 2 governs the accounting treatment of inventory, i. e. inventories should be valued at cost, or if lower, net realizable value. Therefore, historical cost is the normal basis of inventory valuation. The only time when historical cost is not used is in the exceptional cases where the prudence concept requires a lower value to be used.

Inventories might be valued at their expected selling price, less any costs still to be incurred in getting them ready for sale and then selling them. This amount is referred to as the **net realizable value** (**NRV**) of the inventories. NRV is likely to be less than cost in the following situations:

- an increase in costs or a fall in selling price;
- a physical deterioration in the condition of inventory;
- obsolescence of products;
- a decision as part of the company's marketing strategy to manufacture and sell products at a loss.

The reason why inventory is held must be taken into account. Some inventory may be held to satisfy a firm contract and its NRV will therefore be the contract price. Any additional inventory of the same type held at the period end will be assessed according to general sales prices when NRV is estimated. Comparison of cost and NRV normally is performed on an item by item basis but similar or related items may be grouped together. This grouping together is acceptable for items in the same product line but it is not acceptable to write down inventories to NRV based on a whole classification (e. g. finished goods) or a whole company. At the end of each period NRV must be reassessed and compared again with cost. If the NRV has risen for inventories held over the end of more than one period, then the previous write-down must be reversed to the extent that the inventory is then valued at the lower of cost and the new NRV. This may be possible when selling prices have fallen in the past and then risen again.

▶ 核心词汇 Core Words and Expressions

administrative overhead　管理间接成本

aging receivable　应收账款账龄分析

allowance for doubtful accounts　坏账准备

average cost　平均成本法

bad debt　坏账

bank reconciliation　银行存款余额调节表

bank statement　银行对账单

cash book　现金账

cash equivalents　现金等价物

cash on hand　库存现金

cash short and over　现金尾差；现金短溢

cost flow assumption　成本流转假设

count　盘存、盘点

demand deposit　活期存款

deposit in transit　在途存款

deposit to guarantee contract performance　合同履
　行保证金

direct labor　直接人工

direct material　直接材料

dividends receivable　应收股利

equity investment　权益投资

finished goods　产成品

first-in, first-out（FIFO）　先进先出法

fixed production overhead　固定制造费用

import duty　进口税金

interest receivable　应收利息

International Accounting Standard 2—Inventories
　（IAS 2）　国际会计准则第 2 号——存货

IOU（I Owe You）　借据

last-in, first-out（LIFO）　后进先出法

lower of cost and net realizable value　成本与可变

现净值孰低

maturity date　到期日

moving or cumulative weighted average　移动加权
　平均值

net realizable value　可变现净值

notes receivable　应收票据

overdraft　银行透支

overtime premium　加班津贴

past due　过期

periodic system　定期盘存制

perpetual system　永续盘存制

petty cash fund　备用金

prudence concept　谨慎性原则

raw material　原材料

rebate　回扣

redeemable preference shares　可赎回优先股

retail method　零售价格法

reverse　转回

selling cost　销售费用

specific identification　个别认定法

standard cost　标准成本

subsidiary record　明细记录

supplies　物料；价值较低的材料、工具；也指
　文具、纸张等办公用品

trade discount　商业折扣

trade receivable　应收账款，有时也称 accounts
　receivable

variable production overhead　变动制造费用

work in progress　在产品

write down　减记

▶ 知识扩展 More Knowledge

　　根据 IFRS 9（International Financial Reporting Standards 9—Financial instruments，国际财务报告准则第 9 号——金融工具），现金与应收款项均归属于金融资产。

应收账款控制与融资

应收账款控制与融资在为新客户或现有客户制定信用额度前应对企业客户进行评价，通常可以利用"5C"系统进行。"5C"即评估客户信用特征的 5 个方面，包括品质（character）、能力（capacity）、资本（capital）、抵押（collateral）和条件（conditions）。品质：客户的信誉，即履行偿债义务的可能性，企业必须设法了解客户历史的付款记录，了解是否有拖欠的不良记录。能力：客户的偿债能力，包括流动资产的数量和质量以及与流动负债的比例。观察客户的经济状况，尤其关注客户的现金流状况，看其是否有足够的现金支付能力。资本：客户的财务状况和支付能力。通过客户的审计报告、会议纪要等，洞察报表数字后面的隐含因素，调查是否有被抵押和冻结的资产。抵押：客户拒付欠款或无力偿债时能被用以作抵押的资产的数量和质量。条件：可能影响客户付款能力的经济环境。了解社会中介机构对客户的评价，调查客户所在行业的发展趋势和变化政策。根据以上 5 项特性，给客户划定不同的等级，不同的等级给予不同的授信额度。

应收账款保理业务（factoring）是一种金融业务或产品：企业把由于赊销而形成的应收账款有条件地转让给保理商（如银行），保理商为企业提供资金，并负责管理、催收应收账款和坏账担保等业务，企业可借此收回账款，加快资金周转。

资产证券化

资产证券化是资产发起人将缺乏流动性但可预见未来现金流入的资产进行组合，构造和转变成资本市场可销售和流通的金融产品的过程。应收账款证券化的运作方式是先将达到一定金额的若干小额债权集中，交由信托投资机构之类的特殊目的公司（special purpose vehicle，SPV）保管，然后评估等级并由保管者代为发行证券。证券出售后有关旧债权本息的收取、提前偿还的手续、余款的再投资以及新债务的还本付息等，一律由中介机构承办。

▶ **问答题** Questions

1. Describe the methods for establishing and maintaining an allowance for doubtful accounts?

2. In accounting for uncollectible accounts receivable, why is the allowance method, rather than the direct write-off method, required by IFRS?

3. Why is cash on hand both necessary and yet potentially unproductive?

4. Give at least four common sources of differences between the balance on the bank statement and the balance in the cash book?

5. What are the major advantages in using petty cash funds?

6. General Motors' finished goods inventory is composed primarily of automobiles. Are automobiles always classified as "inventory" on the statements of financial position of all companies? Explain.

7. Which better matches the normal physical flow of goods—FIFO or LIFO? Which better matches current costs and current revenues?

8. Why are LIFO and average cost more complicated with a perpetual inventory system than with a periodic system?

9. What differences result from applying lower of cost or net realizable value to individual inventory items instead of to the inventory as a whole?

10. Suppose a company has four items of inventory on hand at the end of its accounting period. Their cost and NRVs are as follows:

Inventory item	Cost	NRV
1	$ 27	$ 32
2	14	8
3	43	55
4	29	40

Determine the value of inventory on the statement of financial position.

11. What amount will be included in "cash and cash equivalents"?

Investment in shares of a public company	$ 12 000
Treasury bills maturing in 30 days	18 000
Bonds of a publicly traded company	10 000
Two-month U. S. dollar term deposits	24 000

12. Philip Corp reported credit sales of $ 240 000 and write-offs of bad debts of $ 57 000 for last year. Accounts receivable had a balance of $ 1 127 000 at the beginning of the year and $ 881 000 at the end of the year. How much cash was collected from customers during the year?

13. Lee Limited began operations on January 1, 20 × 1. The following data relate to the company's first 2 years in business:

Inventory	Reported Amount	Correct Amount
December 31, 20 × 1	25 000	20 000
December 31, 20 × 2	35 000	30 000
Cost of goods sold		
For 20 × 1	400 000	??
For 20 × 2	450 000	??

What is the correct cost of goods sold for 20 × 2?

14. Explain how a manufacturing company can manipulate earnings by including non-production costs in inventories.

▶ 练习题 Exercises

Exercise 1

Accounts receivable of Magily Company on December 31, 20 × 2, had a balance of $ 300 000. Allowance for Doubtful Accounts had a $ 4 200 debit balance. Sales in 20 × 2 were $ 1 690 000 less sales discounts of $ 14 000.

Instructions

Give the adjusting entry for estimated Bad Debt Expense under the following independent assumptions.

1. Of 20 × 2 net sales, 1.5% will probably never be collected.

2. Of outstanding accounts receivable, 3% are doubtful.

3. An aging schedule shows that $ 11 000 of the outstanding accounts receivable are doubtful.

Exercise 2

The accounting department supplied the following data in recording the September 30 bank statement for Rytton, Inc.

Closing cash balance per bank statement	**$ 15 496. 91**
Closing cash balance per cash book	14 692. 71
Deposits in transit	2 615. 23
Bank service charge	25. 00
Outstanding checks	3 079. 51
Note collected by bank including $ 45 interest (Rytton not yet notified)	1 045. 00
Error by bank-check drawn by Rytton Corp. was charged to Rytton's account	617. 08

A sale and deposit of $ 1 729. 00 was entered in the sales journal and cash receipts journal as $ 1 792. 00.

Instructions

Prepare the September 30 bank reconciliation.

Exercise 3

Pomegranite Company's bank balance on its October 31, 20 ×2 bank statement was $ 11 500. Pomegranite's accountant was preparing a bank reconciliation and determined that three checks issued by Pomegranite to its suppliers for a total of $ 6 500 had not yet cleared by the bank. Also, a deposit for $ 700 made by Pomegranite on October 31 did not appear on the bank statement. Bank service charges of $ 240 appear on the bank statement, but have not yet been recorded in the cash book.

Instructions

Given the above information, prepare a bank reconciliation to determine the correct cash balance that should be reflected in Pomegranite's cash book at October 31, 20 ×2.

Exercise 4

The Web Store shows the following information relating to one of its products.

Inventory, January 1	**300 units**	**@ $ 17. 50**
Sales, January 8	**200 units**	
Purchases, January 10	**900 units**	**@ $ 18. 00**
Sales, January 18	**800 units**	
Purchases, January 20	**1 200 units**	**@ $ 19. 50**
Sales, January 25	**1 000 units**	

Instructions

What are the values of closing inventory under a periodic inventory system assuming a (1) FIFO, (2) LIFO and (3) average cost flow? (Round unit cost to 3 decimal places.)

Exercise 5

Richy Corporation had the following transactions relating to Product A during September.

Date		Units	Unit cost
September 1	Opening balance	500	$ 5. 00
6	Purchase	100	4. 50
12	Sale	300	
13	Sale	200	
18	Purchase	200	6. 00
20	Purchase	200	4. 00
25	Sale	200	

Instructions

Determine the closing inventory value under a perpetual inventory system with each of the following costing methods:

1. FIFO

2. LIFO

Exercise 6

The following figures relate to inventory held at the year end.

	A	B	C
cost	$ 20	$ 9	$ 12
Selling price	30	12	22
Modification cost to enable sale	—	2	8
Marketing costs	7	2	2
Units held	200	150	300

Instructions

Determine the value of inventory held on the statement of financial position.

Investments, Plant Assets and Intangibles
投资、固定资产与无形资产

◎ 小案例 Mini Case

For the past three years Olin Company has maintained an investment in Logical Co. reflecting a 15% interest in the voting ordinary shares of Logical. On January 2 of the current year, Olin purchased an additional 10%, with the total ownership interest amounting to 25%. How does this increase in ownership affect the accounting for the investment in Logical? The president of Olin recommends that no depreciation be recorded for the current year because the depreciation rate is 5% per year and price indexes show that prices during the year have risen by more than this figure. Are the remarks of the president right?

正文 Text

6.1 Investments in Equity and Debt Securities

6.1.1 Classifications of Securities

Equity securities are any securities, such as ordinary and preferred shares that represent ownership in a company. Equity securities are attractive investments because of the potential for significant increases in the price of the security.

Debt securities are financial instruments issued by a company that typically have maturity value (representing the amount to be repaid to the debt holder at maturity), interest rate (either fixed or float) and maturity date indicating when the debt obligation will be redeemed.

For accounting purposes, IFRS 9 classifies investments in equity and debt into three categories:

- Financial assets measured at amortized cost.
- Financial assets measured at fair value through other comprehensive income (FVOCI).
- Financial assets measured at fair value through profit or loss (FVPL).

In general, IFRS 9 requires that companies determine how to measure their financial assets based on two criteria:

- The company's business model for managing its financial assets; and
- The contractual cash flow characteristics of the financial asset.

If a company has (a) a business model whose objective is to hold assets in order to collect contractual cash flows and (b) the contractual terms of the financial asset provides specified dates to cash flows that are solely payments of principal and interest on the principal amount outstanding, then the company should use amortized cost. As a result, only debt investments such as receivables, loans, and bond investments that meet the two criteria above are recorded at amortized cost. If a company's business model for debt investments is to profit from changes in value and to collect cash flows to which the company is entitled, these investments are measured at fair value through other comprehensive income. The key difference between investments measured at amortized cost and investments measured at FVOCI is the company's intent. For investments at FVOCI the company may hold the investment to maturity, but if favorable market circumstances arise in the interim, the company may elect to sell the investment at a profit. All other debt investments are recorded and reported at fair value through profit or loss. Equity investments are generally recorded and reported at fair value through profit or loss. Equity investments do not have a fixed interest or principal payment schedule and therefore cannot be accounted for at amortized cost or FVOCI. However, when an investment in an equity instrument is initially recognized, the company may make an irrevocable election to present changes in fair value in other comprehensive income, rather than profit or loss. Thus, the company may classify some investments in equity securities as at FVPL and others at FVOCI-elect.

Fair value is defined in IFRS 13 to be the price that would be received to sell an asset or paid to transfer a liability in an orderly transaction between market participants at the measurement date. Amortized cost is the initial recognition amount of the investment minus repayments, plus or minus cumulative amortization and net of any reduction for uncollectibility.

6. 1. 2　Objectives of Investment in Securities

Companies invest in the debt and equity securities of other companies for a number of reasons. Four of the more common reasons are discussed below.

- Temporary investment of surplus cash. Investing in equity and debt securities of other companies allows a firm to store its cyclical cash surplus and earn a higher rate of return than that of bank deposits by accepting a higher degree of risk.

- Investment solely for a return. Companies investing in equity and debt securities of other companies are simply to earn money (i. e. dividends and interests).

- Investment for influence. Large investments in other companies are often made for business reasons so as to exercise influence over the conduct of that company's operations, for example, to ensure a supply of raw materials or to influence the board of directors.

- Purchase for control. A company may purchase enough shares of another company to be able to control operating, investing and financing decisions. The investor (parent company) is required to prepare consolidated financial statements to report the results of its investee (subsidiary company) of which it owns more than 50% shareholdings. This issue will be more explored in Part 4.

6. 1. 3 Valuations for Investments

A company initially records each category of investments at cost and reports dividend revenue, interest revenue (using effective interest rate method) and realized gains or losses on sales in its income statement. However, the subsequent valuation of the investments on its statement of financial position and the reporting of gains or losses on remeasurement to fair value vary.

When an investor has an ownership interest of less than 20 percent, it is presumed that the investor has little or no influence over the investee. Under IFRS, the presumption is that equity investments are held for trading. That is, companies hold these securities to profit from price changes. The general accounting and reporting rule for these investments is to value the securities at fair value and record unrealized gains and losses in net income. However, some equity investments are held for purposes other than trading. For example, a company may be required to hold an equity investment in order to sell its products in a particular area. In this situation, the recording of unrealized gains and losses in income is not indicative of the company's performance with respect to this investment. As a result, IFRS allows non-trading equity investments are recorded at fair value on the statement of financial position, with unrealized gains and losses reported in other comprehensive income.

Only debt investments can be measured at amortized cost. Companies should amortize premiums or discounts using effective interest rate method. They apply the method to bond investments in a way similar to that for bonds payable. To compute interest revenue, companies compute the effective interest rate or yield at the time of investment and apply that rate to the beginning carrying amount (book value) for each interest period. The investment carrying amount is increased by the amortized discount or decreased by the amortized premium in each period. At each reporting date, debt investments at amortized cost should be reviewed for impairment. As for debt investments at

FVPL or FVOCL, companies follow the same accounting entries as debt investments held-for-collection during the reporting period. That is, they are recorded at amortized cost. However, at each reporting date, companies adjust the amortized cost to fair value, with any unrealized holding gain or loss reported as part of net income (under FVPL), or through OCI (under FVOCI). Therefore, FVPL and FVOCI have the same reporting outcomes on the statement of financial position, but they differ in the statement of comprehensive income. When a company sells investments measured at FVOCI, the total gain or loss flows through income.

6. 1. 4　Equity Method

There is a size of holding not large enough to result in control but large enough to give significant influence, as mentioned in the objectives of investments. IAS 28 lays down the rules for accounting for those investments giving influence but not control. Enterprises in which such investments are held are "associates". A holding of 20% or more of the voting power is presumed to give significant influence, unless it can be clearly demonstrated that it is not the case. A shareholding of between 20% and 50% will normally be an associate. However, the investor must actually exercise significant influence. An investment is probably an associate if the investor is represented on the Board, actually participates in major policy decisions or has material transactions with the investee. Otherwise, the investment should be accounted for as a financial asset in accordance with IFRS 9. Defined in IAS 28 a method of accounting is used to treat investments in associates, i. e. the equity method.

When a company uses the **equity method**, it initially records an investment at its acquisition cost and adjusts thereafter for the post-acquisition change in the investor's share of net assets of the associate. Assume ABC Company purchased 5 000 ordinary shares of Sun Company on January 2 at $20 per share. Sun Company has a total of 25 000 shares outstanding. Thus the 5 000 shares represent a 20% ownership interest. ABC Company can exercise significant influence on Sun Company with a consideration of all relevant factors, as well as the percentage owned. ABC Company received dividend of $0. 80 per share from Sun Company on October 31. On December 31 Sun Company announced earnings for the year of $60 000. Under equity method, ABC Company should make the following journal entries.

January 2	Investment in Sun Company share	$100 000	
	Cash		$100 000
October 31	Cash	$4 000 ($0. 80 × 5 000 shares)	
	Investment in Sun Company share		$4 000
December 31	Investment in Sun Company share	$12 000 (20% × $60 000)	
	Investment income		$12 000

6. 2　Plant Assets and Intangibles

6. 2. 1　Characteristics of Property, Plant and Equipment

Property, plant and equipment are tangible assets held by an enterprise for more than one accounting period for use in the production or supply of goods or services, for rental to others or for administrative purposes. Alternative terms are plant assets, fixed assets and operational assets. Among the most common items are land, buildings, machinery, furniture and fixtures, office equipment and delivery vehicles, etc. To be included in this group, an asset must have three characteristics.

- The asset must be held for use and not for investment. Only the assets used in the normal course of business should be included. However, the asset does not have to be used continuously. Machinery owned in case of breakdowns is included. In contrast, land or buildings held to earn rental income or for capital appreciation should not be included and should be categorized separately as an investment property.

- The asset must have an expected life of more than one year. The asset represents a stream of future services that the company will receive over the life of the asset. Benefits must extend for more than one accounting period (normally expressed in one year) or the operating cycle, whichever is longer.

- The asset must be tangible in nature. There must be a physical substance that can be seen and touched. In contrast, intangible assets such as trademarks or patents do not have a physical substance. Plant asset is also distinct from other tangible assets, such as raw materials, in that plant asset generally does not change its physical substance and is not incorporated into the product.

6. 2. 2　Depreciation, Impairment and Revaluation

An item of property, plant and equipment which qualifies for recognition as an asset should initially be measured at its cost (e. g. purchase price, the cost of site preparation, delivery costs, installation costs, etc). Subsequent expenditure on property, plant and equipment should only be capitalized if it improves the asset beyond its originally assessed standard of performance. All other subsequent expenditure should be written off as incurred. IAS 16 gives some examples of improvements, such as modification of an item of plant to extend its useful economic life, including increased capacity, upgrade of machine parts to improve the quality of output and adoption of a new production process leading to large reductions in operating costs. For example, the cost of an extension to a building should be capitalized while the cost of general repairs should be written off immediately.

It is necessary to apportion the value of an asset used in a period against the revenue it has helped to create. With the exception of land held on freehold or very long leasehold, every plant asset eventually wears out over time. A charge should be made in the income statement to reflect the use that is made of the asset by the company. This charge is called depreciation. Depreciation is the allocation of the depreciable amount of an asset over its estimated useful life. Depreciation for the accounting period is charged to net income for the period directly or indirectly. And the total accumulated depreciation builds up until the asset is fully depreciated. Depreciable amount of a depreciable asset is the historical cost or other amount substituted for historical cost in the financial statements less the estimated residual value. IAS 16 requires the depreciable amount to be allocated on a systematic basis to each accounting period during the useful life of the asset. Although some assets have increased in value over a period, it is irrelevant and depreciation should still be charged based on depreciable amount irrespective of a rise in value. There are several different methods of depreciation, i. e. straight-line method, reducing balance method and sum-of-the-year digits method. It is up to the business concerned to decide which method of depreciation to apply to its plant asset. Once that decision has been made, however, the chosen method of depreciation should be applied consistently from year to year. It is permissible for a company to depreciate different categories of plant assets in different ways. If a company owns three cars, each car would normally be depreciated in the same way (e. g. by the straight-line method); but another category of plant asset, photocopiers, might be depreciated using a different method (e. g. by the reducing balance method).

Carrying amount is the amount at which an asset is recognized after deducting any accumulated depreciation and impairment losses. Under IAS 36 recoverable amount of an asset is measured as the higher value of (a) its fair value less costs to sell and (b) value in use. Recoverable amount should be considered on an individual asset basis or for groups of identical assets. The carrying amount of an item or group of identical items of plant assets should also be reviewed periodically. This is to assess whether the recoverable amount has declined below the carrying amount. When there has been such a decline, the carrying amount should be reduced to the recoverable amount, i. e. impairment losses arising. An impairment loss should be recognized immediately as an expense in the income statement, except that an impairment loss on a revalued asset may first be offset against a revaluation surplus for the asset. Later, a justifiable reversal of impairment loss should be recognized immediately as income in the income statement (or as a revaluation increase to the extent that the original impairment had been charged against the revaluation surplus).

For each class of plant assets, an enterprise must choose between the cost model and the revaluation model. One permitted treatment in IAS 16 is that property, plant and equipment should be valued at cost less accumulated depreciation. The allowed alternative treatment is that plant asset may be carried at a revalued amount less any subsequent accumulated depreciation. If the revaluation alternative is adopted, two conditions must be complied with. Revaluations must subsequently be made with sufficient regularity to ensure that the carrying amount does not differ materially from the fair value at each reporting date. When an item of plant asset is revalued, the entire class of assets to which the item belongs must be revalued. On revaluation, the increase in carrying amount must be credited to equity under the heading of revaluation surplus reserve unless the increase reverses a previous revaluation decrease of the same asset which was recognized as an expense in the income statement. In that case, the increase is credited in the income statement. Conversely if the revaluation decreases the value of the asset, the decrease has to be recognized immediately as an expense in the income statement, unless there is a revaluation reserve representing a surplus on the same asset.

6.2.3 Characteristics of Intangible Assets

An intangible asset is an identifiable non-monetary asset without physical substance. There is generally a higher degree of uncertainty regarding the future benefits that may be derived. The value is subject to wider fluctuations because it may depend, to a considerable extent, on competitive conditions. It may have value to a particular company. And "non-monetary" feature distinguishes intangible assets from other assets without physical substance, such as accounts and notes receivable and investments in securities. So accounting practice restricts the use of the term "intangible" to such items as patents, licenses, copyrights, franchises, trademarks and trade names, etc.

IAS 38 prescribes the required accounting treatment for almost all intangible assets, including research and development activities. However, IAS 38 does not cover goodwill arising on business combinations, which is dealt with in IFRS 3 (explored in Part 4).

6.2.4 Recognition and Amortization

Intangible assets are initially recognized at cost, which could be in cash or the fair value of equity shares given in exchange. Some internally generated items may never be recognized, such as goodwill, brands, mastheads, publishing titles and customer lists.

An enterprise must assess whether the useful life of an intangible asset is finite or indefinite. An asset should be regarded as having an indefinite life if there is no foreseeable limit to the period over which the asset is expected to generate net cash inflows for the enterprise. An intangible asset with a finite useful life must be amortized over that life. Normally the straight-line method should be used with a zero residual value. An intangible asset with an indefinite useful life should not be amortized. It should be tested for impairment annually and more often if there is an actual indication of possible impairment.

6.2.5 Research and Development Costs

The main internally generated asset considered in IAS 38 is development costs. Research is original and planned investigation undertaken with the prospect of gaining new scientific knowledge and understanding. Development is the application of research findings or other knowledge to a plan or design for the production of new or substantially improved materials, devices, products, processes, systems or services before the start of commercial production or use. No intangible asset arising from research should be recognized. An intangible asset arising from development should be recognized if, and only if an enterprise can demonstrate all of the following:

- the technical feasibility of completing the intangible asset so that it will be available for use or sale;
- its intention to complete the intangible asset and use or sell it;
- its ability to use or sell the intangible asset;
- the existence of a market for the output of the intangible asset or the intangible asset itself or, if it is to be used internally, the usefulness of the intangible asset;
- its ability to measure reliably the expenditure attributable to the intangible asset during its development.

▶ 核心词汇 Core Words and Expressions

amortize 摊销

amortized cost 摊余成本

business model 业务模式

capitalize 资本化

carrying amount 账面价值

consolidated financial statements 合并财务报表

contractual cash flow 合同现金流量

control 控制

depreciable amount 应计折旧额

derecognize 终止确认

effective interest rate method 实际利率法，也称
　内含利率法

equity method 权益法

estimated residual value 预计残值

fair value 公允价值

financial asset 金融资产

financial instrument 金融工具

fixed or float interest rate 固定或浮动利率

held on freehold 拥有所有权

held on leasehold 拥有使用权

identifiable 可辨认

impairment 减值

internally generated 自创

International Accounting Standard 16—Property,

plant and equipment（IAS 16）　国际会计准则第16 号——不动产、厂场和设备

International Accounting Standard 28—Investments in associates and joint ventures（IAS 28）　国际会计准则第28 号——在联营企业和合营企业中的投资

International Accounting Standard 36—Impairment of assets（IAS 36）　国际会计准则第36 号——资产减值

International Accounting Standard 38—Intangible assets（IAS 38）　国际会计准则第38 号——无形资产

International Financial Reporting Standard 3—Business combinations（IFRS 3）　国际财务报告准则第3 号——企业合并

International Financial Reporting Standards 9—Financial instruments（IFRS 9）　国际财务报告准则第9 号——金融工具

International Financial Reporting Standards 13 Fair value measurement（IFRS 13）　国际财务报告准则第13 号——公允价值计量

investee　被投资方

investment income　投资收益

investment property 投资性房地产

ordinary shares　普通股

other comprehensive income　其他综合收益

parent company　母公司

physical substance　实物形态

recoverable amount　可收回金额

reducing balance method　余额递减折旧法

research and development costs　研究和开发支出

reserve　公积准备

revaluation surplus　重估增值

revaluation　重估

significant influence　重大影响

straight-line method　直线法或年限平均法

subsidiary company　子公司

sum-of-the-year digits method　年数总和法

surplus cash　现金盈余

value in use　使用价值

write off　核销，记为费用

▶ 知识扩展　More Knowledge

金融工具

金融工具是指形成一个企业金融资产并形成另一个企业金融负债或权益性工具的合同。

金融资产

金融资产是指下列资产：（1）现金；（2）从另一个企业收取现金或其他金融资产的合同权利；（3）在潜在有利的条件下，与另一个企业交换金融工具的合同权利；（4）另一个企业的权益性工具。国际会计准则理事会于2014 年7 月发布的IFRS 9 采用业务模式和合同现金流量特征标准，将金融资产予以分类。为切实解决我国企业金融工具相关会计实务问题、实现我国企业会计准则与国际财务报告准则的持续全面趋同，2017 年3 月31 日，财政部修订发布了《企业会计准则第22 号——金融工具确认和计量》《企业会计准则第23 号——金融资产转移》和《企业会计准则第24 号——套期保值》3 项金融工具会计准则，随后，于2017 年5 月2 日，修订发布了《企业会计准则第37 号——金融工具列报》。修订后的金融工具确认和计量准则规定以企业持有金融资产的"业务模式"和"金融资产合同现金流量特征"作为金融资产分类的判断依据，将金融资产分类为：（1）以摊余成本计量的金融资产；（2）以公允价值计量且其变动计入其他综合收益的金融资产；（3）以公允价值计量且其变动计入当期损益的金融资产，取消了贷款和应收款项、持有至到期投资和可供出售金融资产3

个原有分类，提高了分类的客观性和会计处理的一致性。

金融负债

金融负债是指属于下列合同义务的负债：（1）向另一个企业交付现金或其他金融资产的合同义务；（2）在潜在不利的条件下，与另一个企业交换金融工具的合同义务。金融负债应当在初始确认时划分为下列两类：（1）以公允价值计量且其变动计入当期损益的金融负债，包括交易性金融负债和指定为以公允价值计量且其变动计入当期损益的金融负债；（2）摊余成本计量的金融负债。

权益性工具

权益性工具是指能证明拥有某企业在减除所有负债后的资产的剩余权益的合同。

实际利率法

实际利率法是指计算金融资产或金融负债的摊余成本以及在相关期间分配利息收益或利息费用的方法。实际利率，是指将从现在开始至到期日或下一个以市场为基础的重新定价日预期会发生的未来现金支付额，精确地折现为金融资产或金融负债的当前账面净值所运用的利率。同时实际利率有时被称作是至到期日或下一个重新定价日的平均收益率，是该期间金融资产或金融负债的内含收益率。

金融资产减值

基于减值客观证据的金融资产减值处理会导致信用损失的延迟确认，且不同类别的金融资产减值模型不同，增大人为操纵空间，在 2008 年国际金融危机中被视为重大缺陷，**IFRS 9** 提供了一种全新的减值模式——预期信用损失模式，考虑包括前瞻性信息在内的各种可获得信息，不再采用"已发生损失法"。对于购入或源生的未发生信用减值的金融资产，企业应当判断**金融工具的违约风险自初始确认以来是否显著增加**：（1）如果已显著增加，企业应当采用概率加权法计算确定该金融工具在整个存续期的预期信用损失，以此确认和计提减值准备；（2）如果未显著增加，企业应当按照相当于该金融工具未来 12 个月内预期信用损失的金额确认和计提减值准备。我国修订后的金融工具确认和计量准则也对金融工具减值确认方法提出了上述要求。

投资性房地产

IAS 40（International Accounting Standard 40—Investment property，国际会计准则第 40 号——投资性房地产）指出，投资性房地产是指为赚取租金或为资本增值，或两者兼有而由业主或融资租赁的承租人持有的房地产（土地或建筑物，或建筑物的一部分，或两者兼有），但不包括：（1）用于商品或劳务的生产或供应，或用于管理目的的房地产；或（2）在正常经营过程中销售的房地产。企业可以选择公允价值模式或成本模式计量。在对投资性房地产重估价变动或公允价值变动的处理上，IAS 40 规定采用公允价值模式的房地产的公允价值变动产生的利得和损失需记录在利润表中。

▶ 问答题　Questions

1. Why might a company invest in the securities of another company?

2. Compare the fair value and equity methods of accounting for investments in shares subsequent to acquisition?

3. What criteria must be met for a security to be classified as a trading security?

4. Gift Corp. decides to construct a building for itself and plans to use existing plant facilities to assist with such construction. What costs will enter into the cost of construction?

5. What type of activities is considered to be research and development activities?

6. Under the provisions of IAS 16, what is the credit entry when noncurrent operating assets are written up to reflect an increase in market value?

7. Distinguish among depreciation and amortization expenses.

8. What factors determine the period and method for amortizing intangible assets?

9. Bear Co. purchased $ 500 000 of bonds at par. Bear management has an active trading business model for this investment. At December 31, Bear received annual interest of $ 20 000, and the fair value of the bonds was $ 470 400. In Bear Co. 's year-end statement of financial position what amount will be reported for the bond investment and how much total income/loss will be reported on its income statement?

10. Patton Company purchased $ 400 000 of 10% bonds of Scott Co. on January 1, 2017, paying $ 376 100. The bonds mature January 1, 2027; interest is payable each July 1 and January 1. The discount of $ 23 900 provides an effective yield of 11%. Patton Company uses the effective-interest method and holds these bonds for collection. What interest revenue should Patton Company report from the Scott Co. bonds for the year ended December 31, 2017?

11. Mini Corp. acquires a patent from Maxi Co. in exchange for 2 500 shares of Mini Corp. 's $ 5 par value ordinary shares and $ 75 000 cash. When the patent was initially issued to Maxi Co., Mini Corp. 's shares were selling at $ 7.50 per share. When Mini Corp. acquired the patent, its shares were selling for $ 9 a share. What amount should Mini Corp. record for the patent?

12. In January, 2012, Findley Corporation purchased a patent for a new consumer product for $ 720 000. At the time of purchase, the patent was valid for fifteen years. Due to the competitive nature of the product, however, the patent was estimated to have a useful life of only ten years. During 2017 the product was permanently removed from the market under governmental order because of a potential health hazard present in the product. What amount should Findley charge to expense during 2017, assuming amortization is recorded at the end of each year?

13. During 20 ×0, Noller Co. sold equipment that had cost $ 98 000 for $ 58 800. This resulted in a gain of $ 4 300. The balance in Accumulated Depreciation—Equipment was $ 325 000 on January 1, 20 ×0, and $ 310 000 on December 31. No other equipment was disposed of during 20 ×0. What was the Depreciation expense for 20 ×0?

14. On January 1, 20 ×1, Woon Inc. purchased equipment with a cost of HK $ 4 668 000 a useful life of 12 years and no salvage value. The company uses straight-line depreciation. At December 31, 20 ×1, the company determines that impairment indicators are present. The fair value less cost to sell the asset is estimated to be HK $ 4 620 000. The asset's value-in-use is estimated to be HK $ 4 305 000. There is no change in the asset's useful life or salvage value. What is Loss on Impairment on the 20 ×1 income statement?

▶ 练习题 Exercises ────────────────────────────────

Exercise 1

During 20 ×2, Light Company purchased trading securities as a short-term investment. The costs of the securities and their market values on December 31, 20 ×2, are listed below:

Security	Cost	Market value, December 31, 20 ×2
A	$ 65 000	$ 75 000
B	100 000	54 000
C	220 000	226 000

At the beginning of 20 ×2, Light Company had no investment in trading securities. Before any adjustments related to these trading securities, Light Company had net income of $ 300 000.

Instructions

1. What is net income after making any necessary trading security adjustments? (Ignore income taxes.)

2. What would net income be if the market value of Security B were $ 95 000?

Exercise 2

On January 10, 20 ×2, Booker Inc. acquired 16 000 shares of the outstanding common stock of Pacific Company for $ 800 000. at the time of purchase, Pacific Company had outstanding 80 000 shares with a market value of $ 4 million. On December 31, 20 ×2, the following events took place.

(a) Pacific reported net income of $ 180 000 for the year 20 ×2.

(b) Booker received from Pacific a dividend of $ 0. 75 per share of common stock.

(c) The market value of Pacific Company stock had temporarily declined to $ 40 per share.

Instructions

Prepare the entries that would be required to reflect the purchase and subsequent events on the books of Booker Inc. , assuming the equity method is appropriate.

Exercise 3

A machine is purchased at the beginning of 20 ×2 for $ 36 000. Its estimated life is 6 years. Freight costs on the machine are $ 2 000. Installation costs are $ 1 200. The machine is estimated to have a residual value of $ 500 and a useful life of 40 000 hours. It was used 6 000 hours in 20 ×2.

Instructions

1. What is the cost of the machine for accounting purposes?

2. Compute the depreciation charge for 20 × 2 using (a) the straight-line method and (b) the service-hours method.

Exercise 4

Delta Company purchased a plant building 10 years ago for $ 1 300 000 The building has been depreciated using the straight-line method with a 30-year useful life and 10% residual value. Delta's operations have experienced significant losses for the past 2 years, so Delta has decided that the building should be evaluated for possible impairment. Delta estimated that the recoverable amount of the building is $ 780 000.

Instructions

Determine whether an impairment loss should be recognized.

Exercise 5

Needle Company purchased an asset for $ 17 000 on January 2, 20 ×0. The asset has an expected residual value of $ 1 000. the depreciation expense for 20×0 and 20×1 is shown next for two alternative depreciation methods:

Year	Method A	Method B
20 ×0	$ 4 000	$ 6 400
20 ×1	4 000	4 800

Instructions

1. Which depreciation method is the company using in each example?

2. Compute the depreciation expense for 20×2 and 20×3 under each method.

Exercise 6

On January 1 , 20×0 , the Easy Corporation purchased some machinery. The machinery has an estimated life of 10 years and an estimated residual value of $ 5 000. The depreciation on this machinery was $ 20 000 in 20×2.

Instructions

Compute the acquisition cost of the equipment under the following depreciation methods:

1. Straight-line

2. Sum-of-the-years'-digits

3. Double-declining-balance

Liabilities

负 债

◎ 小案例 Mini Case

Soto Company is seeking a large bank loan for plant expansion. The bank looks very closely at the current ratio. The auditor proposes reclassifications of some items. Among these a note payable issued 4 years ago matures in 6 months from the reporting date. The auditor wants to reclassify it as a current liability. The controller says no because "we are probably going to refinance this note with other long-term debt". If you were the auditor, how would you respond to the controller?

正文 Text

7.1 Current Liabilities

Current liabilities are obligations whose liquidation is reasonably expected to require the use of existing current assets or the creation of other current liabilities within one year or an operating cycle, whichever is longer. The primary types of current liabilities are classified into three groups: current liabilities having a definite amount, current liabilities whose amounts depend on operations and current liabilities requiring amounts to be estimated. Conceptually, all liabilities should be recorded at the present value of the future outlays they will require. However, most current liabilities are measured, recorded and reported at their maturity or face value. Usually the difference between maturity value and present value is not material.

7.1.1 Current Liabilities Having a Contractual Amount

Because of the terms of contracts or the existence of laws, the amount and maturity of some current liabilities are known with reasonable certainty. Examples include trade accounts payable, notes payable, currently maturing portions of long-term debt, dividends payable and accrued liabilities etc.

Trade accounts payable arise from the purchase of inventory, supplies, or services on credit. The amount to be recorded is based on the invoice received from the creditor. Theoretically, a company should record the liability net of any cash discount. However, in practice, the liability is recorded in two ways: using the gross price method (at the invoice price) or using the net price method (at the invoice price less the cash discount). Care must be taken that end-of-year purchases and liabilities are recorded in the proper accounting period, when economic control of (and legal title to) the goods passes.

A note payable, which may be either long-term or short-term, is an unconditional written agreement to pay a sum of money to the bearer on a specific date. Notes arise out of either trade situations (the purchase of goods or services on credit) or bank borrowings. The interest inherent in a note payable may be either stated or implied in different ways. When a note is interest bearing, the principal amount (face value) recorded is the present value of the liability. Interest expense is recorded over the life of the note. When a note is non-interest-bearing, it is made out for the maturity value and discounted, and the borrower receives less than the face amount. The difference between the face amount and the amount received (the interest element or discount) is systematically recognized as interest expense over the life of the note. The discount currently remaining is deducted from Notes Payable in order to report the net amount of the current liquidation value.

A company may declare a cash dividend. When it declares a dividend it reduces retained earnings and recognizes a current liability, entitled Dividends Payable, if there is an intention to distribute the dividend in the coming year or operating cycle. The company eliminates the liability on the date of payment. Under IAS 10 dividends declared on equity instruments after the reporting date are not recognized as liabilities and dividends are debited against retained earnings as they are paid.

Unearned items (sometimes called deferred revenues) are amounts which a company has collected in advance but has not earned or recorded as revenues. Unearned items should be properly classified as current or long-term liabilities. Examples include advance collections of interest, rent, subscriptions or tickets. Such items are current unless more than one year (or one operating cycle, if longer) is required in the earning process, or if non-current assets primarily are used to earn the revenue.

7. 1. 2　Current Liabilities Whose Amounts Depend on Operations

A sales tax is levied on most goods and services. It is a form of indirect taxation imposed in many countries. Examples include Value Added Tax (VAT) and Goods & Service Tax (GST). Although it is eventually borne by the final consumer, sales tax is collected at each stage of the production and distribution chain. The majority of traders act as collection agents for the tax authorities, accounting for the tax levied on their sales (or outputs) less tax suffered on their purchases (or inputs). All taxes suffered on inputs are debited in sales tax account while all taxes charged on outputs are credited in sales tax account. The balance on the account will represent the net amount due to or from the tax authorities. As the balance on this account represents a normal trade liability, it can be included in accounts payable on the statement of financial position.

Payroll taxes are paid by both the company (employer) and employee. These withholdings are current liabilities of the employer until remitted. In most countries, the employer must also pay taxes including employer's social security and unemployment insurance taxes. Employer payroll taxes are an expense and a liability. Bonuses may be given to certain employees, particularly officers and managers, as incentives. As additional salaries, bonuses are an operating expense of the corporation and are deductible in computing taxable income. A bonus obligation is recorded as an expense and a current liability when it has been earned by the employee and is pending payment.

The income of corporations is subject to income tax separate from that of individuals. In accruing its applicable income taxes for either interim or end-of-period financial statement purposes, the corporation records a debit to Income Tax Expense and a credit to a current liability, Income Taxes Payable.

7. 1. 3　Current Liabilities Requiring Amounts to be Estimated

Product warranties require the seller, for a specified period of time after the sale, to replace faulty goods or to rectify defects. Theoretically, according to the matching principle a company estimates and records warranty expense and warranty obligation in the period of the sale. The warranty obligation is a provision as required by IAS 37, which is liability of uncertain timing or amount.

7. 2　Bonds Payable and Convertible Bonds

Companies prefer to issue debt rather than other types of securities for five basic reasons:
- Debt financing may be the only available source of funds if the company is too risky to attract equity investments.
- Debt financing may have a lower cost because of the lesser risk associated with debt investments.

- Debt financing offers an income tax advantage because the interest payments are a tax deductible expense.
- The voting privilege of shareholders is not shared with debt holders.
- Debt financing offers the opportunity for leverage.

7. 2. 1　Bonds Payable

A bond is a type of note in which a company (the issuer) agrees to pay the holder (the lender) the face value at the maturity date and usually to pay periodic interest at a specified rate (the contract rate). Companies may issue several types of bonds with different characteristics, such as:

- debenture bonds which are not secured by specific property;
- mortgage bonds which are secured by a lien against specific property of the company;
- registered bonds which require registration of ownership with the company and notification to the company in the event of transfer of ownership for interest to be paid;
- zero-coupon bonds (deep discount bonds) which pay interest only at maturity;
- callable bonds which the bondholders can be required by the company to return before the maturity date for a predetermined price and interest to date;
- convertible bonds which can be exchanged by bondholders for a predetermined number of shares;
- serial bonds which are issued at one time but which mature in installments at future dates.

When the bonds are sold, the actual rate of interest that must be paid in order to sell the bonds may be different from the contract (stated) rate because of changing market conditions. This actual rate is also called the effective rate, or yield. The selling price of the bonds is adjusted to achieve the demanded yield. If the yield and the contract rate are the same, the bonds are sold at par (their face value). If the yield demanded is greater than the contract rate, the selling price is less than the face value, and the bonds are sold at a discount. If the yield demanded is less than the contract rate, the selling price will be more than the face value, and the bonds are sold at a premium.

When a company sells bonds, it credits the face value of the bonds to a Bonds Payable account. If the bonds are sold at a premium, the company credits the premium to an account entitled Premium on Bonds Payable, an adjunct account which is shown as an addition to Bonds Payable on the company's statement of financial position. If the bonds are sold at a discount, the company debits the discount to an account entitled Discount on Bonds Payable, a contra account which is shown as a deduction from Bonds Payable on the company's statement of financial position. The book value (carrying value) of a bond issue is the face value plus any unamortized premium or minus any unamortized discount.

A company must amortize any premium or discount over the life of the bonds. IFRS 9 requires bonds payable, being financial liabilities, should be measured at amortized cost using the effective interest rate method. When the effective interest method of amortization is used, the amount of discount or premium to be amortized is determined by finding the difference between the amount of interest expense and the actual cash payment. The amount of annual interest expense is calculated by multiplying the effective interest rate (yield) times the book value of the bonds (if semiannual interest payments are made, one-half the yield is multiplied times the book value). The effective interest rate is equal to the discount rate which equates the present value of the face value of the bonds plus the present value of the future interest payments with the cash proceeds. Because the book value is the face value plus any unamortized premium or minus any unamortized discount, the book value changes with each successive premium or discount amortization and thus reflects the present value of the remaining cash interest payments plus the present value of the future principal. This is consistent with the method of determining the issuance price of the bonds by discounting the future interest payments and the future principal using the effective interest rate. A bond is issued for $ 1 000 and redeemable at $ 1 250. The term of the bond is five years and interest is paid at 5.9% per annum. The effective rate of interest on the bond can be calculated to be 10% per annum, making the present value of future payments (3.791 × $ 59 + 0.621 × $ 1 250) equal the proceeds of $ 1 000.

7.2.2　Extinguishment of Liabilities

On the maturity date, a company repays the face value of the bonds to the bondholders. By this time, the book value equals the face value because any discount or premium has been completely amortized. When bonds are to be retired at maturity, the company reclassifies the bonds as a current liability on the statement of financial position immediately before retirement. The entry to record the retirement includes a debit to Bonds Payable and a credit to Cash. Bonds may be retired prior to the scheduled maturity date either as a result of a call provision, which allows the company to recall the debt issue at a restated percentage of the face value, or by purchasing the bonds on the open market. If the debt is not replaced with another issue, the extinguishment is called a debt retirement; if the debt is replaced with another debt issue, this type of extinguishment is called a refunding. The retirement or refunding of bonds prior to maturity usually results in either a gain or loss as measured by the difference between the current book value of the bonds (plus any unamortized bond issue costs) and the call price (or market price). A company recognizes the gain or loss in the period of recall (the current period) and includes the gain or loss in its income from continuing operations for that period.

7.2.3 Convertible Bonds

A company may choose to issue bonds carrying the right, at some future time, to convert them into ordinary shares. From the lender's point of view, the idea is attractive because the conversion right can be exercised if the company prospers and the bonds retained if the company does badly. Convertible bond is a compound instrument, which has both a liability and an equity component. The economic effect of issuing convertible bonds is substantially the same as the simultaneous issue of a debt instrument with an early settlement provision and warrants to purchase shares. As required by IAS 32, convertible bonds should be included in financial statements, split between their liability component and equity component.

▶ **核心词汇** Core Words and Expressions ─────────────────

adjunct account 附属账户，附加账户

at par 平价

bonus 奖金

book value（carrying value） 账面价值

callable bonds 可提前赎回债券

cash discount 现金折扣

cash dividend 现金股利

compound instrument 混合工具

convertible bonds 可转换债券

deferred revenue 递延收入

discount rate 折现率

discount 折价

face value 面值

Goods & Service Tax（GST） 货物和劳务税

gross price method 总价法

income tax 所得税

indirect taxation 间接课税

installment 分期

interest-bearing 带息、附息

International Accounting Standard 10—Events after the reporting period（IAS10） 国际会计准则第 10 号——报告期后事项

International Accounting Standard 37—Provisions,

contingent liabilities and contingent assets（IAS 37） 国际会计准则第 37 号——准备、或有负债和或有资产

leverage 杠杆，此处指财务杠杆

lien 留置权、质权

mortgage bonds 抵押债券

net price method 净价法

notes payable 应付票据

payroll tax 工资薪金税

premium 溢价

provision 准备

retained earnings 留存收益

sales tax 销售税

social security and unemployment insurance tax 社会保障税和失业保险金

tax authorities 税务机关

tax deduction 税前抵扣

Value Added Tax（VAT） 增值税

warrant 认股权证

warranty 产品质保

yield 收益率

zero-coupon bonds（deep discount bonds） 零息债券（巨额贴现债券）

▶ 知识扩展 More Knowledge

金融负债与权益工具的区分：强制赎回的优先股

假设甲企业发行 10 年后按面值强制赎回的优先股；由于发行人存在支付现金偿还本金的合同义务，因而该优先股应分类为金融负债，相应地，该优先股股利应作为利息费用处理。

混合工具：可转换债券的列报

某企业在 20×1 年年初发行了 2 000 份可转换债券。债券期限为 3 年，按照面值平价发行（每份债券 $1 000），总计收到价款 $2 000 000。利息每年年末按照票面利率 6% 支付。每份债券到期前均可转换成 250 股普通股。债券发行时，不带转换权的类似债务的市场利率为 9%。

可转换债券的负债部分（主合同）和权益部分（嵌入衍生工具）应分开确认。先计量负债部分，再将债券发行收入与负债部分公允价值之差计入权益部分。负债部分的公允价值采用现值计量（折现率为 9%，1 年折现系数为 0.917，2 年折现系数为 0.842，3 年折现系数为 0.772）。

3 年后支付本金 $2 000 000 的现值 = 0.772 × $2 000 000 = $1 544 000

3 年内每年年末支付利息 $120 000 的现值 = (0.917 + 0.842 + 0.772) × $120 000

= $303 720

负债部分现值 = $1 544 000 + $303 720 = $1 847 720

权益部分 = $2 000 000 − $1 847 720 = $152 280

资产负债表列报（节选）如下：

权益：转换权　　　　　　　　　　　　$152 280
长期借款：可转换债券　　　　　　　　$1 847 720

▶ 问答题 Questions

1. Distinguish between current and noncurrent liabilities.

2. Define legal and nonlegal liabilities and give some examples.

3. What is meant by market rate of interest, stated or contract rate and effective or yield rate? Which of these rates changes during the lifetime of the bond issue?

4. What are the distinguishing features of convertible debt securities? What questions relate to the nature of this type of security?

5. How does the accounting for convertible debt under IAS 32?

6. The appropriate method of amortizing a premium or discount on issuance of bonds is the effective interest method. What is the effective interest method amortization and how is it different from and similar to the straight-line method of amortization?

7. On September 1, Hydra purchased $9 500 of inventory items on credit with the terms 1/15, net 30, FOB destination. Freight charges were $200. Payment for the purchase was made on September 18. Assuming Hydra uses the perpetual inventory system and the net method of accounting for purchase discounts, what amount is recorded as accounts payable from this purchase?

8. Vista newspapers sold 4 000 of annual subscriptions at $125 each on September 1. How much unearned

revenue will exist as of December 31?

9. On January 1, Martinez Inc. issued $3 000 000, 11% bonds for $3 195 000. The market rate of interest for these bonds is 10%. Interest is payable annually on December 31. Martinez uses the effective-interest method of amortizing bond premium. At the end of the first year, what amount should Martinez report for bonds payable?

10. Mann, Inc., which owes Doran Co. $600 000 in notes payable with accrued interest of $54 000, is in financial difficulty. To settle the debt, Doran agrees to accept from Mann equipment with a fair value of $570 000, an original cost of $840 000, and accumulated depreciation of $195 000. What is the gain or loss to Mann on the settlement of the debt? What is the gain or loss to Mann on the transfer of the equipment?

▶ 练习题 Exercises

Exercise 1

On December 1, 20×2, Sun Company purchased merchandise, invoice price $25 000, and issued a 12%, 120-day note to Moon Company. Sun uses the calendar year as its fiscal year and uses the periodic inventory system.

Instructions

Prepare journal entries on Sun Company's books to record the preceding information, including the adjusting entry at the end of the year and payment of the note at maturity.

Exercise 2

During August, Mountain Company had following summary transactions:

1. Cash sales of $210 000, subject to sales taxes of 6%.

2. Sales on account of $260 000, subject to sales taxes of 6%.

3. Paid the sale taxes to the tax authority.

Instructions

Prepare journal entries to record the preceding transactions.

Exercise 3

On August 1, 20×1 Apple Company had ready for sale 2 000 large scientific calculators. During the next 5 months, 1 600 calculators were sold at $460 each with a 1-year warranty. Apple Company estimated that the warranty cost on each calculator would probably average $10 per unit. In current period, Apple Company incurred warranty costs of $9 200. Cost for 20×2 were $7 000.

Instructions

Prepare journal entries for the preceding transactions, using the sales warranty accrual method.

Exercise 4

Listed below are several issuances of bonds.

(a) Company A sold 1 500 of its $1 000, 8% stated-rate bonds when the market rate was 7%.

(b) Company B sold 500 of its $2 000, 8.5% bonds to yield 9%.

(c) Company C sold 5 000 of its 12% contract-rate bonds with a stated value of $ 1 000 at an effective rate of 12%.

Instructions

In each of the above independent cases, state whether the bonds were issued at par, a premium or a discount? Explain your answers.

Exercise 5

On January 1, 20 ×1, Tree Company sold $ 100 000 of 10-year, 8% bonds at 92.5, an effective rate of 9%. Interest is to be paid on July 1 and December 31.

Instructions

Compute the premium or discount to be amortized in 20 ×1 and 20 ×2 using (a) the straight-line method and (b) the effective-interest method. Make journal entries to record the amortization when the effective-interest method is used.

Owners' Equity

所有者权益

◎ 小案例 Mini Case

Alibaba Group was established in 1999 by 18 people led by Jack Ma, a former English teacher from Hangzhou, China. On September 18 of 2014, Alibaba Group (NYSE: BABA) announced the pricing of its initial public offering (IPO) of 320 106 100 American depositary shares ("ADSs"), each representing one of its ordinary shares, at a price to the public of US $ 68 per ADS for a total offering size of approximately US $ 21. 77 billion, assuming the underwriters do not exercise their option to purchase additional ADSs. See its 2014 annual report to find more information about this IPO, and compare its equity structure in recent financial reports.

正文 Text

Businesses have two principal financing alternatives. They can raise debt capital by borrowing funds, or they can raise equity capital by selling ownership interest to outside parties. This chapter focuses on the latter one.

8. 1 Contributed Capital

8. 1. 1 Ownerships of Business Entities

In general, businesses take one of the three alternative legal forms: proprietorships, partnerships and corporations.

1. Proprietorships and Partnerships

A proprietorship is a business that is owned by one person and is not organized as a corporation. A partnership is an unincorporated association of two or more persons to carry on a business for profit as co-owners. Proprietorships and partnerships are not separate entities; they do not exist apart from the owners. And the owners are personally responsible for the liabilities of the entities. This means that the personal assets of the owner (s) are available to satisfy the claims of the business creditors. Proprietorships and partnerships are not subject to income taxes. Instead, the income is taxed as personal income of the owner (s), whether the owner (s) withdraw (s) cash from the business or not.

In case of a proprietorship, the owners' equity is reported by means of a single capital account. In a partnership, capital accounts are established for each partner. Investments by owners' are credited to Capital account. Withdraws and distributions are debited to Capital account, or to separate contra-equity accounts, closing to Capital account at the end of the accounting period.

2. Corporations

A corporation is a separate legal entity chartered (or incorporated) under laws in different jurisdiction. The ownership (or equity) of a corporation is divided into units called shares of stock, and the individuals or organizations that own these shares are called shareholders or stockholders. The advantages of corporations are:

a. Corporations are separate legal entities. This characteristic means that a corporation is responsible for its own acts and its own debts as a person. However, because a corporation is not a person, it can only through its agents, who are managers.

b. Corporations have continuity of life. A corporation's life may continue indefinitely because it is not tied to the physical lives of its owners.

c. Shareholders are not liable for the corporation's debts. This limited liability feature is a major reason why corporations are able to obtain resources from investors who are not active participants in managing the affairs of the business.

d. Stockholders are not agents of the corporation. Instead, they participate in the affairs of the corporation only by voting in the stockholders' meeting.

e. Ownership rights can be easily transferred. Also, the transfer of shares from one stockholder to another usually has no effect on the corporation or its operations[1].

There are also disadvantages to incorporating a business. The income of a corporation is taxed twice, first as income of the corporation and again as personal income to the stockholders when cash is distributed to them as dividends. Another disadvantage is that corporations are generally subject to more reporting regulations than other businesses, such as Securities Law and Company Law.

1　如果股份转让导致公司控制权转换，则可能会给公司带来很大变化。

8. 1. 2 Rights and Privilege of Shareholders

Ownership interest in a corporation is made up of common and, optionally, preferred shares.

1. Rights and Privilege of Common Shareholders

The most important legal privilege of common shareholders is the right to vote on key corporate matters, including the election of a board of directors. Secondly, common shareholders generally have a preemptive right to purchase enough shares to retain their proportional ownership interest in a corporation when the company issues additional common shares. They also have the right to share proportionately in any dividends or distribution of earnings. Finally, if a corporation goes out of business and its assets are liquidated, common shareholders are entitled to share proportionately in the assets that remain after the satisfaction of all claims of creditors and senior classes of equity.

2. Rights and Privilege of Preferred Shareholders

Preferred shareholders are owners who have certain rights superior to those of common shareholders. These rights will pertain either to the earnings or the assets of the corporation. Preferences as to earnings exist when the preferred shareholders have a stipulated dividend rate. Preferences as to assets exist when the preferred shareholders have a stipulated liquidation value. Preferred shares may also have the following features: participation in earnings beyond the stipulated dividend rate; a cumulative feature, affording the preferred shareholders the protection that their dividends in arrear, if any, will be fully satisfied before the common shareholders participate in any earnings distribution; and convertibility or callability by the corporation.

In exchange for the preferences, the preferred shareholders' rights are limited. The right to vote, and the right to participate without limitation in the earnings of the corporation, may be restricted to common shareholders.

8. 1. 3 Issuance of Shares

The accounting for the sale of shares by a corporation depends on whether the stock has a par value. If there is a par value, the amount of the proceeds representing the aggregate par value is credited to the common or preferred stock account. The aggregate par value is generally defined as legal capital not subject to distribution to shareholders. Proceeds in excess of par value are credited to an additional paid-in capital account. The additional paid-in capital represents the amount in excess of the legal capital that may, under certain defined conditions, be distributed to shareholders.

For example, a company sells 200 000 shares of $ 2 par value common stock for $ 2. 5 per share cash. The journal entry is

Cash   500 000
    Common stock   400 000
    Additional paid-in capital   100 000

If the company sells 200 000 shares of no-par common stock for $2.5 per share cash, the journal entry is

Cash   500 000
    Common stock   500 000

Preferred stock will often be assigned a par value because in many cases the preferential dividend rate is defined as a percentage of par value. For example, 10% $100 par value preferred stock will have a required annual dividend of $10. Assume the company sells 1 000 shares for $120 per share cash. The journal entry is

Cash   120 000
    Preferred stock   100 000
    Additional paid-in capital   20 000

8.2 Retained Earnings

Retained earnings represent the accumulated amount of earnings of the corporation from the date of inception less the cumulative amount of distributions made to shareholders and other charges to retained earnings (e.g. from treasury stock transactions). The distributions to shareholders generally take the form of dividends.

8.2.1 Dividends

Dividends are the proportional distribution of earnings to the owners of the corporation. Generally speaking, corporations are not allowed to declare dividends in excess of the amount of retained earnings. Common types of dividends are cash dividends and stock dividends.

1. Cash Dividends

Cash dividends become a liability of the corporation only when they are declared by the board of directors. There are three important dividend dates: the declaration date, the record date, and the payment date. The declaration date governs the incurrence of a legal liability by the corporation. The record date refers to that point in time when a determination is made as to which specific registered stockholders will receive dividends and in what amounts. Finally, the payment date relates to the date when the distribution of the dividend takes place.

Assume that on June 2, 20 ×5, the directors of Mars Corp. declare a $0.10 per share dividend on its 100 000 outstanding common shares. The dividend is payable June 30 to holders of record June 20. The journal entries are as the following:

June 2	Dividends	10 000	
	Dividends payable		10 000
June 20	No entry		
June 30	Dividends payable	10 000	
	Cash		10 000

2. Stock Dividends

Stock dividends do not represent an actual distribution of the assets of a corporation. Therefore, a stock dividend is not considered a legal liability. In accounting for stock dividends, a distinction is made between a small or a large stock dividend. As a general guide, a stock dividend of less than 20% to 25% of the outstanding shares prior to declaration is considered a small stock dividend. With a small stock dividend, companies must transfer from retained earnings to capital stock and additional paid-in capital an amount equal to the fair value of the additional shares issued. Such a transfer is consistent with the general public's view of a stock dividend as a distribution of corporate earnings at an amount equal to the fair market value of the shares received.

Assume that equity of Mars Corp. on July 1 is as follows:

Common stock, $1 par, 100 000 shares outstanding	$100 000
Additional paid-in capital	50 000
Retained earnings	80 000

The company declares a 10% stock dividend, or a dividend of 1 share of common for every 10 shares held. Before the dividend, the stock is selling for $3.3 per share. After the dividend, each original share worth $3.3 will become 1.1 shares, each with a value of $3. The journal entries are as follows:

Declaration of dividends:

Retained earnings	30 000	
Stock dividends distributable		10 000
Additional paid-in capital		20 000

Distribution of dividends:

| Stock dividends distributable | 10 000 | |
| Common stock | | 10 000 |

When stock dividends are large in magnitude, the accounting treatment depends on the legal requirements. If regulation requires that earnings be capitalized in an amount equal to the aggregate of the par value of the stock dividends declared, companies must transfer from retained earnings to capital stock an amount equal to the par value of the additional shares issued. If regulation requires treatment as a stock split, there is no formal entry to record the split but merely a notation that the number of shares outstanding has increased and the par value per share has decreased accordingly.

To illustrate, assume that Mars Corp. declares a large dividend of 50% , or a dividend of one share for every two held. Legal requirements call for the transfer to capital stock of an amount equal to the par value of the shares issued. Entries for the declaration of the dividend and the issuance of the 50 000 shares are as follows:

Declaration of dividends:

Retained earnings	50 000	
Stock dividends distributable		50 000

Distribution of dividends:

Stock dividends distributable	50 000	
Common stock		50 000

8. 2. 2　Treasury Stock

Treasury stock consists of a corporation's own stock that has been issued, subsequently reacquired by the firm, and not yet reissued or canceled. If corporate executives believe their company's common stock is selling for less than its actual value, the firm may purchase large blocks of the stock. Corporations typically resell such shares at a later date when the stock's market price has risen. Another reason for companies buy back their own shares is to sell them to company employees as part of stock option or incentive compensation plans.

Treasury stock does not reduce the number of shares issued but does reduce the number of shares outstanding, as well as total equity. These shares are not eligible to receive cash dividends.

Two approaches exist for the treatment of treasury stock: the cost and par value method.

1. Cost Method

Under the cost method, the gross cost of the shares reacquired is charged to a contra equity account, Treasury Stock. When the treasury shares are reissued, proceeds in excess of cost are credited to Additional Paid-In Capital account. Any deficiency is charged to Retained Earnings, unless Additional Paid-In Capital from previous treasury share transactions exists, in which case the deficiency is charged to that account, with any excess charged to Retained Earnings. If many treasury stock purchases are made, a cost flow assumption (e. g. FIFO or others) should be adopted to compute excesses and deficiencies on subsequent share reissuances. The cost method avoids identifying the amounts related to the original issuance of the shares; therefore it is the easier and more frequently used method.

2. Par Value Method

Under the par value method, the Treasury Stock account is charged only for the aggregate par value of the shares reacquired. Additional Paid-In Capital account is reduced in the proportion to the amounts recognized on the original issuance of the shares. When treasury stock is subsequently resold, the excess of the sale price over par value is credited to Additional Paid-In Capital.

3. Example of Accounting for Treasury Stock

200 shares ($10 par value) that were sold originally for $20 per share are later reacquired for $25 each. The carring amount of Additional Paid-in Capital is $2 000.

Subsequently, 100 shares are resold for $30 per share; other 100 shares are resold for $18 per share.

Table 8-1

Cost method		Par value method	
To record the acquisition		To record the acquisition	
Treasury stock　5 000		Treasury stock　2 000	
Cash	5 000	Additional paid-in	
		Capital-common stock　2 000	
		Retained earnings　1 000	
		Cash	5 000
To record the resale at $30 per share		To record the resale at $30 per share	
Cash　6 000		Cash　6 000	
Treasury stock	5 000	Treasury stock	1 000
Additional paid-in		Additional paid-in	
Capital-treasury stock	1 000	Capital-common stock	5 000
To record the resale at $18 per share		To record the resale at $18 per share	
Cash　3 600		Cash　3 600	
Additional paid-in		Treasury stock	1 000
capital-treasury stock 1 000		Additional paid-in	
Retained earnings　400		Capital-common stock	2 600
Treasury stock	5 000		

▶ 核心词汇 Core Words and Expressions

additional paid-in capital　股本溢价

callability　可赎回（优先股），公司可以在约定的条件下按照约定的价格购回

cash dividend　现金股利

common shares, common stock, ordinary shares　普通股

convertibility　可转换（优先股），在约定的条件下可以按照约定的价格转换为普通股

cost flow assumption　成本流假设

cost method　成本法

cumulative　累积（优先股），没有分配的约定优先股股利可以累积到以后期间，在分配普

通股股利前得到补偿

declaration date　股利宣告日

fair market value　公允市价

legal capital　法定资本（股本），一般约定可以发行的股份总数

limited liability　有限责任

liquidate　清算

par value method　面值法

par value　面值

participation　参加（优先股），除了获得约定优先股股利外，还可以在一定范围内参与剩余利润的分配

payment date　股利支付日

preferred shares, preferred stock　优先股

record date　股权登记日

Securities Law　证券法

shareholders or stockholders　股东

shares outstanding　流通在外的股份

stock dividend　股票股利

stock dividends distributable　应付股票股利，属于所有者权益类账户

stock option　股票期权

stock split　股票分割，例如 1 : 2 分割，即每一股分割为两股，面值相应降至原来的 1/2

treasury stock　库存股

▶ 知识扩展　More Knowledge

直接计入所有者权益的利得或损失

按照国际财务报告准则，利得和损失通常计入当期损益，即当期净利润。但是，有一些特殊利得和损失应当直接计入所有者权益，这些项目主要有以下几个方面。

1. 资产重估增值

如 IAS 16 允许一些企业采用重估法或者成本法对固定资产进行计价。如果以重估法计价，资产的增值部分直接计入所有者权益，在处置该资产时将资产重估增值转出，计入当期损益。

2. 金融资产公允价值变动损益

IAS 39 要求特定的金融资产以公允价值计价且变动计入其他综合收益，也就是说，将由于公允价值变动产生的利得或损失计入所有者权益，在该金融资产终止确认的时候，将累积的公允价值变动损益计入当期损益。

3. 外币折算差额

在编制报表时，企业可能需要对境外经营从一种货币折算为另一种货币，产生的外币折算差额不计入当期损益，直接列示为所有者权益的一个项目。只有当投资者处置其在境外经营的权益时才能计入利润表。

▶ 问答题　Questions

1. What basic rights are held by common stockholders?

2. Distinguish between common and preferred stock.

3. Why might a company purchase its own stock?

4. Why is the distinction between paid-in capital and retained earnings important?

5. Describe the accounting entry for a stock dividend, if any.

6. Dividends are sometimes said to have been paid "out of retained earnings." What is the error, if any, in that statement?

▶ 练习题 Exercises

Exercise 1

John's Corporation issued 600 shares of $10 par value common stock for $8 100.

Instructions

Prepare John's Corporation journal entry.

Exercise 2

Paul Corporation issued 1 200 shares of no-par common stock for $20 200.

Instructions

Prepare Paul's journal entry if (a) the stock has no stated value, and (b) the stock has a stated value of $2 per share.

Exercise 3

Mick Inc. has outstanding 10 000 shares of $10 par value common stock. On July 1, 20×5, Mick reacquired 100 shares at $85 per share. On September 1, Mick reissued 60 shares at $90 per share. On November 1, Mick reissued 40 shares at $83 per share.

Instructions

Prepare Mick's journal entries to record these transactions using (a) the cost method, (b) the par value method.

Exercise 4

Micro Machines Inc. declared a cash dividend of $1.50 per share on its 1 million outstanding shares. The dividend was declared on August 1, payable on September 9 to all stockholders of record on August 15.

Instructions

Prepare all journal entries necessary on those three dates.

Exercise 5

Horen Corporation has outstanding 200 000 shares of $10 par value common stock. The corporation declares a 5% stock dividend when the fair value of the stock is $65 per share.

Instructions

Prepare the journal entries for Horen Corporation for both the date of declaration and the date of distribution.

Exercise 6

Use the information from Exercise 5, but assume Horen Corporation declared a 100% stock dividend rather than a 5% stock dividend.

Instructions

Prepare the journal entries for both the date of declaration and the date of distribution.

第 9 章
Chapter 9

Performance
经营成果

◎ 小案例 Mini Case

Wealth, a maker of notebook computers, sells its products to dealers who in turn sell to the final customers. Wealth allows its dealers to take up to 90 days to pay. As the end of the fiscal year nears, Wealth needs to increase its profit to meet the expectation of shareholders. The president of the company has asked that all dealers should be shipped extra inventory other than ordered. Should the extra inventory be accounted for as sales? Why?

正文 Text

Performance is usually measured by profit (or loss) which is the difference between income and expenses during a reporting period.

9.1 Income

According to the IASB's *Framework*, income is "increases in assets, or decreases in liabilities, that result in increases in equity, other than those relating to contributions from holders of equity claims (par. 4.68)". This definition encompasses both revenue and gains.

9.1.1 Revenue versus Gains

Revenue arises in the course of the ordinary operating activities of an entity. To illustrate, a manufacturing company earns its revenue from selling the products made in its factories. A wholesaling or retailing company earns its revenue from reselling merchandise that it has purchased. As businesses diversify, the distinction between ordinary operating activities and other operating activities becomes less clear. For example, department stores that have installment sales programs often make a sizable portion of their income from the interest paid by customers.

Gains represent other items that meet the definition of income and may, or may not, arise in the course of the ordinary activities of an entity. Rather, gains arise from transactions that are incidental to the entity's main revenue-generating activities. Gains represent increases in economic benefits and as such are not really different in nature from revenue. Hence, the IASB does not treat them as separate financial statement elements.

9.1.2 Measurement of Revenue

1. Amount Collected as an Agent

The amount of revenue to be recognized usually depends on the terms of the contract between the entity and the buyer or user of the asset. Revenue shall be measured at the transaction price.

Revenue encompasses only the gross benefits inflow received or receivable by the entity, on its own account. This implies that amount collected on behalf of others does not qualify as revenue, such as in the case of sales tax or value-added tax, which also flows to the entity along with the revenue from sales. These other collections should not be included in an entity's reported revenue. Similarly, in an agency relationship the amounts collected on behalf of the principal are not regarded as revenue for the agent. Instead, the commission earned on such collections qualifies as revenue of the agent. For example, the collections from ticket sales of a travel agency do not qualify as revenue. Instead, the commission on the tickets sold will constitute that entity's gross revenue.

2. Significant Financing Component in the Contract

In most cases, the consideration is in the form of cash or cash equivalents. When the inflow of the consideration is deferred for a certain period of time, the consideration will be normally an amount higher than the cash selling price. In these circumstances, the contract may contain a significant financing component. The difference between the amount of promised consideration and the cash selling price represents the time value of money and should be recognized as interest revenue.

For example, Han's is a car dealer introducing a special offer deal for a new model. The offer is either a cash payment in full of $40 000 or an extended credit term of one year of $42 000.

This arrangement effectively constitutes a financing transaction. The cash price of $40 000 would be regarded as the amount of consideration attributable to the sale of the car, other than the nominal value $42 000. The difference between the cash price and the amount payable in one year, which is $2 000, is interest revenue and is to be recognized over the credit period. The journal entries would be as follows:

Accounts receivable	42 000	
Sales		40 000
Unearned interest revenue		2 000

To record the credit sale.

| Cash | 42 000 | |
| Accounts receivable | | 42 000 |

To record the payment for accounts receivable.

| Unearned interest revenue | 2 000 | |
| Interest revenue | | 2 000 |

To record the interest earned.

3. Trade Discounts and Cash Discounts

Trade discounts depend on the volume of the business or size of order from the customer. In effect, the trade discount reduces the list sales price to the net sales price actually charged to the customer. This net price is the amount at which the receivable and corresponding revenue should be recorded.

Cash discounts are offered to customers by some companies to encourage prompt payment of bills. Cash discounts can be taken by the customer only if payment is made within a specified period of time. Revenues and receivables are recorded at their gross amounts, without regard to any cash discount offered. If payment is received within the discount period, Sales Discounts (a contra-revenue account) is debited for the difference between the recorded amount of the receivable and the total cash collected.

Assume that a company sells $2 000 goods with credit terms of "2/10, n/30", which means 2% discount if paid within 10 days, amount due in 30 days.

| Accounts receivable | 2 000 | |
| Sales | | 2 000 |

To record sale of $2 000, terms 2/10, n/30.

Cash	980	
Sales discounts	20	
Accounts receivable		1 000

To record the partial payment of $1 000, received within discount period.

| Cash | 1 000 | |
| Accounts receivable | | 1 000 |

To record the partial payment of $1 000, received after discount period.

4. Sales Returns and Allowances

Most companies grant customers a full cash refund if they need or want to return merchandise. Additionally, customers also may be granted a price reduction, referred to as sales allowance, to persuade them to keep the goods damaged during shipment, spoiled or otherwise defective, or shipped of an incorrect quantity or type. Such refunds and price reductions are recorded together in another contra-revenue account entitled Sales Returns and Allowances.

To illustrate, assume that on May 10, Lex Company sells Max shop 20 specially monogrammed shirts, costing $25 each, at $40. On May 13, Max returns 2 shirts to Lex because of blots. On May 14, Max asks for a price reduction of $60 on the remaining shirts because the logo was slightly smaller than ordered; Lex agrees to the price reduction. On May 25, Max remits the amount owned. Journal entries of Lex Company are as follows:

Accounts Receivable	800	
Sales		800
Cost of Goods Sold	500	
Inventory		500

To record sale on account.

Sales Returns and Allowances	80	
Accounts Receivable		80
Inventory	50	
Cost of Goods Sold		50

To record return of shirts on credit.

Sales Returns and Allowances	60	
Accounts Receivable		60

To record an allowance given for a monogramming error.

Cash	660	
Accounts Receivable		660

To record payment on account receivable.

9.2 Expenses

According to the IASB's *Framework*, "expenses are decreases in assets, or increases in liabilities, that result in decreases in equity, other than those relating to distributions to holders of equity claims (par. 4.69)". The term expenses include losses as well. Losses may or may not arise in the course of ordinary activities, whereas other expenses arise from ordinary activities.

Generally, expenses are recognized on the basis of a direct association between the costs incurred and the earnings of specific items of income. This process commonly is referred to as the matching of costs with revenues.

The matching principle requires that all expenses incurred in the generating of revenue be recognized in the same accounting period as the revenues are recognized. Some expenses are directly associated with revenues and can thus be recognized in the same period as the related revenues. Other expenditures are not recognized currently as expenses because they relate to future revenues and therefore are reported as assets. Still other expenses are not associated with specific revenues and are recognized in the period when paid or incurred. Thus, the matching principle is broken down into three pervasive measurement principles: (1) associating cause and effect, (2) systematic and rational allocation, and (3) immediate recognition.

9. 2. 1 Associating Cause and Effect

Costs such as materials and direct labor consumed in the manufacturing process are relatively easy to identify with the related revenues. These cost elements are included in inventory and expensed as cost of sales when the product is sold and revenue from the sale is recognized. Similarly, shipping costs and sales commissions usually relate directly to revenues.

Anticipated expenses could also associate with revenues of the current period except those that have already been incurred. After delivery of goods to customers, there are still costs of collection, bad debt losses from uncollectible receivables, and possible warranty costs for product deficiencies. These expenses are directly related to revenues and should be estimated and matched against recognized revenues for the period.

9. 2. 2 Systematic and Rational Allocation

Some costs are more closely associated with specific accounting periods. In the absence of a cause and effect relationship, the assets' costs, such as buildings and equipment, should be allocated to benefiting accounting periods in a systematic and rational manner. This form of expense recognition involves assumptions about the expected length of benefit and the relationship between benefit and cost of each period. Depreciation of fixed assets, amortization of intangibles, and allocation of rent and insurance are examples of costs that would be recognized by the use of a systematic and rational method.

9. 2. 3 Immediate Recognition

All other costs are generally expensed in the period in which they are incurred. This would include those costs for which no clear-cut future benefits can be identified, costs that were recorded as assets in prior periods but for which no remaining future benefits can be identified, and those other elements of administrative or general expense for which no rational allocation scheme can be devised. For example, expenditures for new technical research may provide significant future benefits, but these benefits are usually so uncertain that the costs are written off in the period in which they are incurred. Other examples include office salaries, utilities, and advertising expenses. Most losses also fit in the immediate recognition category because they do not relate directly to revenues. Examples include losses from disposition of used equipment, losses from disposition of investments, and losses from natural disasters such as earthquakes or tornadoes.

▶ 核心词汇 Core Words and Expressions

associating cause and effect　因果关系配比

cash discount　现金折扣

commission　（销售）佣金

consideration　对价

cost of sales　销售成本

dealer　经销商

direct labor　直接人工

immediate recognition　立即确认

installment sales　分期收款销售

matching　配比

nominal value　名义价值

ordinary operating activities　日常经营活动

refund　退款

sales allowances　销售折让

sales returns　销售退回

shipping cost　运费

systematic and rational allocation　系统合理分摊

trade discount　销售折扣，通常指打折，如八折表示按照标价的 80% 作为实际售价，包括数量折扣

value-added tax　增值税

volume rebate　数量折扣，指针对购买数量多的顾客给予的价格折扣

warranty cost　产品质量保证费用，如包修、包换等费用

written off　注销，即计入当期费用

▶ 知识扩展 More Knowledge

国际财务报告准则第 15 号——客户合同收入

《国际财务报告准则第 15 号——客户合同收入》（下称 IFRS 15）取代了原来的 IAS 16 收入准则和 IAS 11 建造合同准则。IFRS 15 的目的在于提供一套更加坚实的框架来阐述收入问题，并且期望改进不同企业、行业、法律和资本市场中收入确认实务的可比性。

收入确认的核心原则

IFRS 15 的核心原则是，确认收入的方式应体现企业向客户转让商品或服务的模式，确认收入的金额应反映企业预计因交付商品或服务而有权获得的金额。

收入确认五步法

IFRS 15 规定，企业在确认收入时需遵循以下五步：

第一，识别与客户订立的合同。该合同是两方或多方之间签订的可强制执行的权利和义务的协议。合同必须具有商业实质，而且企业应当很可能收回合同对价。

第二，识别合同中交付商品或服务的履约义务。企业必须识别出合同中包含了哪些履约义务。当交付商品或服务的承诺能够与其他承诺（如售后服务）区分开来，并且该商品或服务能够单独使客户受益（或商品或服务在使用时需要的其他资源是客户易于获得的），那么企业向客户转让的商品

或服务就是可以区分的履约义务,应单独核算。

第三,确定交易价格。交易价格是指企业预计因交付合同所承诺的商品或服务而有权获得的对价金额,可以是固定金额,也可以是可变金额(如与客户收益挂钩)。如果合同中包含重大融资成分,交易价格还需考虑货币的时间价值。

第四,将交易价格分摊至单独的履约义务。如果单项合同内识别出多项履约义务,交易价格应当基于单独售价的比例分摊至每一项单独的履约义务。如果单独售价无法直接观察,则企业需要对其做出估计。

第五,履行每一项履约义务时确认收入。当客户获得商品或服务的控制权时,企业针对这一项履约义务确认收入。控制权可在某一时点转移或某一时间段内转移。控制权在某一时间段内转移的,企业需要使用恰当方法确认收入,以体现履约义务的完成进度(如完工百分比法)。

影响

IFRS 15 是以原则为导向的综合收入准则,针对不同行业的特定情况,在执行过程中需要进行相应的判断。在某些行业,如电信、房地产、高科技行业等,因为其提供商品和服务的特殊性,需要对原有系统做重大调整,也会对企业经营产生重大影响。

根据我国财政部在 2010 年发布的《中国企业会计准则与国际财务报告准则持续趋同路线图》,我国会计准则与国际财务报告准则保持持续趋同,因此,我国在 2017 年发布了修订后的《企业会计准则第 14 号——收入》,完全采用了 IFRS 15 的做法。

▶ 问答题 Questions

1. Distinguish between revenue and gain.

2. What is income and when is income recognized?

3. What are the reasons that a company gives trade discounts? Why are trade discounts not recorded in the accounts like cash discounts?

4. How is the matching principle applied to expenses recognition?

5. Sales contract with expanded collection period generally include interest. How should the interest be treated for accounting purposes?

▶ 练习题 Exercises

Exercise 1

Gail Devers Corporation sells farm machinery on the installment plan. On July 1, 20×5, Devers entered into an installment-sale contract with Gwen Torrence Inc. for a 10-year period. Equal annual payments under the installment sale are $100 000 and are due on July 1. The first payment was made on July 1, 20×5.

Additional information:

1. The amount that would be realized on an outright sale of similar farm machinery is $676 000.

2. The cost of the farm machinery sold to Gwen Torrence Inc. is $500 000.

3. The finance charges relating to the installment period are $324 000 based on a stated interest rate of 10%, which is appropriate.

4. Circumstances are such that the collection of the installments due under the contract is reasonably assured.

Instructions

What income or loss before income taxes should Devers record for the year ended December 31, 20×5, as a result of the transaction above?

Exercise 2

On June 3, David Company sold to Kim merchandise having a sale price of $5 000 with terms of 2/10, n/60, f. o. b. shipping point. Upon receipt of the goods, June 5, Kim notified David Company that merchandise costing $400 contained flaws that rendered it worthless. The same day David Company issued a credit memo covering the worthless merchandise and asked that it be returned at company expense. The freight on the returned merchandise was $24, paid by David Company on June 7. On June 12, the company received a check for the balance due from Kim.

Instructions

(a) Prepare journal entries on David Company books to record all the events noted above.

(b) Prepare the journal entry, assuming that Kim did not remit payment until August 5.

Exercise 3

On November 1, Magi Company sold goods for $5 000. The terms of the sale were 3/10, n/40. Payment in satisfaction of $2 000 of this amount was received on November 9. Payment in satisfaction of the remaining $3 000 was received on December 9.

Instructions

1. How much cash did Magi collect from this $5 000 account?

2. What journal entries would Magi make on November 9 and December 9?

Exercise 4

Scooby Music sold CDs to retailers and recorded sales revenue of $800 000. During 20×5, retailers returned CDs to Scooby and were granted credit of $78 000. Past experience indicates that the normal return rate is 15%.

Instructions

Prepare Scooby's entries to record (a) the $78 000 of returns and (b) estimated returns at December 31, 20×5.

Exercise 5

On July 23, Louis Company sold goods costing $3 000 on account for $4 500. The terms of the sale were n/30. Payment in satisfaction of $3 000 of this amount was received on August 17. Also on August 17, the customer returned goods costing $1 000 (with a sales price of $1 500). The customer reported that the goods did not meet the required specifications.

Instructions

1. Make the journal entry necessary on July 23 to record the sale. Louis uses a perpetual inventory system.

2. Make the journal entry necessary on August 17 to record the cash collection.

3. Make the journal entry necessary on August 17 to record the return of the goods.

Financial Statement Analysis
财务报表分析

◎ 小案例 Mini Case

Esther is considering investing $2 000 and wishes to know which of the following two companies offers the better alternative. The Mark Company earned net income of $45 000 last year on average total assets of $200 000 and average shareholders' equity of $150 000. The company's shares are selling for $10 per share; 45 000 shares of common stock are outstanding. The Luke Company earned net income of $23 500 last year on average total assets of $100 000 and average shareholders' equity of $75 000. The company's shares are selling for $8 per share; 25 000 shares of common stock are outstanding. Which stock should Esther buy?

正文 Text

Financial statement analysis examines: (1) the relationships among financial statement numbers, and (2) the trends in those numbers over time. Financial statement analysis has two purposes. One purpose is to use the past performance of an entity to predict its future profitability and cash flows. Another purpose is to evaluate the performance of an entity with an eye toward identifying problem areas.

This chapter summarizes the framework of financial statement analysis, and then discusses the financial ratios commonly used.

10. 1　Framework for Financial Statement Analysis

10. 1. 1　Context for Financial Statement Analysis

Financial statement analysis must be done in a wide context; it is not merely a mechanical exercise using various techniques. We outline some of the factors that are directly relevant to an analysis of business performance.

The size of the business. The fact that a business is the size of Sinopec (China Petroleum & Chemical Corporation) makes it less vulnerable to the decisions of people outside the organization. For example, the banker is likely to ask for security from a small business whereas with Sinopec the name itself is enough security.

The business risk. The nature of the business needs to be taken into account: gold prospecting has a different level of risk and return from a bank. Other factors which affect the risk, known as business risk, are reliance on a small number of products, degree of technological innovation, and vulnerable to competition.

The economic environment. The way in which the economic environment affects industry is pervasive. Examples can be found in virtually any daily newspaper. For example, if the Yuan rises relative to the American dollar, imports and exports will be affected and firms will gain or suffer accordingly. Changes in interest rates often have sharp effects on firms that are financed by a large amount of borrowing.

Industry trends, effects of changes in technology. In order to make any judgments about the performance of a business, and more especially about the future, it is vital to understand the way the industry is headed.

10. 1. 2　Information Sources to the Business

In the case of public companies, the annual reports provide the vital information needed in financial analysis. The information provided includes the followings:

Chairman's statement. A chairman's statement contains summarized information for the year, as well as some predictions for the future. However, the statement may be biased for the positive side is often highlighted. It is as important to ascertain what is left out as it is to ascertain what has been included.

Directors' report. This is a statutory requirement for all companies and the information to be contained in is laid down in the Corporation Law. The statutes, however, lay down a minimum and therefore that is normally all the information given.

The statement of financial position. This statement gives information about the financial position at a point in time. The information is only valid at that point of time; and the median time for publication by list companies is over three months after the reporting date.

Statements of comprehensive income and changes in equity. As with the statement of financial position, the information in the statements of comprehensive income and changes in equity are behind the times. Another question is that the statement of comperhensive income is summarized: the weak performance of parts of the business may be offset by the strong performance parts.

Statement of cash flows. The cash flow statement shows the gross cash inflows and outflows associated with operating, financing and investing activities of the business. This statement will allow users to assess an entity's ability to meet its obligations and continue to operate as a going concern.

Notes to the statements. Notes are vital to any financial analysis because they contain the detailed information. Without the information provided in notes, such as accounting policies, it would be impossible to understand the statements and compare the results of different companies.

Auditors' report. Auditors' report states whether the statements show a "true and fair" view in their opinion. If the report is qualified, the events mentioned must be taken into consideration.

External sources. It should be clear that, although annual reports contain some of the required information, a lot more information will have to be obtained from other sources. These other information sources include government statistics, financial press, and online databases about companies, industries, and economic indicators. And specialist agencies can provide an industry-wide analysis, credit-scoring services, and other services.

10. 2　Techniques of Analysis

Many techniques are used in financial analysis; they range from simple techniques, such as studying the financial statements and forming a rough opinion of what is happening, to sophisticated statistical techniques. Ratio analysis technique will be introduced later.

10. 2. 1　Comparison of Financial Statements over Time

A simple comparison of the rate and direction of change over time can be very useful. This can be done both in terms of absolute amount and in percentage terms. Both are important in reaching any conclusions. And it must be borne in mind that other changes might have affected the figures; for example, the industry in which the company operates may change from growth to recession; the company might have changed its accounting policies, such as decided to depreciate its equipment over 8 years instead of 5. Having taken account of these warnings, let us now look at how we can make the comparisons.

Trend Analysis

Trend analysis is normally used for periods more than two or three years in order to make results easier to understand and interpret. It involves two steps: (1) select a base year and assign each item on the base year statement a weight of 100%; (2) express each item from the statements for the other years as a percentage of its base year amount. To illustrate, assume the following data for Matthew Company as Table 10-1.

Table 10-1

	20 × 5	20 × 4	20 × 3	20 × 2	20 × 1
Net sales	$ 5 937	$ 4 649	$ 3 753	$ 2 759	$ 1 843
Cost of sales	877	763	633	467	362
Gross profit	$ 5 060	$ 3 886	$ 3 120	$ 2 292	$ 1 481

Using 20 × 1 as the base year, the percentage trends for these items appear as Table 10-2.

Table 10-2

	20 × 5	20 × 4	20 × 3	20 × 2	20 × 1
Net sales	322. 1%	252. 3%	203. 6%	149. 7%	100%
Cost of sales	242. 3	210. 8	174. 9	129. 0	100
Gross profit	341. 7	262. 4	210. 7	154. 8	100

Figure 10-1 presents the same data in a graph. Note that through 20 × 5, cost of sales increased at a rate somewhat less than the increase in net sale. The different trends in these two items had a clear effect on the percentage changes in gross profit. That is, gross profit increased at a faster rate.

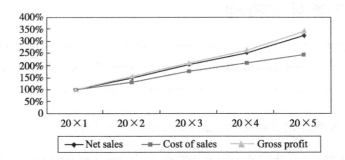

Figure 10-1　Trends lines showing percentage changes in net sales, cost of sales and gross profit

10. 2. 2 Common-Size Statements

Common-size statements technique emphasizes the relative importance of each financial statement item, and deals with the problem of comparing companies of different sizes. In common-size statements, each item is expressed as a percentage of a base amount. For a common-size statement of financial position, the base amount is the amount of total assets, which is assigned a value of 100%. Then, each asset, liability, and stockholders' equity item is shown as a percentage of total assets. In this way, changes in the mixture of the assets or liabilities and equity are more readily apparent. In producing a common-size statement of profit or loss, the amount of net sales is usually the base amount and is assigned a value of 100%. Then each statement item appears as a percentage of net sales. Common-size percentages help the analyst see any potentially important changes in a company's expenses.

This is illustrated by looking at Apple Inc (see Appendix in Chapter 3), the common-size comparative statement of profit or loss and statement of financial position of which are shown in Table 10-3 and Table 10-4. Note that, operating income decreased from 2016, 27.84% to 2017, 26.76%, because cost of sales and operating expenses increased slightly. At the same time, current liabilities increased from 24.56% to 26.86%, and long-term debt increased from 23.45% to 25.90%.

Table10-3   Common-Size Consolidated Statements of Operations

Apple Inc.

	Original Data ($ in millions)		Common Size	
	2017	2016	2017	2016
Net sales	229 234	215 639	100.00%	100.00%
Cost of sales	141 048	131 376	61.53%	60.92%
Gross margin	88 186	84 263	38.47%	39.08%
Operating expenses:				
Research and development	11 581	10 045	5.05%	4.66%
Selling, general and administrative	15 261	14 194	6.66%	6.58%
Total operating expenses	**26 842**	**24 239**	**11.71%**	**11.24%**
Operating income	**61 344**	**60 024**	**26.76%**	**27.84%**
Other income/ (expense), net	2 745	1 348	1.20%	0.63%
Income before provision for income taxes	**64 089**	**61 372**	**27.96%**	**28.46%**
Provision for income taxes	15 738	15 685	6.87%	7.27%
Net income	**48 351**	**45 687**	**21.09%**	**21.19%**

Table10-4   Common-Size Consolidated Statement of Financial Position

Apple Inc.

	Original Data ($ in millions)		Common Size	
	2017	2016	2017	2016
ASSETS:				
Current assets:				
Cash and cash equivalents	20 289	20 484	5.41%	6.37%
Short-term marketable securities	53 892	46 671	14.36%	14.51%
Accounts receivable, less allowances of $58 and $53, respectively	17 874	15 754	4.76%	4.90%
Inventories	4 855	2 132	1.29%	0.66%
Vendor non-trade receivables	17 799	13 545	4.74%	4.21%
Other current assets	13 936	8 283	3.71%	2.57%
Total current assets	**128 645**	**106 869**	**34.28%**	**33.22%**

(continued)

	Original Data ($ in millions)		Common Size	
	2017	2016	2017	2016
Long-term marketable securities	194 714	170 430	51. 88%	52. 98%
Property, plant and equipment, net	33 783	27 010	9. 00%	8. 40%
Goodwill	5 717	5 414	1. 52%	1. 68%
Acquired intangible assets, net	2 298	3 206	0. 61%	1. 00%
Other non-current assets	10 162	8 757	2. 71%	2. 72%
Total assets	**375 319**	**321 686**	**100. 00%**	**100. 00%**
Liabilities and Shareholders' equity:				
Current liabilities:				
Accounts payable	49 049	37 294	13. 07%	11. 59%
Accrued expenses	25 744	22 027	6. 86%	6. 85%
Deferred revenue	7 548	8 080	2. 01%	2. 51%
Commercial paper	11 977	8 105	3. 19%	2. 52%
Current portion of long-term debt	6 496	3 500	1. 73%	1. 09%
Total current liabilities	**100 814**	**79 006**	**26. 86%**	**24. 56%**
Deferred revenue, non-current	2 836	2 930	0. 76%	0. 91%
Long-term debt	97 207	75 427	25. 90%	23. 45%
Other non-current liabilities	40 415	36 074	10. 77%	11. 21%
Total liabilities	**241 272**	**193 437**	**64. 28%**	**60. 13%**
Shareholders' equity:				
Common stock and additional paid-in capital	35 867	31 251	9. 56%	9. 71%
Retained earnings	98 330	96 364	26. 20%	29. 96%
Accumulated other comprehensive income/ (loss)	(150)	634	(0. 04%)	0. 20%
Total shareholders' equity	**134 047**	**128 249**	**35. 72%**	**39. 87%**
Total liabilities and shareholders' equity	**375 319**	**321 686**	**100. 00%**	**100. 00%**

10. 3　Ratio Analysis

Ratio analysis involves assessing how various line items in a firm's financial statements relate to one another. In ratio analysis, the analyst can (1) compare ratios for a firm over several years (a time-series comparison), (2) compare ratios for the firm and other firms in the industry (cross-sectional comparison), and/or (3) compare ratios to some absolute benchmarks. In a time-series comparison, the analyst can hold firm-specific factors constant and examine the effectiveness of a firm's strategy over time. Cross-sectional comparison facilitates examining the relative performance of a firm within its industry, holding the industry-level factors constant. For most ratios there are no absolute benchmarks. The exceptions are measures of rates of return, for example, return on equity, which can be compared to the cost of equity capital associated with the investment.

Return on equity (ROE, net income ÷ equity) is a starting point for a systematic analysis of a firm's performance. ROE provides an indication of how well managers are employing the funds invested by the firm's shareholders to generate returns. It can be interpreted as the number of cents of net income an investor earns in one year by investing one dollar in the company. On average over long periods, large publicly traded firms in the US generate ROEs from the range of 11 to 13 percent. ROEs for Apple Inc for the year 2017 and 2016 are computed below.

Table10-5　Direct ROE Computation of Apple Inc

	2017	2016
Net Income ($)	48 351	45 687
Stockholders' equity ($)	134 047	128 249
Return on equity (%)	36. 07	35. 62

ROE is a comprehensive ratio and needs to be decomposed to identify general factors of ROE deviation. Two decomposition approaches, the traditional DuPont system of financial ratio analysis and an alternative approach, will be discussed.

10. 3. 1　DuPont System

The DuPont system, named after a system of ratio analysis developed internally at DUPONT around 1920, provides a framework for calculation of financial ratios to yield more in-depth analysis of a company's areas of weakness and strength.

In DuPont system, a firm's ROE is affected by two factors: how profitably it employs its assets and how big the firm's asset base is relative to shareholders' investment. So ROE can be decomposed into return on assets (ROA) and a measure of financial leverage. ROA tells us how much profit a company is able to generate for each dollar of assets invested. Financial leverage indicates how many dollars of assets the firm is able to deploy for each dollar invested by its shareholders.

$$\text{ROE} = \frac{\text{Net income}}{\text{Assets}} \times \frac{\text{Assets}}{\text{Shareholders'equity}}$$

$$= \text{ROA} \times \text{Financial Leverage}$$

The ROA itself can be decomposed as a product of two factors:

$$\text{ROA} = \frac{\text{Net income}}{\text{Sales}} \times \frac{\text{Sales}}{\text{Assets}}$$

The ratio of net income to sales is called net profit margin or return on sales (ROS); the ratio of sales to assets is known as asset turnover. The profit margin indicates how much the company is able to keep as profits for each dollar of sales it makes. Asset turnover indicates how many sales dollars the firm is able to generate for each dollar of its assets.

The three drivers of ROE are profitability, efficiency and leverage. Ratios for Apple Inc are displayed as Table 10-6.

Table10-6　DuPont ROE Computation of Apple Inc

Ratio（%）	2017	2016
Net profit margin（ROS）: profitability（%）	21.09	21.19
Assets turnover: efficiency（%）	61.08	67.03
Financial leverage	2.80	2.51
Return on equity（%）	36.07	35.62

10.3.2　An Alternative Approach

Even though the DuPont system is popularly used to decompose a firm's ROE, it has several limitations. In the computation of ROA, the denominator includes the assets claimed by all providers of capital to the firm, but the numerator includes only the earnings available to equity holders. The assets themselves include both operating assets and financial assets, such as cash and short-term investments. Further, net income includes income from operating activities, as well as interest income and expense, which are consequences of financing decisions. Often it is useful to distinguish between these two sources of performance. These issues are addressed by an alternative approach to decomposing ROE discussed below.

The terminology used in this approach should be defined first. This terminology is given in Table 10-7.

Table10-7　Definitions of Accounting Items Used in Ratio Analysis

Item	Definition
Net interest expense after tax	（Interest expense – Interest income）×（1 – Tax rate）[①]
Net operating profit after taxes（NOPAT）	Net income + Net interest expense after tax
Operating working capital	（Current assets – Cash and marketable securities）–（Current liabilities – Short-term debt and current portion of long-term debt）
Net long-term assets	Total long-term assets – Non-interest-bearing long-term liabilities
Net debt	Total interest bearing liabilities – Cash and marketable securities
Net assets	Operating working capital + Net long-term assets
Net capital	Net debt + Shareholders' equity

①利息费用可以在应税收益中抵扣，因此计算税后净利息费用时扣除所得税的影响。所得税率采用实际税率，即以当期所得税费用除以当期税前利润。

These terms are used to decompose ROE in the following manner:

$$ROE = \frac{NOPAT}{Equity} - \frac{Net\ interest\ expense\ after\ tax}{Equity}$$

$$= \frac{\text{NOPAT}}{\text{Net assets}} \times \frac{\text{Net assets}}{\text{Equity}} - \frac{\text{Net interest expense after tax}}{\text{Net debt}} \times \frac{\text{Net debt}}{\text{Equity}}$$

$$= \frac{\text{NOPAT}}{\text{Net assets}} \times \left(1 + \frac{\text{Net debt}}{\text{Equity}}\right) - \frac{\text{Net interest expense after tax}}{\text{Net debt}} \times \frac{\text{Net debt}}{\text{Equity}}$$

$$= \text{Operating ROA} + (\text{Operating ROA} - \text{Effective interest rate after tax})$$

$$\times \text{Net financial leverage}$$

In the above equation, operating ROA less effective interest rate after tax reflects the positive economic effect of borrowing: as long as the return on operating assets is greater than the cost of borrowing.

Operating ROA can be further decomposed into NOPAT margin and operating asset turnover as follows:

$$\text{Operating ROA} = \frac{\text{NOPAT}}{\text{Sales}} \times \frac{\text{Sales}}{\text{Net assets}}$$

The decomposition of ROE, distinguishing operating and financing components for Apple Inc is presented in Table 10-8 and Table 10-9.

Table10-8   ROE Decomposition for Apple Inc: Distinguishing Operating and Financing Components

Item	2017	2016
Sales ($)	229 234	215 639
Net income ($)	48 351	45 687
Equity ($)	134 047	128 249
Interest expense① ($)	2 538	1 644
interest income② ($)	1 476	1 162
Effective tax rate③ (%)	24. 56%	25. 56%
Net interest expense after tax ($)	801	359
Net operating profit after taxes (NOPAT) ($)	49 152	46 046
Operating working capital④ ($)	(39 854)	(35 792)
Net long-term assets⑤ ($)	203 423	175 813
Net debt⑥ ($)	29 522	11 772
Net assets ($)	163 569	140 021
Net capital ($)	163 569	140 021
Effect interest rate after tax (%)	2. 71%	3. 05%

① The information of interest expenses is cited from the notes of 2017 financial report of Apple inc. , P117, Exhibit 12. 1.

② The interest incomes are calculated from the information of notes of 2017 financial report of Apple inc. , P27.

③ Effective tax rate = Provision for income taxes ÷ Income before provision for income taxes.

④ Operating working capital = Total current assets-Cash and cash equivalents – Short-term marketable securities- (Total current liabilities – Current portion of long-term debt).

⑤ Net long-term assets = Total assets – Total current assets.

⑥Net debt = Current portion of long-term debt + total long-term liabilities – Cash and cash equivalents – Short-term marketable securities.

Table10-9　ROE Decomposition for Apple Inc

Ratio	2017	2016
Net operating profit margin	21.44%	21.35%
× Net operating asset turnover	1.40	1.54
= Operating ROA	30.05%	32.89%
Operating ROA – Effective interest rate after tax	27.34%	29.84%
× Net financial leverage	0.22	0.09
= Financial leverage gain	6.02%	2.74%
ROE = Operating ROA + Financial leverage gain	36.07%	35.62%

▶ 核心词汇 Core Words and Expressions

accounting policy　会计政策

asset turnover　资产周转率

auditors' report　审计报告

base amount　基数

base year　基期或基年

business risk　经营风险

chairman's statement　董事长报告

common-size statement　统一度量式财务报表，
　或称为同比报表

comparative statements　比较报表

credit scoring　信用评级

cross-sectional comparison　同行业比较

directors' report　董事会报告

DuPont system　杜邦分析系统

economic environment　经济环境

financial asset　财务资产

financial leverage　财务杠杆

financial ratio　财务比率

government statistics　政府统计数据

net income to sales　销售净利率，销售利润率

net profit margin　边际净利率

operating asset　经营资产

ratio analysis　比率分析

return on assets（ROA）　资产报酬率

return on equity（ROE）　权益报酬率

return on sales（ROS）　销售报酬率

sales to assets　资产销售率

time-series comparison　时间序列比较

trend analysis　趋势分析

working capital　营运资本

▶ 知识扩展 More Knowledge

在财务报表分析中常用的比率

1. 反映偿债能力的财务比率

（1）短期偿债能力。短期偿债能力是指企业偿还短期债务的能力。一般来说，企业应该以流动资产偿还流动负债，所以用流动资产与流动负债的数量关系来衡量短期偿债能力。比率高一般表明企业短期偿债能力较强。常用比率有：

$$流动比率 = 流动资产/流动负债$$

$$速动比率 = （流动资产 - 存货 - 待摊费用）/流动负债$$

$$现金比率 = （现金 + 有价证券）/流动负债$$

（2）长期偿债能力。长期偿债能力是指企业偿还长期利息与本金的能力。通常以负债比率和利

息保障倍数两项指标衡量企业的长期偿债能力。负债比率越高,债权人所受的保障就越低。利息保障倍数考察企业的营业利润是否足以支付当年的利息费用,它从企业经营活动的获利能力方面分析其长期偿债能力。

$$负债比率 = 负债总额/资产总额$$

$$利息保障倍数 = 经营净利润/利息费用$$

$$= (净利润 + 所得税 + 利息费用)/利息费用$$

2. 反映营运效率的财务比率

营运效率是以企业各项资产的周转速度来衡量企业资产利用的效率。周转速度越快,表明企业的各项资产进入生产、销售等经营环节的速度越快,其形成收入和利润的周期就越短,经营效率越高。常用比率有:

$$应收账款周转率 = 赊销收入净额/应收账款平均余额$$

$$存货周转率 = 销售成本/存货平均余额$$

$$流动资产周转率 = 销售收入净额/流动资产平均余额$$

$$固定资产周转率 = 销售收入净额/固定资产平均净值$$

$$总资产周转率 = 销售收入净额/总资产平均值$$

3. 反映盈利能力的财务比率

盈利能力是各方面关心的核心,也是企业成败的关键,只有长期盈利,企业才能真正做到持续经营。常用比率有:

$$毛利率 = (销售收入 - 成本)/销售收入$$

$$营业利润率 = 营业利润/销售收入 - (净利润 + 所得税 + 利息费用)/销售收入$$

$$净利润率 = 净利润/销售收入$$

$$总资产报酬率 = 净利润/总资产平均值$$

$$权益报酬率 = 净利润/权益平均值$$

$$每股收益 = 净利润/流通股总股份$$

▶ 问答题　Questions

1. What are the purposes of financial statement analysis?

2. In analyzing a company' performance, what factors should be taken into account?

3. Public companies provide the annual reports according to the securities regulations. Discuss the information you would find in the annual reports of a public company.

4. There are many other sources providing information useful in financial statement analysis. Discuss the information you would find other than the annual report.

5. What is common-size statement? How to prepare the common-size statement?

6. In ratio analysis, how to compare the ratios?

7. What is DuPont system?

▶ 练习题 Exercises ────────────────────────

Exercise

The following data is subtracted from the annual report of one listing company ($ in millions) .

Statement of Profit or Loss

	20×7	20×6	20×5
Total Revenue	**98 786**	91 424	91 134
Total Cost	**57 057**	53 129	54 602
Gross Profit	**41 729**	38 295	36 532
Expense and Other Income:			
Selling, general and administrative	**22 060**	20 259	21 314
Research, development and engineering	**6 153**	6 107	5 842
Intellectual property and custom development income	**(958)**	(900)	(948)
Other (income) and expense	**(626)**	(766)	(2 122)
Interest expense	**611**	278	220
Total Expense and Other Income	**27 240**	24 978	24 306
Income from Continuing Operations Before Income Taxes	**14 489**	13 317	12 226
Provision for income taxes	**4 071**	3 901	4 232
Income from Continuing Operations	**10 418**	9 416	7 994
Discontinued Operations:			
(Loss) /earnings from discontinued operations, net of tax	**(00)**	76	(24)
Income before cumulative effect of change in accounting principle	**10 418**	9 492	7 970
Cumulative effect of change in accounting principle, net of tax	—	—	(36)
Net Income	**10 418**	9 492	7 934

Statement of Finacial Position

AT DECEMBER 31:	20×7	20×6
Assets		
Current assets:		
Cash and cash equivalents	14 991	8 022
Marketable securities	1 155	2 634
Notes and accounts receivable—trade (net of allowances)	11 428	10 789
Short-term financing receivables (net of allowances)	16 289	15 095
Other accounts receivable (net of allowances)	1 072	964
Receivables	28 789	26 848
Inventories	2 664	2 810
Deferred taxes	1 687	1 806
Prepaid expenses and other current assets	3 891	2 539
Total current assets	**53 177**	**44 660**
Plant, rental machines and other property	38 584	36 521
Less: Accumulated depreciation	23 503	22 082
Plant, rental machines and other property—net	15 081	14 440

(continued)

AT DECEMBER 31:	20 ×7	20 ×6
Long-term financing receivables	11 603	10 068
Prepaid pension assets	17 417	10 629
Investments and sundry assets	6 761	8 381
Goodwill	14 285	12 854
Intangible assets—net	2 107	2 202
Total Assets	**120 431**	**103 234**
Liabilities and Stockholders' Equity		
Current liabilities:		
Taxes	3 673	4 670
Short-term debt	12 235	8 902
Accounts payable	8 054	7 964
Compensation and benefits	4 645	4 595
Deferred income	9 802	8 587
Other accrued expenses and liabilities	5 901	5 372
Total current liabilities	**44 310**	**40 091**
Long-term debt	23 039	13 780
Retirement and nonpension postretirement benefit obligations	13 582	13 553
Deferred income	3 060	2 502
Other liabilities	7 970	4 801
Total Liabilities	**91 962**	**74 728**
Stockholders' equity:		
Common stock, and additional paid in capital	35 188	31 271
Retained earnings	60 640	52 432
Treasury stock, at cost	(63 945)	(46 296)
Accumulated gains and (losses) not affecting retained earnings	(3 414)	(8 901)
Total Stockholders' Equity	**28 470**	**28 506**
Total Liabilities and Stockholders' Equity	**120 431**	**103 234**

Instructions

1. Analyze the trend of revenue, cost, gross profit and net income.

2. Prepare common-size statement of profit or loss for 20 ×7 and 20 ×6.

3. Calculate the ROE, and decompose the ROE of the company. (using DuPont system)

4. Decompose the ROE of the company using the alternative approach.

5. Briefly discuss the profitability, efficiency, financial leverage of this company.

Cost and Management Accounting
成本与管理会计

Modern cost accounting takes the perspective that collecting cost information is a function of the management decisions being made. Cost accounting also provides key data to managers for planning and controlling, as well as costing products, services and customers. Cost accountants are increasingly becoming integral members of decision-making teams instead of just data providers. Thus, the distinction between management accounting and cost accounting is not so clearcut. This is the reason why this part introduces cost accounting and management accounting together.

Chapter 11   An Introduction to Cost terms and Concepts
成本术语与概念介绍
Chapter 12   Costing Systems 成本核算系统
Chapter 13   Management Accounting 管理会计

03

An Introduction to Cost terms and Concepts

成本术语与概念介绍

◎ 小案例 Mini Case

What does the word "cost" mean to you? Is it the price you pay for something of value? A cash outflow? Something that affects profitability? You will find that the word is rarely used without a preceding adjective to specify the type of cost being considered. There are many different types of costs. In different enterprises, what are the elements of the costs of goods sold and how to calculate the costs?

正文 Text

Whereas the retailer/wholesaler purchases goods for sale, the manufacturer makes them. A manufacturing company has a more complex income statement than service or retail/wholesale company. For decision making, it is not enough to know how much was paid for a good; the manufacturer must also know the different costs associated with making it. In order to know the different costs of goods, we need assign manufacturing costs to each product.

11.1　Cost Objects and Cost Assignment

Cost assignment is a general term for assignment costs, whether direct or indirect, to a cost object. **Cost object** is an end to which a cost is assigned, for example, a unit of inventory, a department, a product line, a work-in-progress or a finished good.

Direct costs of a cost object are related to the particular cost object and can be specifically and exclusively traced to it in an economically feasible (cost-effective) way because they can be physically identified with a particular object, such as the wood used to manufacture desks. The term **cost tracing** is used to describe the assignment of direct costs to a particular cost object.

Indirect costs of a cost object are related to the particular cost object but cannot be traced to it in an economically feasible (cost-effective) way because they are incurred in providing benefits to several different product lines or users, such as manufacturing overhead. The term **cost allocation** is used to describe the assignment of indirect costs to a particular cost object.

Figure 11-1 depicts direct costs and indirect costs and both forms of cost assignment—cost tracing and cost allocation.

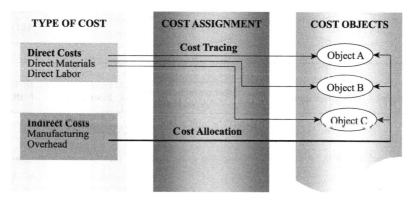

Figure 11-1   Cost Assignment to a Cost Objects

11. 2 Elements of Cost

The manufacturer purchases materials (for example, unassembled parts), hires workers to convert the materials to a finished good, and then offers the product for sale. **Costs of goods manufactured**, **costs of finished goods**, or **manufacturing costs**, refer to the costs of goods brought to completion, whether they were started before or during the current accounting period, including the following major categories or elements.

a. **Direct materials** are raw materials that can feasibly be identified directly with the product. Materials that cannot be identified with a specific product (for example, glue or grease) are included in manufacturing overhead. **Direct material costs** are the acquisition costs of all materials that eventually become parts of the cost object and that can be traced to the cost object in an economically feasible way. Acquisition costs of direct materials also include freight-in (inward delivery) charges, sales taxes and custom duties. Examples of direct material costs are the aluminum used to make Pepsi cans and the paper used to print *China Daily*.

b. **Direct labor** is the labor of workers who transform the materials into a finished product. **Di-**

rect labor cost is the cost of labor directly related to the finished product, including the compensation of all manufacturing labor that can be traced to the cost object (work in process and then finished goods) in an economically feasible way. Examples include wages and fringe benefits paid to machine operators and assembly-line workers who convert direct materials purchased into finished goods.

c. All other costs of transforming the materials to a finished good, often referred to in total as **manufacturing overhead.**

There are also many other types of costs. What we introduced is frequently used by manufacturing firms. Figure 11-2 shows the relationship between the two kinds of cost categories.

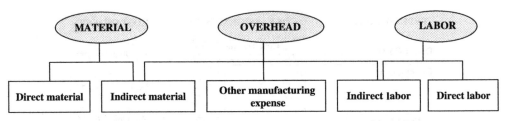

Figure 11-2   RELATIONS BETWEEN COST CATEGORIES

Source: Al Aseervatham and D. Anandarajah. Management Accounting Principles. Thomas Nelson Australia Publishing, 1996, page 7.

11.3   Materials and Labor

11.3.1   Materials

Most companies have substantial sums of money tied up in materials, so it is essential that materials are purchased in the most economical quantities and that there are enough individual materials on hand to meet production demands. Sloppy recording and storage systems may lead to obsolete stock remaining in the storeroom from one year to the next, and the result is a cost to the business far in excess of the implementation costs of an efficient internal control system. In any manufacturing business the ultimate profit is determined by the efficient operation of the receiving and issuing of materials which suits their particular business.

Materials cost is a major part of the total cost of goods manufactured. All materials purchased for production are recorded in the material purchases account. When a material control account is in use, purchase could be recorded at the same time that entries are made in the stores ledger card. The issue of raw materials to production from the stores is first recorded in the stores ledger card instead of the material control account. At the end of the accounting period, the total value of the issues is recorded in the material control account, and in the work-in-process account. The methods of valuing the raw materials issued to production were discussed in Chapter 5, Part 2. Any return of surplus material from the factory to the stores is recorded in the reverse manner. The journal entry for the issue of raw materials is as follows:

> Work-in-process account　　　　　　　× × ×
> 　　Material control account　　　　　　　　　× × ×

Raw materials are those materials that actually become part of the product. Since they are directly traceable to the product, they are commonly referred to as **direct materials**. For example, steel in an automobile, wood in furniture, alcohol in cologne, and denim in jeans would all be classified as direct materials.

Indirect materials are generally those materials necessary for production but do not become a physical part of the finished product. Lubricating oil for machinery used in production is an example of an indirect material. The oil is necessary to maintain the machinery but is not directly traceable to any single product. The recording of the issue of consumable supplies or indirect materials is similar to that of raw materials, except that the recording is in the factory overhead account instead of the work-in-process account.

On the other hand, materials that form an insignificant part of the final product are usually lumped into the overhead category as a special kind of indirect material. This is justified on the basis of cost and convenience. The glue used in furniture or toys is an example.

11. 3. 2　Labor

Labor costs are a significant part of the total manufacturing cost. The cost of labor may be classified as either direct or indirect in a similar way to materials. **Direct labor costs** include the wages that can be directly traced to the cost of producing the finished product, and are usually a major part of the cost of finished goods. Production-related labor costs that cannot be directly traced to finished goods are classified as **indirect labor costs**, and include the wages of supervisors, department heads, cleaners and other support personnel. Indirect labor is accounted for as part of manufacturing overhead, which will be discussed later. But managers' salaries usually are not classified as indirect labor costs, which should be classified as administration overhead.

In the following, we will discuss accounting procedures which record the payment of wages and distribution of labor costs, i. e., payroll systems.

Payroll Systems

Each day employee clock cards and time cards are forwarded to the timekeeping department where the hours spent at work are reconciled with the clock cards. The sum of the time spent on production orders should be less than the attendance time indicated on the clock cards. Once this has been established, the time cards are then used to determine the distribution of costs to work-in-process or factory overhead. This is achieved by examining the time cards to identify hours spent on production orders, idle time, overtime, cleaning, supervision, etc.

Clock cards are forwarded to the payroll department where, together with the master file for each employee, they provide the basic information required to prepare the payroll register and other payroll reports. The payroll summary, representing the totals of employee pay details from the payroll register, is the source document to record the payroll entries in the ledger.

Wages payments are recorded through a payroll clearing account. Although this account can be described in several ways, its main functions are to control the distribution of gross wages and account for the distribution of net wages and deductions. The source document for recording wages is the payroll summary provided by the payroll system. The gross wages is classified as factory, marketing, administrative, etc. In general, **gross wages** consist of pay for normal hours worked, pay for overtime worked, shift loading, incentive pay and other allowances. **Net pay** is the amountremaining after subtracting tax and other deductions from the gross wages. It is the net amountpaid to the employee on pay day.

The time sheet of an employee should provide information as to the type of work performed, which is used to separate direct labor and indirect labor, so that indirect labor can be charged to overhead and that direct labor can be traced to manufacturing goods directly. The total labor cost is calculated by adding gross wages and labor-related cost.

At the end of each month the factory labor incurred is identified from the labor cost summary. This report is prepared from data recorded on time cards and is the source for allocating labor costs to production. The double entry recording direct and indirect labor incurred is represented in the following entry:

Work-in-process account	× × ×	
Factory overhead control account	× × ×	
Factory labor accrued		× × ×

11. 4 Manufacturing Overheads

In a manufacturing organization, overheads are incurred in all sections or departments. Overhead is generally classified, for control reasons, by the internal functions of the organization. The main functions under which overheads may be grouped are:

- production or manufacturing overhead
- office administration
- selling and distribution
- research and development

In this part, we will consider only production overhead as a major part of the cost of a product.

Manufacturing overheads are all indirect costs that are related to the cost object (work-in-progress and then finished goods) but that cannot be traced to that cost object in an economically feasible way, which are also called as *indirect manufacturing costs*, *factory burden*, *factory overhead*, *factory expenses*, and the unmodified word, *overhead* in practice. The overhead cost category contains a wide variety of items. Many inputs other than direct labor and direct materials are needed to make a product. All factory-related indirect costs also belong to the overhead category. Examples include supplies, indirect materials such as lubricants, indirect manufacturing labor such as plant maintenance and cleaning labor, plant rent, plant insurance, property taxes on the plant, plant depreciation, and the compensation of plant managers.

The procedure to calculate the allocation rate for each department and to allocate department overhead is set out as follows:

Step 1: Allocate the indirect costs to departments. This is done by proportionally distributing costs based on an appropriate measure of usage.

Step 2: Reallocate service departments' costs to production departments.

Step 3: Calculate the allocation rate for the production departments using an appropriate basis (labor hours, machine hours) and allocate production departments overhead to each cost object.

11.4.1　Direct allocation and apportionment of indirect overhead

Direct materials and labor can be readily identified with a product, but it is not so easy to economically and feasibly trace manufacturing overhead to the cost of finished goods. Some overhead can be associated directly with a particular cost center, while others are common to a number of cost centers. Methods of dealing with overhead are described below.

In circumstances where a particular overhead cost is associated directly with a cost center, it is allocated to that cost center. This is called **direct allocation**. Direct allocation becomes possible when a cost center has specifically caused the overhead to be incurred and the amount of the overhead is known.

However, in most business there will be overhead costs which are not directly identifiable and cannot be allocated to a specific cost center. These overhead costs belong to a number of cost centers. It is necessary to determine the share of the overhead applicable to each cost center. This is done by dividing the total overhead among the cost centers in proportion, using some equitable basis. This division is called **the apportionment of indirect overhead.**

For example, Stick-up Ltd, a manufacturer of adhesives, wants to account for factory overheads on a department basis. Production takes place in two departments—the mixing department, where the various raw materials are combined, and the bottling department where the product is packaged in special applicators. The plant operation is supported by two service departments. The store controls the receipt and issue of all materials, while the maintenance department ensures that all plant and equipment in the factory is operating efficiently. Table 11-1 shows the information and statistics prepared for January, 20×9.

Table11-1　Stick-up Ltd cost information for January, 20×9

Costs	Total	Mixing	Bottling	Maintenance	Store
Indirect labor	$95 000	$33 600	$30 400	$13 000	$18 000
Indirect materials	46 800	23 450	18 645	1 475	3 230
Depreciation—plant	18 000	9 000	6 000	1 000	2 000
Rates	3 600				
Power	33 600				
Insurance—buildings	22 500				
— plant	10 500				
	$230 000				
Other information:					
Area (m²)	4 500	1 500	2 000	400	600
Kilowatt hours	6 000	3 500	1 800	300	400
Value of plant	$200 000	$100 000	$70 000	$10 000	$20 000
No. of material requisitions	5 000	2 000	1 000	2 000	
Maintenance hours	2 000	350	1 400		250
Direct labor costs	$390 000	$110 000	$280 000		
Machine hours	25 000	20 000	5 000		

Calculate an overhead allocation rate for the two production departments on the following basis:

Mixing department: $ per machine hour

Bottling department:% direct labor costs

Solution　The first step is to allocate the indirect costs to departments. The allocated indirect costs are shown in Table 11-2 and Table 11-3.

Table　11-2

Rates—basis of allocation: area		
Mixing	(1 500 ÷ 4 500) × $3 600	$1 200
Bottling	(2 000 ÷ 4 500) × $3 600	1 600
Maintenance	(400 ÷ 4 500) × $3 600	320
Stores	(600 ÷ 4 500) × $3 600	480
		$3 600
Power—basis of allocation: kilowatt hours		
Mixing	(3 500 ÷ 6 000) × $33 600	$19 600
Bottling	(1 800 ÷ 6 000) × $33 600	10 080
Maintenance	(300 ÷ 6 000) × $33 600	1 680
Stores	(400 ÷ 6 000) × $33 600	2 240
		$33 600

(continued)

Insurance (buildings) —basis of allocation: area		
Mixing	$(1\ 500 \div 4\ 500) \times \$22\ 500$	$7 500
Bottling	$(2\ 000 \div 4\ 500) \times \$22\ 500$	10 000
Maintenance	$(400 \div 4\ 500) \times \$22\ 500$	2 000
Stores	$(600 \div 4\ 500) \times \$22\ 500$	3 000
		$22 500
Insurance (plant) —basis of allocation: value of plant		
Mixing	$(100\ 000 \div 200\ 000) \times \$10\ 500$	$5 250
Bottling	$(70\ 000 \div 200\ 000) \times \$10\ 500$	3 675
Maintenance	$(10\ 000 \div 200\ 000) \times \$10\ 500$	525
Stores	$(20\ 000 \div 200\ 000) \times \$10\ 500$	1 050
		$10 500

Table11-3　Departmental Overhead Distribution Sheet

Costs (fixed/variable)		Total	Mixing	Bottling	Maintenance	Stores
Indirect labor	V	95 000	33 600	30 400	13 000	18 000
Indirect materials	V	46 800	23 450	18 645	1 475	3 230
Depreciation—plant	F	18 000	9 000	6 000	1 000	2 000
Rates	F	3 600	1 200	1 600	320	480
Power	V	33 600	19 600	10 080	1 680	2 240
Insurance—buildings	F	22 500	7 500	10 000	2 000	3 000
—plant	F	10 500	5 250	3 675	525	1 050
Total		230 000	99 600	80 400	20 000	30 000

11. 4. 2　Reallocation of service departments' overheads

After the overhead costs have been determined for all departments, it is necessary to reallocate the expenses from the service departments to the production departments. The aim of the reallocation is to get all expenses attached to products so that the sale price can be calculated to recover all costs. Although service departments do not actually work on the products, they are essential for the efficient operation of the production process. Since production departments are the only ones actually making products for sale, they must recover not only their own specific expenses but also those of the service departments as well.

Some service departments in an organization exist solely to provide a support service to the production departments. The costs incurred by these departments therefore form part of the production overheads. However, the services provided by a service department may relate to more than one production department. One service department may also render services to other service departments, and vice-versa. There are three methods of reallocation of service department overheads: direct method, step-down method, and the reciprocal method.

Direct or simple reallocation

Service department overheads are reallocated to production departments only. Though this method is easy to perform, it may not be accurate because sometimes service departments also service other service departments as well as production departments.

In the above example, the store department costs are allocated on the number of material requisitions: 2 000 for mixing and 1 000 for bottling. The maintenance department's costs are allocated on the basis of maintenance hours. The allocation of costs is shown in Table 11-4 and Table 11-5.

Table11-4　Allocating Service Departments' Costs Using Direct Method

Store		
Mixing	$(2\ 000 \div 3\ 000) \times \$30\ 000$	20 000
Bottling	$(1\ 000 \div 3\ 000) \times \$30\ 000$	10 000
		30 000
Maintenance		
Mixing	$(350 \div 1\ 750) \times \$20\ 000$	4 000
Bottling	$(1\ 400 \div 1\ 750) \times \$20\ 000$	16 000
		20 000

Table11-5　Manufacturing Overhead Reallocated Using Direct Method

	Mixing	Bottling	Maintenance	Store
Indirect Production Costs	99 600	80 400	20 000	30 000
Storage Cost	20 000	10 000		(30 000)
Maintenance Cost	4 000	16 000	(20 000)	—
Total	123 600	106 400	0	0

Step-down reallocation

Service department overheads are reallocated to other service departments as well as to production departments. It is important to correctly organize the sequence in which service departments are dealt with, since this method does not allow a reallocation of service department overheads to a service department which has already had its overhead reallocated. The technique is to start with that service department which provides the most services to other departments, and move progressively to the service department which provides the least services. The method is more accurate than the first, though it takes longer to do. It is referred to as step or step-down reallocation or repeated distribution.

In the above example, the step allocation begins with the stores department, as it performs the highest percentage of service work to other service departments. The allocation of service department costs is shown in Table 11-6 and Table 11-7 separately. In maintenance department, the cost to be allocated will be $20 000 plus the share of the store costs of $12 000 in Table 11-6.

Table11-6   Reallocation of Storage Cost Using Step-Down Method

	Number of requisition	**Proportion**	**Cost allocation**
Mixing	2 000	0. 40	$ 12 000
Bottling	1 000	0. 20	6 000
Maintenance	2 000	0. 40	12 000
	5 000	1. 00	$ 30 000

Table11-7   Reallocation of Maintenance Cost Using Step-Down Method

	Maintenance hours	**Proportion**	**Cost allocation**
Mixing	350	0. 20	$ 6 400
Bottling	1 400	0. 80	25 600
	1 750	1. 00	$ 32 000

Table11-8   Manufacturing Overhead Reallocated Using Step-Down Method

	Mixing	**Bottling**	**Maintenance**	**Store**
Indirect Production Costs	99 600	80 400	20 000	30 000
Storage Cost	12 000	6 000	12 000	(30 000)
Maintenance Cost	6 400	25 600	(32 000)	—
Total	118 000	112 000	0	0

Reciprocal reallocation

This method takes into account the fact that some service departments provide reciprocal services. It therefore employs a circular reallocation process or uses simultaneous equations. This method usually does not warrant the extra effort needed to use it. This procedure, which is often tedious and time-consuming, can be simplified by the use of algebra.

Let X = total costs to be allocated from the maintenance department

Y = total costs to be allocated from the store

Store—percentage of total service to maintenance based on requisition

$$\frac{2\ 000}{5\ 000} \times 100\% = 40\%$$

Maintenance—percentage of total service to the store based on maintenance hours

$$\frac{250}{2\ 000} \times 100\% = 12.5\%$$

The total costs for each service department to be allocated are represented by the following equations:

$$X = \$ 20\ 000 + 0.40Y \qquad (1)$$

$$Y = \$ 30\ 000 + 0.125X \qquad (2)$$

The result of the equations is:

$$X = \$ 33\ 684.21$$
$$Y = \$ 34\ 210.53$$

The total costs to be distributed to the production departments are therefore $33 684.21 in the maintenance department and $34 210.53 in the store. Then, these costs will now be distributed, based on the direct usage of their respective services. The reallocation rate of service cost is calculated as follows:

For the store, the reallocation rate $= \dfrac{34\ 210.53}{5\ 000} = 6.842\ 1$

For the maintenance department, the reallocation rate $= \dfrac{33\ 684.21}{2\ 000} = 16.842\ 1$

The manufacturing overhead reallocated is shown in Table 11-9.

Table11-9 Manufacturing Overhead Reallocated Using Reciprocal Method

	Mixing	Bottling	Maintenance	Store
Indirect Production Costs	99 600	80 400	20 000	30 000
Storage Cost	13 684.21	6 842.11	13 684.21	(34 210.53)
Maintenance Cost	5 894.74	23 578.94	(33 684.21)	4 210.53
Total	119 178.95	110 821.05	0	0

11.4.3 Calculation of the allocation rate for production department overheads

After allocating overheads to each production department, we should calculate an allocation rate of department overheads to allocate overheads to each product or cost object. We will discuss this step in more details in the next chapter.

So far, discussion of overheads has been centered on a plant-wide view of allocating overheads to work in process. This approach is suitable for a small manufacturer or a business which produces everything in one workshop. In the next chapter, we will turn to a situation where the production flows through more than one manufacturing department.

▶ 核心词汇 Core Words and Expressions

allocation rate 分配率	direct method 直接分配法
clock card 工时卡	gross wages 工资总额
cost allocation 成本分配	indirect labor 间接人工
cost object 成本对象	indirect material 间接材料
cost tracing 成本汇集、成本追溯	manufacturing overhead 制造费用
department overhead 部门制造费用	net pay 实发工资
direct labor 直接人工	payroll system 工资系统
direct material 直接材料	reciprocal method 交互分配法

step-down method　顺序分配法

► 知识扩展 More Knowledge

产品成本项目与直接成本和间接成本的关系

如图 11-2 所示，产品成本项目包括直接材料、直接人工和制造费用，产品成本分为直接成本和间接成本。首先，虽然直接材料和直接人工的名字中包含"直接"二字，但并不意味着企业生产发生的材料费和人工费一定是直接成本，也就是发生的材料费不一定归入直接材料，发生的人工费也不一定归入直接人工，也可能是间接成本。其次，直接材料和直接人工成本项目也不意味着直接材料和直接人工成本不需要成本分配。有时不同产品生产耗用同一原材料或者同一生产线工人的加工时间，则直接材料和直接人工成本的归集也需要经过一定的分配流程，即某些直接材料和直接人工成本项目也可能是间接成本。

► 问答题 Questions

1. Compare direct costs and indirect costs.

2. Compare cost allocation and cost tracing.

3. Which one of the following should be classified as indirect labor?

（1）Assembly workers on a car production line.

（2）Bricklayers in a house building company.

（3）Machinists in a factory producing clothes.

（4）Truck drivers in the stores of an engineering company.

（5）Machine operators in a factory producing furniture.

（6）Lawyers in a legal firm.

（7）Maintenance workers in a power generation organization.

（8）Lorry drivers in a road haulage company.

4. Explain the elements of cost of goods produced.

5. A manufacturing organization incurs costs relating to the following transactions:

（1）Commission payable to salespersons.

（2）Inspecting all products.

（3）Packing the products at the end of the manufacturing process prior to moving them to the warehouse.

Which of these costs are classified as production costs?

6. The following statements relate to labor costs, Which is/are correct?

There would be an increase in the total cost for labor as a result of

（1）additional labor being employed on a temporary basis.

（2）a department with spare capacity being made to work more hours.

（3）a department which is at full capacity switching from the production of one product to another.

7. Explain the procedures of allocating manufacturing overhead to products.

8. Explain the methods of allocating service departments' costs to production departments.

9. Which of the following would NOT be classified as a service cost centre in a manufacturing company?

(1) Product inspection department

(2) Materials handling department

(3) Maintenance department

(4) Stores

▶ 练习题 Exercises

Exercise 1

PC plc sells computers. On January 1 of this year, it had a beginning merchandise inventory of $500 000, including transportation-in costs. It purchased $2 600 000 of merchandise, had $260 000 of transportation-in costs, and had marketing and administration costs of $160 000 during the year. The ending inventory of merchandise on December 31 of this year was $400 000, including transportation-in costs.

Instructions

Prepare a schedule of cost of goods sold.

Exercise 2

The balance in the Work in Process Inventory account on April 1 was $31 600, and the balance on April 30 was $22 600. Costs incurred during the month were as follows:

Direct materials	41 250
Direct Labor	17 300
Manufacturing Overhead	32 600

Instructions

What was the amount transfer to Finished Goods Inventory account during April?

Exercise 3

A factory consists of two production cost centers (P and Q) and two service cost centers (X and Y). The total allocated and apportioned overhead for each is as follows:

P	Q	X	Y
$95 000	$82 000	$46 000	$30 000

It has been estimated that each service cost centre does work for the other cost centers in the following proportions:

	P	Q	X	Y
Percentage of service cost center X to	40	40	—	20
Percentage of service cost center Y to	30	60	10	—

Instructions

Reapportion service cost centre costs using direct method and the reciprocal method seperately, and calculate the total overhead for production cost center P.

Exercise 4

A business operates with two production centers and three service centers. Costs have been allocated and apportioned to these centers as follows:

Production Centers		Service Centers		
1	2	A	B	C
$ 2 000	$ 3 500	$ 300	$ 500	$ 700

Information regarding how the service centers work for each other and for the production centers is given as:

	Work done for:				
	Production Centers		Service Centers		
	1	2	A	B	C
By A	45%	45%	—	10%	—
By B	50%	20%	20%	—	10%
By C	60%	40%	—	—	—

Information concerning production requirements in the two production centers is as follows:

	Center 1	Center 2
Units produced	1 500 units	2 000 units
Machine hours	3 000 hours	4 500 hours
Labor hours	2 000 hours	6 000 hours

Instructions

(a) **Using the reciprocal method calculate the total overheads in production centers 1 and 2 after reapportionment of the service centre costs.**

(b) **Using the most appropriate basis establish the overhead absorption rate for production centre 1. Briefly explain the reason for your chosen absorption basis.**

Chapter 12

Costing Systems
成本核算系统

◎ 小案例 Mini Case

Most companies—such as Oracle, JP Morgan Chase, and Honda—offer more than one product (or service). To guide decision making, their costing systems must be able to recognize that different products may vary in their use of resources. Consider Dell Computer as an example, It broadened its line of personal computers to include desktops, laptops, and servers. The three basic activities for manufacturing personal computers are (a) designing computers, (b) ordering component parts, and (c) configuring the assembly line so that the manufacturing process is as efficient as possible. Finished machines are then packed and shipped to buyers. That sounds simple. And it is, but not simple enough to make managers assume that the cost to manufacture each type of computer is the same. So Dell Computer's accountant should provide managers the information they need with an appropriate costing system. Which costing system is appropriate for Dell Computer?

正文 Text

We need to introduce and explain two terms to discuss costing systems:

Cost pool. A cost pool is a grouping of individual cost items. Cost pools can range from broad, such as all manufacturing-plant costs, the costs of operating metal-cutting machines, etc. Cost pools are often organized in conjunction with cost-allocation bases.

Cost-allocation base. How should a company allocate costs to operate metal-cutting machines—collected in a single cost pool—among different products? One way would be to allocate the costs on the basis of the number of machine-hours used to produce the different products. The **cost-allocation base**, or **cost diver**, (in our example, the number of machine-hours) links in a systematic way an indirect cost or group of indirect costs (in our example, operating costs of all metal-cutting machines) to a cost object (different products in our example). Companies often use the cost diver of indirect costs (number of machine-hours) as the cost-allocation base because of the cause-and-effect link between changes in the level of the cost diver and changes in indirect costs. A cost-allocation base can be either financial (such as direct labor cost) or non-financial (such as the number of machine-hours). When the cost object is a job, product, or customer, the cost-allocation base is also called **a cost-application base.**

Costing systems should be tailored to the underlying operations, not vice versa. Any significant change in operations is likely to justify a corresponding change in the costing system. There are two basic types of costing systems used to assign costs to products or services: a job-costing system and a process-costing system.

12. 1　Job Costing and Process Costing

Manufacturing firms can be divided into two major industrial types based on different manufacturing processes: job-order manufacturing and process manufacturing. Two different cost assignment or accumulation systems have been developed, each corresponding to one of these systems.

12. 1. 1　Job Costing

Job costing is a method that gathers the cost elements at different cost centers through which the cost object passes. In a job-costing system, the cost object is an individual unit (or batch) of a distinct product or service, called a **job.** The product or service is often custom-made, such as a construction job or an advertising campaign, Where the products and services are distinct, and direct and indirect costs are assigned to each job.

Job costing uses a seven-step procedure to assign costs to individual jobs.

- Identify the job that is chosen to be cost object.
- Identify the direct costs of the job.
- Select the cost-allocation base (s) to use in allocating indirect costs to the job.
- Identify the indirect costs associated with each cost-allocation base.
- Compute the rate per unit of each cost-allocation base used to allocate indirect costs to the job.
- Compute the indirect costs allocated to the job.
- Compute the total costs of the job by adding the direct and indirect costs assigned to it.

Assume a custom-made machine is the chosen cost object. For each direct cost traced to the job, the actual quantity used was multiplied by the actual cost rate. To illustrate, assume 700 gallons of direct materials were used at an actual cost of $10 per gallon, then the direct material cost of the job is $7 000 (=700 × $10) . 100 direct labor hours were used to produce the machine with $25 per hour, then the direct labor cost is $2 500 (=100 × $25).

Machine-hour was selected as the only cost-allocation base for allocating indirect manufacturing costs (manufacturing overhead) to the job. All $220 000 of the company's indirect manufacturing costs were grouped in a single cost pool and allocated based on a total of 20 000 machine-hours. The indirect-cost allocated rate is $11 (= $220 000 ÷ 20 000). Eight hundred machine-hours were used to produce the custom-made machine, so indirect manufacturing costs of $8 800 (800 × $11) are allocated to the job. The total costs of the job are as follows:

Direct material costs	$7 000
Direct labor costs	2 500
Manufacturing overhead costs	8 800
Total manufacturing costs of the job	$18 300

12. 1. 2　Process Costing

Firms in process industries mass-produce large quantities of similar or homogeneous products. Each product is essentially indistinguishable from its companion products.

A processing-costing system determines the cost of a product (or service) by assigning costs to masses of identical or similar units of the output. Process firms accumulate manufacturing costs by process or by department for a given period of time. In a process-costing system, the cost object is masses of identical or similar units of a product or service. Examples are barrels of oil refined or bank deposits processed. Costs are separated into cost categories according to the timing of when costs are introduced into the process. In each period, the total costs of producing this type of product or service are divided by the total number of units produced to obtain the average costs per unit. Industries using process costing include chemical, pharmaceutical, and semiconductor.

Units produced in a process firm typically pass through a series of manufacturing steps or processes. Each process is responsible for one or more operations that bring a product one step closer to completion. In each process, materials, labor, and overhead inputs may be needed. Upon completion of a particular process, the partially completed goods are transferred to another process. After passing through the final process, the goods are finished and are transferred out to the warehouse.

Two typical process patterns are **sequential processing** and **parallel processing**. In a sequential process, units pass from one process to another in a sequential pattern with each unit processed in the same series of steps. Figure 12-1 shows the sequential pattern of manufacturing process in a medical factory.

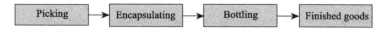

Figure 12-1 Sequential processing Illustrated

Another processing pattern is parallel processing, in which two or more sequential processes are required to produce a finished good. Partially completed units (e. g. two subcomponents) can be worked on simultaneously in different processes and then brought together in a final process for completion. Consider, for example, the manufacture of a mass storage (hard disk) system for personal computers. In one series of processes, read-write heads and cartridge disk drive are produced, assembled, and tested. In a second series of processes, printed circuit boards are produced and tested. These two major subcomponents then come together for assembly in the final process. Figure 12-2 portrays this type of process pattern. Notice that processes one and two can occur independently or parallel to processes three and four.

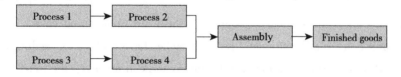

Process 1: Production and assembly of write-head and disk drive

Process 2: Testing of write-head and disk drive

Process 3: Production of circuit board

Process 4: Testing of circuit board

Figure 12-2 Parallel Processing Illustrated

Regardless of which processing pattern exists within a firm, all units produced share a common property. Since units are homogeneous and subjected to the same operations for a given process, each unit produced in a period should receive the same unit cost. Understanding how unit costs are computed requires an understanding of the manufacturing cost flows that take place in a process-costing firm.

1. Process Costing: Cost Flows

The manufacturing cost flows for a process costing system are generally the same as those for a job-order system. As raw materials are purchased, the cost of these materials flows into a Raw Materials Inventory account. Similarly, raw materials, direct labor, and applied overhead costs flow into a Work in Process account when they are used in production. When goods are ultimately completed, the cost of the completed goods is transferred from Work in Process to the Finished Goods account. Finally, as goods are sold, the cost of the finished goods is transferred to the Cost of Goods Sold account. The journal entries generally parallel those described in a job-order costing system.

Although job-order and process costing flows are generally similar, some differences exist. In process costing, each processing department has its own Work in Process account. As goods are completed in a process, they are transferred to the next process. The costs transferred from a prior process to a subsequent process are referred to as **transferred-in costs**. These transferred-in costs are (from the viewpoint of the subsequent process) a type of raw material cost because the subsequent process receives a partially completed unit that must be subjected to additional manufacturing activity, which includes more direct labor, more overhead, and, in some cases, additional raw materials.

2. Accounting for Process Costs

The presence of beginning work in process inventories complicates the computation of the unit cost. Since many firms have partially completed units in process at the beginning of a period, there is a clear need to address the issue. The work done on these partially completed units represents prior-period work, and the costs assigned to them are prior-period costs. In computing a current period unit cost for a department, two approaches have evolved for dealing with the prior-period output and prior-period costs found in beginning work in process: the weight average method and the first-in, first-out (FIFO) method. Basically, **the weighted average method** combines beginning inventory costs with current-period costs to compute unit cost as if they belong to the current period. **The FIFO method**, on the other hand, transfers out beginning inventory cost as a dollar amount and computes unit cost based only on current-period cost and output. If product costs do not change from period to period, the FIFO and weighted average methods yield the same result.

Both the weighted average and FIFO approaches follow the same general pattern for costing out production. This general pattern is described by the following five steps:

- Analysis of the flow of physical units;
- Calculation of equivalent units;
- Computation of unit cost;
- Valuation of inventories (goods transferred out and ending work in process);
- Cost reconciliation.

In the following discussion, we will follow the five steps listed above to account for process cost using the weighted average costing method.

Assume Department A has the following data for October:

Units, beginning work in process	—
Units completed	1 000
Units, ending work in process (25% complete)	600
Total manufacturing costs	$ 11 500

What is the output for this department? 1 000? 1 600? Somehow output must be measured so that it reflects the effort expended on both completed and partially completed units. The solution is to calculate equivalent units of output. **Equivalent units of output** are the complete units that could have been produced given the total amount of manufacturing effort expended for the period under consideration. Determining equivalent units of output for transferred-out units is easy, each transferred-out unit is an equivalent unit. Units remaining in ending work in process inventory, however, are not complete. Thus, someone in production must "eyeball" ending work in process to estimate its degree of completion. In the example, the 600 units in ending work in process are 25 percent complete. Therefore, the equivalent units of ending work in process are 150 fully completed units (600 × 25%). The equivalent units for October would be the 1 000 completed units plus 150 equivalent units in ending work in process, a total of 1 150 units of output.

Knowing the output for a period and the manufacturing costs for the department for that period ($ 11 500), we can calculate a unit cost, $ 10 ($ 11 500/1 150). The unit cost is used to assign a cost of $ 10 000 ($ 10 × 1 000) to the 1 000 units transferred out and a cost of $ 1 500 ($ 10 × 150) to the 600 units in ending work in process. This unit cost is $ 10 per equivalent unit. Thus, when valuing ending work in process, the $ 10 unit cost is multiplied by the equivalent units, not the actual number of partially completed units.

In reality, the details are more complicated than the basics just described. Nonetheless, understanding these basics is essential to understand the nature of process costing.

Furthermore, many companies have costing systems that are neither pure job costing nor pure process costing but have elements of both. Costing systems, therefore, need to be tailored to the underlying operations.

12. 2　Absorption and Marginal Costing

This part examines a type of cost accounting choices for inventories that affect the operating income of manufacturing companies. The inventory cost choice determines which manufacturing costs are treated as inventoriable costs. Inventoriable costs are all costs of a product that are regarded as assets when they are incurred and expensed as costs of goods sold when the product is sold. There are two common methods of inventory costing: absorption costing and marginal costing.

12. 2. 1　Absorption Costing

Absorption Costing, or **full costing**, is a method for sharing all manufacturing overheads between different products on a fair basis. The objective of absorption costing is to include in the total cost of a product an appropriate share of the organization's total overhead. The full absorption cost "full absorbs" the variable and fixed costs of manufacturing a product. However, the full absorption cost excludes non-manufacturing costs, so marketing and administrative cost are not included in finished product cost. An appropriate share is generally taken to mean an amount which reflects the amount of time and effort that has gone into producing a unit or completing a job.

Absorption costing is the costing method compatible with the functional approach to income determination and is recommended for external reporting in financial accounting by the *Inventory* (IAS 2). IAS 2 states that cost should include all costs of purchase (including taxes, transport, and handling) net of trade discounts received, costs of conversion (including fixed and variable manufacturing overheads) and other costs incurred in bringing the inventories to their present location and condition. These costs incurred will include all related production overhead, even though these overheads may accrue on a time basis. In other words, in financial accounting, closing stocks should be valued at full factory cost, and it may therefore be convenient and appropriate to value stocks by the same method in the cost accounting system. The costing system discussed in 12. 1 is absorption costing system.

12. 2. 2　Marginal Costing

Marginal costing or **variable costing** is an alternative method of costing to absorption costing. In marginal costing, only variable costs are charged as cost of sales and the contribution is calculated (sales revenue minus variable cost of sales). Closing stocks of work in process or finished goods are valued as marginal (variable) production costs. Fixed costs are treated as period costs, excluded from inventoriable costs and are charged in full to the income statement of the accounting period in which they are incurred. The definition of variable cost and fixed cost will be discussed in the next chapter.

In a word, how fixed manufacturing costs are accounted for is the main difference between marginal costing and absorption costing. The easiest way to understand the difference between marginal costing and absorption costing is with an example.

During the most recent year, Fairchild Company had the following data associated with the product it makes:

Table 12-1

Units, beginning inventory	—
Unit produced	10 000
Units sold ($300 per unit)	8 000
Normal volume	10 000
Variable costs per unit:	
Direct labor	$100
Direct materials	50
Variable overhead①	50
Variable selling and administration	10
Fixed costs:	
Fixed overhead	$250 000
Fixed selling and administration	100 000

①*Estimated and actual overhead are equal.*

The unit cost obtained under each method differs as shown in Table 12-2.

Table 12-2

	Variable Costing	Absorption Costing
Direct labor	$100	$100
Direct materials	50	50
Variable overhead	50	50
Fixed overhead ($250 000/10 000)		25
Total cost per unit	$200	$225

Under variable costing, each product is reported in the balance sheet at $200 per unit; under absorption costing, the unit cost is $225. The $25 difference is attributable to the way fixed overhead is treated. Under absorption costing, fixed overhead is spread over all the units produced, whereas variable costing assigns no fixed overhead to production. Note that none of the selling and administration costs, either variable or fixed, are assigned to the product under either method. Both methods treat these costs as period costs.

Differences in the computation of product cost produce differences in income figures. Under marginal costing, the total fixed manufacturing overhead of the period is deducted from the revenues of the period. Under absorption costing, fixed overhead is unitized and becomes part of the product cost. Only the fixed overhead attached to the units sold is deducted from the period revenues. If the fixed overhead attached to the units sold is different from the total fixed overhead of the period, the two income figures will be different. The difference arises because of the different amount of fixed overhead recognized as an expense under the two methods.

In the above example, Fairchild produced 10 000 units and sold 8 000 units. The 2 000 units not sold went into inventory. Income statements appear in Table 12-3 and Table 12-4. These income statements reveal that absorption costing income is $50 000 higher than marginal costing income due to some of the period's fixed overhead flowing into inventory when absorption costing is used.

Table12-3　Fairchild Company
Variable-Costing Income Statement

Sales		$ 2 400 000
Less: variable expenses		
Variable cost of goods sold	$ 1 600 000	
Variable selling and administrative	80 000	(1 680 000)
Contribution margin		$ 720 000
Less: fixed expenses		
Fixed overhead	$ 250 000	
Fixed selling and administrative	100 000	(350 000)
Net income		$ 370 000

Table12-4　Fairchild Company
Absorption-Costing Income Statement

Sales	$ 2 400 000
Less: cost of goods sold	(1 800 000)
Gross margin	$ 600 000
Less: selling and administrative expenses	(180 000)
Net income	$ 420 000

12.3　Activity Based Costing

An **activity-based costing (ABC) system** is one that first traces costs to activities and then to products. Conventional product costing discussed above also involves two stages, but in the first stage, costs are traced not to activities but to organizational unit such as the plant or department. ABC refines costing systems by focusing on individual activities as the fundamental cost objects. An **activity** is an event, task, or unit of work with a specified purpose (for example, setting up machines for production runs). ABC calculates the cost of these individual activities and assigns costs to cost objects such as products or services on the basis of the activities undertaken to produce each product or service.

A key step in implementing ABC is to identify activities that help explain why an organization incurs its particular costs. Activities are classified into categories that have an easy and clear physical interpretation and that correspond to manageable segments of the production process. The logic of ABC system is that more finely structured activity-cost pools with activity-specific cost-allocation bases, which are cost drivers for the cost pools, lead to more-accurate costing of activities. Allocating costs to products by measuring the cost-allocation bases of different activities used by different products leads to more accurate product costs. Once a cost pool is defined, the cost per unit of the cost diver is computed for that pool. This is called the **pool rate**. Thus, the overhead assigned from each cost pool to each product is computed as follows.

Applied overhead ＝ Pool rate × Cost driver units used by the product

Assume that a company has annual manufacturing overhead costs of $ 2 000 000—of which $ 200 000 is directly involved in setting up the production machines. During the year the company expects to perform 400 machine setups. Let's also assume that the batch sizes vary considerably, but the setup efforts for each machine are similar.

The cost per setup is calculated to be $ 500 （ $ 200 000 of cost per year divided by 400 setups per year）. Under activity based costing, $ 200 000 of the overhead will be viewed as a batch-level cost. This means that $ 200 000 will first be allocated to batches of products to be manufactured （referred to as Stage 1 allocation）, and then be assigned to the units of product in each batch （referred to as Stage 2 allocation）. For example, if Batch X consists of 5 000 units of product, the setup cost per unit is $ 0. 10 （ $ 500 divided by 5 000 units）. If Batch Y has 50 000 units, the cost per unit for setup will be $ 0. 01 （ $ 500 divided by 50 000 units）. For simplicity, let's assume that the remaining $ 1 800 000 of manufacturing overhead is caused by the production activities that correlate with the company's 100 000 machine hours.

For our simple two-activity example, let's see how the rates for allocating the manufacturing overhead would look with activity based costing and without activity based costing:

Table　12-5

	With ABC	Without ABC
Mfg overhead costs assigned to setups	$ 200 000	$ 0
Number of setups	400	Not applicable
Mfg overhead cost per setup	$ 500	$ 0
Total manufacturing overhead costs	$ 2 000 000	$ 2 000 000
Less: Cost traced to machine setups	200 000	0
Mfg O/H costs allocated on machine hours	$ 1 800 000	$ 2 000 000
Machine hours （MH）	100 000	100 000
Mfg overhead costs per MH	$ 18	$ 20
Mfg overhead cost allocations	$ 500 setup cost per batch × number of setup used + $ 18 per MH × number of MH used	$ 20 per MH × number of MH used

Our example with just two activities （production and setup） illustrates how the cost per unit using the activity based costing method is more accurate in reflecting the actual efforts associated with production.

Activity based costing has grown in importance in recent decades because （1） manufacturing overhead costs have increased significantly, （2） the manufacturing overhead costs no longer correlate with the productive machine hours or direct labor hours, （3） the diversity of products and the diversity in customers' demands have grown, and （4） some products are produced in large batches, while others are produced in small ones.

▶ 核心词汇 Core Words and Expressions

absorption costing 完全成本法

activity 作业、活动

cost diver 成本动因

cost pool 成本库

cost-allocation base 成本分配基础

equivalent units 约当产量

fixed overhead 固定间接费用

job costing 分批法

marginal costing 变动成本法

parallel processing 平行分步生产

process costing 分步法

sequential processing 顺序分步生产

variable overhead 变动性制造费用

▶ 知识扩展 More Knowledge

变动成本法与完全成本法的比较

变动成本法与完全成本法的计算结果用途是不同的。变动成本法用于管理会计，主要是对内提供有效的成本控制信息。完全成本法是财务会计核算使用的方法，用于对外提供信息。两者的利润差异可以以一个简化的公式计算得出：两种计算方法的利润差额 = 产品销售成本差额 = 完全成本法期末存货分摊的固定性制造费用 – 完全成本法期初存货分摊的固定性制造费用。

完全成本法的利润 = 变动成本法利润 + 期末存货分摊的固定制造费用 – 期初存货分摊的固定制造费用。

▶ 问答题 Questions

1. Explain the methods of allocating production departments' costs to products.

2. The following statements refer to organizations using job costing：

   （1）Work is done to customer specification.

   （2）Work is usually completed within a relatively short period of time.

   （3）Products manufactured tend to be all identical.

   Which of these statements is/are CORRECT?

3. Identify the main differences between process costing and job costing.

4. Explain two typical processing pattern and costing system used in each pattern.

5. Define and contrast marginal costing and absorption costing

6. When inventory increases, is absorption-costing or marginal-costing income higher? Why?

7. Which of the following is correct when considering the allocation, apportionment and reapportionment of overheadsin an absorption costing situation?

   （1）Only production related costs should be considered.

   （2）Allocation is the situation where part of an overhead is assigned to a cost centre.

   （3）Costs may only be reapportioned from production centers to service centers.

   （4）Any overheads assigned to a single department should be ignored.

8. How to identify activities in activity-based costing system.

9. Explain how Activity Based Costing differs from traditional absorption costing, giving an example.

▶ 练习题 Exercises

Exercises 1

A company operates a job costing system. Job number 1012 requires $45 of direct materials and $30 of direct labor. Direct labor is paid at the rate of $7.50 per hour. Production overheads are absorbed at a rate of $12.50 per direct labor hour and non-production overheads are absorbed at a rate of 60% of prime cost.

Instructions

What is the total cost of job number 1012?

Exercises 2

The final stage of production adds Material Z to units that have been transferred into Process D and converts them to the finished product. There are no losses in Process D. Data for Process D in the latest period are shown below:

	Units
Opening work in progress	225
Material Z: 80% complete	
Conversion costs: 80% complete	
Units transferred in	500
Units transferred out	575
Closing work in progress	150
Material Z: 60% complete	
Conversion costs: 40% complete	

Instructions

Assuming first-in-first-out (FIFO) costing, calculate the equivalent units to be used in calculation of the cost per equivalent unit for Material Z and Conversion Costs.

Exercises 3

A company operates a process costing system using the first in first out (FIFO) method of valuation. No losses occur in the process.

The following data relate to last month:

	Units	Degree of completion	Value
Opening work in process	100	60%	$680
Completed during the month	900		
Closing work in process	150	48%	

The cost per equivalent unit of production for last month was $12.

Instructions

Calculate the value of the closing work in process and the total value of the units completed in last month.

Exercises 4

Duddon Ltd makes a product that has to pass through two manufacturing processes, Ⅰ and Ⅱ. All the material is input at the start of process Ⅰ. No losses occur in process Ⅰ and Ⅱ.

Process Ⅰ is operated only in the first part of every month followed by process Ⅱ in the second part of the month. All completed production from process Ⅰ is transferred into process Ⅱ in the same month. There is no work in process in process Ⅱ.

Information for last month for each process is as follows:

Process

Opening work in process	200 units (40% complete for conversion costs) valued in total at $ 16 500
Input into the process	1 900 units with a material cost of $ 133 000
Conversion costs incurred	$ 93 500
Closing work in process	50% complete for conversion costs

Process

Transfer from process Ⅰ	1 800 units
Conversion costs incurred	$ 78 450

Instructions

(a) **Calculate for process　:**

(i) **the value of the closing work in process; and**

(ii) **the total value of the units transferred to process**

(b) **Prepare the process　account for last month.**

Exercises 5

The following information relates to the single product of a manufacturing company for the last period:

	Units		$
Production	14 000	Fixed production costs	63 000
Sales	12 000	Fixed selling costs	12 000

There is no beginning inventory.

Using absorption costing the profit for last period has been calculated as $ 36 000.

Instructions

What would the profit for last period be using marginal costing?

Exercises 6

A company which uses marginal costing has a profit of $ 37 500 for a period. Opening stock was 100 units and closing stock was 350 units. The fixed production overhead absorption rate is $ 4 per unit.

Instructions

What is the profit under absorption costing?

Exercises 7

Oat Limited, which manufactures a single product, is considering whether to use marginal or absorption costing to report its budgeted profit in its management accounts. The following information is available:

	$/unit
Direct materials	4
Direct labor	15
	19
Selling price	50

Fixed production overheads are budgeted to be $ 300 000 per month and are absorbed on an activity level of 100 000 units per month.

For the month in question, sales are expected to be 100 000 units although production units will be 120 000 units.

Fixed selling costs of $ 150 000 per month will need to be included in the budget as will the variable selling costs of $ 2 per unit.

There are no opening stocks.

Instructions

(a) **Prepare the budgeted profit and loss account for a month for Oat Limited using absorption costing. Clearly show the valuation of any stock figures.**

(b) **Prepare the budgeted profit and loss account for a month for Oat Limited using marginal costing. Clearly show the valuation of any stock figures.**

Exercises 8

Sargent Company uses activity-based costing to determine the costs of its two products: A and B. The estimated total cost and expected activity for each of the company's three activity cost pools are as follows:

Activity Cost Pool	Estimated Cost	Expected Activity		
		Product A	Product B	Total
Activity 1	$ 32 000	2 200	1 800	4 000
Activity 2	$ 28 000	400	300	700
Activity 3	$ 37 600	800	300	1 100

Instructions

(a) **What is the cost driver rate under the activity-based costing system for Activity 2?**

(b) **How much total cost will be assigned to Products A and B for Activity 2?**

第13章
Chapter 13

Management Accounting
管理会计

◎ 小案例 Mini Case

Do you remember the anxiety you felt in school on report card day? You had planned to make straight A's, but your report card contained a B in one subject and a C in another. What happened? You probably evaluated reasons for the difference and made changes so that your grade expectations for the next report card stood a greater chance of being met. Businesses also have report cards in the form of performance reports. Managers prepare budget describing the expected performance for a period. At the end of the period, actual performance is compared against the budgets, and any variance is explained. Then, corrective action is taken. When a company's performance report in a period is disappointing, would you shed some light on what happened and give some suggestions?

正文 Text

Management accounting measures, analyzes, and reports financial and non-financial information that helps managers make decisions to fulfill the goals of an organization. Managers use management accounting information to choose, communicate and implement strategy. They also use management accounting information to coordinate product design, production, and marketing decisions. In the chapter above, we have discussed some basic concepts of management accounting, such as marginal cost and ABC. In this chapter, we will discuss some management systems used in enterprises.

13. 1　Cost Behavior and CVP Analysis

13. 1. 1　Cost Behavior

There are different costs for different purposes. This theme is the management accountant's version of the "one size does not fit all" notion. A cost concept for the external-reporting purpose of accounting may not be an appropriate concept for internal, routing reporting to managers. In order to adequately predict costs and make decisions, their behavior must be understood. From a behavioral view, costs are classified as fixed or variable.

A **variable cost** changes in proportion with changes in the activity level. For example, if the number of units produced doubles, direct materials (a variable cost) would double in total. Note, however, that the variable cost per unit stays the same.

Fixed costs do not change due to changes in the activity level. If units produced doubles, fixed costs remain the same in total. However, when expressed on a per-unit basis, fixed costs would decline with an increase in activity. Relevant range is the range of activity within which costs behave as predicted. Outside this level of activity, costs behave differently.

Costs are not inherently fixed or variable; it depends on the defined cost object. They may be variable with respect to the level of one activity and fixed for another.

In dealing with costs, it is important to distinguish between behaviors of costs when expressed as unit costs and when dealing with total costs. Unit costs (also called average costs) are normally used in making decisions such as product mix and pricing. However, managers should usually think in terms of total costs for most decisions.

Fixed costs, when expressed on a unit basis can be misleading. For example, if fixed costs are $50 000 and you manufacture 5 000 units, fixed costs are $10 per unit. When production increases to 6 250 units, total fixed costs remain at $50 000, but the unit cost declines to $8. Managers should avoid using the higher unit cost including fixed costs per unit when production level decreases.

Costs can also be measured in different ways, such as prime cost, conversion cost or relevant cost. The management accountant should define and understand the ways costs are measured in a particular company or situation. **Prime cost** is a term used to describe all direct costs or direct materials plus direct labor. **Conversion cost** is direct materials plus factory overhead. It is the cost of converting the materials into a finished product.

Relevant costs are expected future costs that differ among alternative courses of action being considered. Relevant revenues are expected future revenues that differ among alternative courses of action being considered. The question is always "what difference will an action make?" Understanding which costs are relevant costs and which are irrelevant helps the decisions maker concentrate on obtaining only the pertinent data and saves time.

13. 1. 2　CVP analysis

Cost-volume-profit（CVP）analysis examines the behavior of total revenues, total costs, and operating income as changes occur in the units sold, the selling price, the variable cost per unit, or the fixed costs of a product.

Contribution margin is the difference between total revenues and total variable costs. This is an indication of the reason operating income changes as the number of units sold changes. **Contribution margin per unit** is the difference between selling price and variable cost per unit; i. e. , contribution margin per unit is the change in operating income for each additional unit sold after covering up all fixed costs.

$$\text{Contribution margin} = \text{Revenue} - \text{Variable costs}$$

$$\text{Operating income} = \text{Contribution margin} - \text{Fixed costs}$$

The **contribution margin ratio** equals contribution margin divided by total revenue. This is an indication of the percent of each sales dollar that is available to pay fixed costs and return a profit.

There are a number of assumptions that must be made in conducting CVP analysis. Although these assumptions do not always precisely hold, they can allow meaningful analysis.

- Changes in the levels of revenues and costs arise only because of changes in the number of units sold. Thus, number of units sold is the only revenue and cost driver.
- Total costs can be separated into fixed and variable components.
- Total revenues and total costs are linear; that is, when graphed they can be represented as a straight line.
- Selling price, variable cost per unit, and total fixed costs are known and constant.
  Companies are frequently interested in knowing their **breakeven point（BEP）**, the quantity of output sold at which revenues exactly equal expenses. There are three approaches to determining the breakeven point:
- **Contribution Margin Method.** Under this approach fixed costs are divided by the unit contribution margin to give the breakeven point in units. Or breakeven revenues are fixed costs divided by the contribution margin ratio.

$$\text{Breakeven units} = \frac{\text{Fixed cost}}{\text{Contribution margin per unit}}$$

$$\text{Breakeven revenues} = \frac{\text{Fixed cost}}{\text{Contribution margin ratio}}$$

- **Equation Method.** The equation method is based on the following formula:

Operating income = (Selling price × Quantity of units sold) − (Variable cost per unit × Quantity of units sold) − Fixed costs

- **Graph Method.** The graph method represents total costs and total revenues graphically. The breakeven point is the point of intersection of total costs line and total revenues line in the graph, as the graph in Figure 13-1.

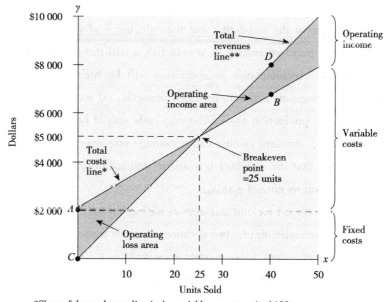

*Slope of the total costs line is the variable cost per unit= $120
**Slope of the total revenues line is the selling price= $200

Figure 13-1 Cost-Volume-Profit Graph

Resource: Horngren, C. T., Datar, S. M., Foster, G., Rajan M., Ittner C. M.. *Cost Accounting: A Managerial Emphasis* (13th Edition). Prentice Hall, 2009.

However, many companies are beyond this point and are not interested in knowing the breakeven; instead, they are concerned with how they can achieve their goals for operating profit.

Target operating income (TOI) analysis can help managers determine the level of sales needed to attain a specified dollar amount of operating income. In order to determine TOI, managers may simply treat the desired operating income as a fixed cost in the breakeven calculation.

$$\text{Quantity of units to be sold} = \frac{\text{Fixed costs} + \text{Target operating income}}{\text{Contribution margin per unit}}$$

13.2 Standard Costing and Variance Analysis

13.2.1 Standard Costing

Chapter 12 focused on accounting for mass production using actual costs for the period. However, for maximum control over costs, the most effective means of accounting for this type of production is standard costing. Standard costing can also be used in accounting for certain types of job order costing but it is usually more appropriate in accounting for mass production.

Standard costing requires management to determine the amount that the product should cost. The predetermined unit cost so calculated is used for inventory valuation. The predetermined unit cost should be based on efficient use of the company's factory resources (e. g. machinery and manpower), and provides a base for measuring actual results. This costing method involves the comparison of actual results against the standard, and the calculation of variances.

The main objective of standard costing is to establish a realistic goal for evaluating and controlling actual performance. Inefficiencies in operations will be highlighted at the end of each month, and this allows appropriate action to be taken promptly. If standard costing is to provide a base which sets out specific production goals, the standards should be determined carefully.

When used effectively, standard costing can encourage employees to work efficiently, but it is first necessary to ensure that the standard is realistic and includes allowances for unavoidable idle time and wastage as well as normal spoilage.

Standards could be developed for unit amounts as well as for total amounts. To determine the **unit standard cost** for a particular input, two decisions must be made: (1) how much of the input should be used per unit of output (the quantity decision) and (2) how much should be paid for the quantity of the input to be used (the pricing decision). The quantity decision produces **quantity standards**, and the pricing decision produces **price standards**. The unit standard cost can be computed by multiplying these two standards.

Historical experience, engineering studies, and input from operating personnel are three potential sources of quantitative standards. Although historical experience may provide an initial guideline for setting standards, it should not be used without caution. Often, processes are operating inefficiently; adopting input-output relationships from the past thus perpetuates these inefficiencies. Engineering studies can determine the most efficient way to operate and can provide very rigorous guidelines, however, engineered standards are often too rigorous. They may not be achievable by operating personnel. Since operating personnel are accountable for meeting the standards, they should have significant input in setting standards. The same principles pertaining to participative budgeting pertain to setting unit standards.

Once set, the standard cost is updated as necessary, but is usually reviewed at least annually.

13. 2. 2 Variance Analysis

Variance analysis involves managers identifying differences between actual and budgeted or recovered costs, isolating the causes of the variance, and taking action to reduce them. Variance analysis takes place for materials, labor and overhead. Variance analysis usually involves:

- determining standard costs;
- comparing the standard and actual costs, and recording the variances (differences);
- analyzing all variances, and taking appropriate action.

Variances are labeled as favorable or unfavorable. A **favorable variance** increases operating income relative to the budget amount. An **unfavorable variance** decreases operating income relative to the budget amount.

Total variances include price variances and volume variances. **Price variances** are sometimes called **rate variances**, especially when those variances are for direct labor. **Volume variances** are sometimes called **usage variances** or **efficiency variances**. The formula for computing the price and efficiency variances are below.

$$\text{Price variance} = \left(\begin{array}{c} \text{actual price} \\ \text{of input} \end{array} - \begin{array}{c} \text{budget price} \\ \text{of input} \end{array} \right) \times \text{actual quantity of input}$$

$$\text{Volume variance} = \left(\begin{array}{c} \text{actual quantity} \\ \text{of input used} \end{array} - \begin{array}{c} \text{budgeted quantity of input} \\ \text{allowed for actual output} \end{array} \right) \times \begin{array}{c} \text{budgeted price} \\ \text{of input} \end{array}$$

1. Material Cost Variance

Material cost variance is the comparison between the expected cost of materials and the actual cost of such items. If the actual cost is less than the expected cost, the variance is favorable. This means that there has been a cost advantage in the purchase of the materials. Conversely, an adverse variance is the result of actual cost being higher than the expected cost of materials.

This variance is caused by either the price paid for the materials used or the quantity of materials used differing from the standard.

$$\text{Material cost variance} = \text{actual material cost} - \text{standard material cost}$$
$$= AQ \times AP - SQ \times SP$$

Where　SQ——Standard quantity for actual production units

SP——Standard price

AQ——Actual quantity

AP——Actual price

Material cost variance can also be expressed as:

Material cost variance = material price variance + material usage variance

Material price variance = actual material quantity at standard price − actual material cost
$$= AQ \times (AP - SP)$$
$$= AQ \times AP - AQ \times SP$$

Material usage variance = (actual material quantity − standard cost of material for actual

production units) × standard price
$$= (AQ - SQ) \times SP$$

$$= AQ \times SP - SQ \times SP$$

2. Labor Cost Variance

When the standard labor cost, allocated for the production, is compared with the actual labor cost incurred, the difference is known as the **labor cost variance.**

Labor cost variance = actual cost of labor - standard cost of labor

$$= AH \times AR - SH \times SR$$

Where　SH——Standard hours for actual production units

SR——Standard rate of pay

AH——Actual hours

AR——Actual rate of pay

This variance can be subdivided into labor rate variance and labor efficiency variance. Labor rate variance is caused by the actual rate of pay differing from the standard. Labor efficiency variance is the other portion of the labor cost variance. It is due to the difference between the standard cost of the labor and the standard rate of pay for actual hours worked, that is, the difference in hours evaluated at the standard rate.

Labor cost variance = labor rate variance + labor efficiency variance

Labor rate variance $= (AR - SR) \times AH$

$$= AH \times AR - AH \times SR$$

Labor efficiency variance $= (AH - SH) \times SR$

$$= AH \times SR - SH \times SR$$

3. Overhead Variance

Total overhead variance is the difference between actual overhead costs and recovered (or applied) overhead costs. Total overhead variance comprises fixed and variable overhead variances.

(1) Fixed overhead variance

Fixed overhead variance is the result of comparison between recovered overhead and actual overhead related to fixed costs. Since variance can be due to differences in expenditure or level (capacity) of activity, fixed overhead variance is in turn subdivided into fixed overhead expenditure variance and fixed overhead volume variance.

Fixed overhead expenditure variance is the difference between budgeted fixed overhead and actual fixed overhead expenditure. This is caused by the total budgeted fixed overhead differing from the total amount spent on fixed overhead. **Fixed overhead volume variance** is the difference between actual fixed overhead cost recovered by the standard absorption rate per unit and budgeted fixed overhead cost. The fixed overhead volume variance can be further split between capacity and efficiency variances.

$$\text{Fixed overhead variance} = \text{actual fixed overhead} - \begin{array}{c} \text{standard fixed overhead} \\ \text{for actual production units} \end{array}$$

$$\begin{array}{c} \text{Fixed overhead} \\ \text{expenditure variance} \end{array} = \text{actual fixed overhead} - \text{budgeted fixed overhead}$$

$$\begin{array}{c} \text{Fixed overhead} \\ \text{volume variance} \end{array} = \text{budgeted fixed overhead} - \begin{array}{c} \text{standard fixed overhead} \\ \text{for actual production units} \end{array}$$

$$= \left(\text{budget hours} - \begin{array}{c} \text{standard hours for} \\ \text{actual production units} \end{array} \right) \times \begin{array}{c} \text{standard (or budgeted) fixed} \\ \text{overhead allocated rate} \end{array}$$

$$= \begin{array}{c} \text{fixed overhead} \\ \text{capacity variance} \end{array} + \begin{array}{c} \text{fixed overhead} \\ \text{efficiency variance} \end{array}$$

$$\begin{array}{c} \text{Fixed overhead} \\ \text{capacity variance} \end{array} = \text{budgeted fixed overhead} - \text{actual hours} \times \begin{array}{c} \text{standard fixed} \\ \text{overhead allocated rate} \end{array}$$

$$\begin{array}{c} \text{Fixed overhead} \\ \text{efficiency variance} \end{array} = \left(\text{actual hours} - \begin{array}{c} \text{standard hours for} \\ \text{actual production units} \end{array} \right) \times \begin{array}{c} \text{standard fixed} \\ \text{overhead allocated rate} \end{array}$$

(2) Variable Overhead Variance

The **variable overhead variance** is the outcome of the comparison between recovered overhead expenditure and actual expenditure related to variable costs. Variable overhead variance is comprised of variable overhead expenditure variance and variable overhead efficiency variance. **Variable overhead expenditure variance** is the difference between the budgeted variable overhead cost and actual variable overhead cost. This is caused by the changes in price of the items comprising variable overhead since setting the budget. **Variable overhead efficiency variance** is the difference between the amount calculated by applying the standard cost of recovery to the actual production hours, and the amount calculated by applying the standard rate to the standard production hours. In the calculation, the variable overhead expenditure is recovered into the cost of the product by employing a cost per hour or per unit of activity.

The total recovered overhead is obtained by applying this rate to the total hours expended in production. However, the actual total hours might have differed from the standard units specified, on which the total budgeted variable overhead cost is based.

$$\begin{aligned} \text{Variable overhead expenditure variance} = &\text{ actual units of activity} \times \text{ (Actual variable overhead} \\ &\text{rate} - \text{standard variable overhead rate)} \end{aligned}$$

$$\begin{aligned} \text{Variable overhead efficiency variance} = &\text{ actual units of activity} \times \text{standard variable overhead rate} \\ &- \text{standard units of activity on actual unit} \times \text{standard} \\ &\text{variable overhead rate} \end{aligned}$$

$$\begin{aligned} \text{Variable overhead variance} = &\text{ Variable overhead expenditure variance} \\ &+ \text{Variable overhead efficiency variance} \end{aligned}$$

The most important task in variance analysis is to identify the causes of variances and use this knowledge to promote continuous improvement. Managers consider many possible causes for variances. Here are some examples:

- A favorable material-price variance occurs if the purchasing manager negotiated more skillfully with suppliers than is expected.
- An unfavorable labor-price variance is caused by an unexpected increase in wage rates for highly skilled workers.
- A favorable labor-efficiency variance occurs because budgeted time standards for highly skilled workers are set too low.

Often the causes of variances are interrelated. For example, an unfavorable materials-efficiency variance is likely to be related to a favorable material-price variance if a purchasing manager buys lower-priced, lower-quality materials. It is always best to consider possible interdependencies among variances rather than to interpret them in isolation of each other.

13. 3　Master Budgets

The **master budget** is a comprehensive expression of management's operating and financial plans for a future time period (usually a year) that is summarized in a set of budgeted financial statements. It is the initial plan of what the company intends to accomplish in the budget period. It evolves from both operating and financial decisions made by managers:

- operating decisions deal with how to best use the limited resources of an organization;
- financing decisions deal with how to obtain the funds to acquire those resources.

Therefore, the two main parts of the master budget are the **operating budget** and the **financial budget**. Figure 13-2 provides an overview of master budget.

13. 3. 1　Operating Budget

The operating budget includes the budgeted income statement and its supporting budget schedules. Nine steps are used to develop the operating budget for a manufacturing company:

- Prepare the revenues budget;
- Prepare the production budget (in units);
- Prepare the direct materials usage budget and direct materials purchases budget;
- Prepare the direct manufacturing labor budget;
- Prepare the manufacturing overhead budget;
- Prepare the ending inventories budget (direct materials and finished goods);
- Prepare the cost of goods sold budget;

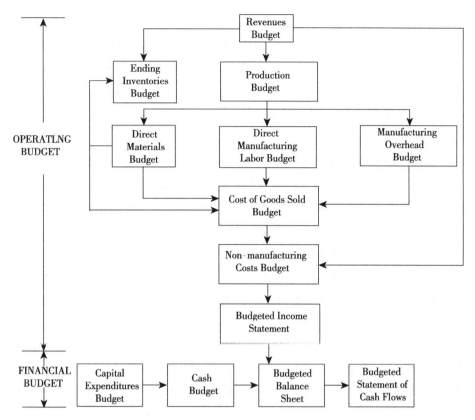

Figure13-2   Overview of Master Budget

- Prepare the non-manufacturing costs budget;
- Prepare the budgeted income statement.

The **sales forecast** is the basis for the revenues budget, which, in turn, is the basis for all of the other operating budgets and most of the financial budgets. Accordingly, the accuracy of the sales forecast strongly affects the soundness of the entire master budget.

Once a sales forecast is generated, a revenues budget is prepared. The revenues budget and the sales forecast are not necessarily synonymous. The sales forecast is merely the initial estimate. The **revenues budget**, or the **sales budget**, is the projection that describes expected sales in units and dollars.

The **production budget** describes how many units must be produced in order to meet sales needs and satisfy ending inventory requirements. Usually, the production budget must consider the existence of beginning and ending inventories since traditional manufacturing firms use inventories as a buffer against demand or production line fluctuations. To compute the units to be produced, both sales requirements and finished goods inventory information are needed.

Units to be produced = finished goods in ending inventory + Expected sales
– finished goods in beginning inventory

After the production schedule is completed, it is possible to prepare budgets for direct materials, direct labor, and overhead. The **direct materials budget** reveals the expected usage of materials in production and the purchasing needs of the firm. Expected usage is directly related to production requirements and determined by the technological relationship between direct materials and output. Once expected usage is computed, purchases (in units) can be computed as follows:

Purchases = Desired direct material, ending inventory + Expected usage
- Direct materials beginning inventory

In the formula, the quantity of direct materials in inventory is determined by the firm's inventory policy.

The **direct labor budget** shows the total direct labor hours needed and the associated cost for the number of units in the production budget. As with direct materials, the usage of direct labor is determined by the technological relationship between labor and output. Given the direct labor used per unit of output and the units to be produced from the production budget, the direct labor budget can be computed.

The **overhead budget** shows the expected cost of all indirect manufacturing items. Unlike direct materials and direct labor, there is no readily identifiable input-output relationship for overhead items. However, that overhead consists of two types of costs: variable overhead and fixed overhead. These relationships can be exploited to facilitate budgeting. **Non-manufacturing costs** budgets are prepared according to the same rules as overhead budget.

With direct materials budget, direct labor budget, and overhead budget, the costs of goods available for sale can be computed. Then, the **cost of goods sold budget** can be prepared.

With the completion of the budgeted cost of goods sold schedule, we have all the operating budgets needed to prepare an estimate of operating income. Operating income is not equivalent to the net income of a firm. To yield net income, interest expenses and taxes must be subtracted from operating income. The interest expense deduction is taken from the cash budget in financial budget.

13. 3. 2 Financial Budget

The remaining budgets found in the master budget are the financial budget. The financial budget consists of the capital expenditures budget, cash budget, budgeted balance sheet, and budgeted statement of cash flows.

13. 4 Performance Measurement

Performance measurement is not a new discipline, having being espoused in the management theory of the early 20th Century through time and motion studies and scientific management princi-ples. It is only recently, however, that larger numbers of organizations have paid particular at-tention to fully integrating performance measurement to the corporate culture. This has been prompted in part by the 1980s drive for improved quality, initially from the US and Japan, con-tinuous improvement and quality circles. In order to achieve agreed quality standards and obtain accreditation, many organizations began to realize the benefits of measuring performance at each key stage of the business process and consider how to measure the results of each production stage. Increased competition during the 1990s prompted greater performance comparison or benchmarking against competitors and a more urgent need to adopt "best practice" solutions.

13. 4. 1 Responsibility Accounting

Responsibility accounting is a system that measures the plans (by budget) and actions (by actual results) of each responsibility center. The performance report for each responsibility center shows by line item the actual result, the budgeted amount, and the variance.

Responsibility centers

Each manager, regardless of his or her level within an organization, is in charge of a respon-sibility center. A **responsibility center** is an area of operations over which a manager has a signif-icant amount of control and responsibility. Responsibility centers can be classified according to the nature of their activities, as shown below:

Cost center—the manager is accountable for costs only.

Revenue center—the manager is accountable for revenues only.

Profit center—the manager is accountable for revenues and costs.

Investment center—the manager is accountable for investments, revenues, and costs.

The principles on which responsible accounting is based are as follows:

- Managers are responsible only for the activities which they are able to control.

- Managers are expected to achieve the targets which are set for the section of the organiza-tion for which they are responsible.

- The target-setting process should involve the managers concerned.

- The targets set should be attainable by managers within the resources at their disposal.

- The reports which provide information to the managers should be timely so that they are able to take the necessary corrective action.

- Rewards and punishment should form part of the policy of the organization and are to be applied fairly and consistently.

- The relationship of the responsibility accounting to the organization's reward and punish-ment structure should be made known to the managers.

13. 4. 2 Balanced Scorecard

The **balanced scorecard** translates an organization's mission and strategy into a set of performance measures that provides the framework for implementing its strategy. [1] Developed by Robert Kaplan and David Norton, the balanced scorecard does not focus solely on achieving financial objectives. It also highlights the non-financial objectives that an organization must achieve to meet its financial objectives. It balances the use of financial and non-financial performance measures to evaluate short-run and long-run performance in a single report, so it is called the balanced scorecard.

The scorecard measures an organization's performance from four perspectives: financial, customer, internal business processes, and learning and growth. A company's strategy influences the measures it uses to track performance in each of these perspectives.

a. The financial perspective evaluates the profitability of the organization's strategy. Under the strategy of product differentiation, the financial perspective focuses on how much operating income and return on capital resulting from charging premium selling prices. Under the strategy of cost leadership, the financial perspective focuses on how much operating income and return on capital resulting from reducing costs and selling more units of output.

b. The customer perspective identifies the targeted market segments and measures the organization's success in these segments. Performance measures for this perspective include market share, number of new customers, and customer satisfaction ratings in the targeted segments.

c. The internal business process perspective focuses on internal operations that further the customer perspective (by creating value for customers) and the financial perspective (by increasing shareholder wealth). Performance measures for this perspective include production yield and on-time order delivery rate.

d. The learning and growth perspective identifies the capabilities in which the organization must excel in order to achieve superior internal processes that create value for customers and shareholder wealth. Performance measures for this perspective include employee education and skill levels, employee satisfaction ratings, and number of suggestions per employee.

These four perspectives are linked in a cause-and-effect chain, moving backward from (d) to (a). That is, gains in learning and growth lead to improvements in internal business processes, which in turn lead to higher customer satisfaction and market share, and finally result in superior financial performance. In this chain, many non-financial measures serve as leading indica-

---

[1] See R. S. Kaplan and D. P. Norton, *The Balances Scorecard* (Boston: Harvard Business School Press, 1996); R. S. Kaplan and D. P. Norton, *The Strategy-Focused Organization: How Balanced Scorecard Companies Thrive in the New Business Environment* (Boston: Harvard Business School Press, 2000); R. S. Kaplan and D. P. Norton, *Strategy Maps: Converting Intangible Assets into Tangible Outcomes* (Boston: Harvard Business School Press, 2004).

tors of future financial performance.

▶ 核心词汇 Core Words and Expressions

breakeven point　盈亏平衡点	material cost variance　材料成本差异
budgeted balance sheet　预算资产负债表	material price variance　材料价格差异
budgeted statement of cash flows　预算现金流量表	material usage variance　材料使用差异
capital expenditures budget　资本支出预算	operating budget　经营预算
cash budget　现金预算	overhead budget　间接费用预算
contribution margin　边际贡献	price standards　价格标准
contribution margin ratio　边际贡献率	price variance　价格差异
conversion cost　加工成本	prime cost　主要成本
cost center　成本中心	production budget　生产预算
cost of goods sold budget　产品销售成本预算	profit center　利润中心
cost-volume-profit analysis　本量利分析	quantity standards　数量标准
direct labor budget　直接人工预算	responsibility center　责任中心
direct materials budget　直接材料预算	relevant cost　相差成本
efficiency variance　效率差异	revenue budget　收入预算
favorable variance　有利差异	revenue center　收入中心
financial budget　财务预算	sales forecast　销售预测
fixed cost　固定成本	unfavorable variance　不利差异
fixed overhead capacity variance　固定性制造费用能量差异	unit standard cost　标准单位成本
	variable cost　变动成本
fixed overhead expenditure variance　固定性制造费用耗费差异	variable overhead efficiency variance　变动性制造费用效率差异
fixed overhead variance　固定性制造费用差异	variable overhead expenditure variance　变动性制造费用耗费差异
investment center　投资中心	
labor cost variance　人工成本差异	variable overhead variance　变动性制造费用差异
labor efficiency variance　人工效率差异	volume variance　数量差异
labor rate variance　人工工资率差异	

▶ 知识扩展 More Knowledge

标准成本分类

　　标准成本按其制定时所根据的生产技术和经营管理水平，分为理想标准成本和正常标准成本；按其适用期，分为现行标准成本和基本标准成本。

　　理想标准成本是指在最优的生产条件下，利用现有的规模和设备能够达到的最低成本。制定理想标准成本的依据，是理论上的业绩标准、生产要素的理想价格和可能实现的最高生产经营能力利用水平。它的主要用途是提供一个完美无缺的目标，揭示实际成本下降的潜力。因其提出的要求太高，不能作为考核的依据。

正常标准成本是指在效率良好的条件下，根据下期一般应该发生的生产要素消耗量、预计价格和预计生产经营能力利用程度制定出来的标准成本。

现行标准成本是指根据其适用期间应该发生的价格、效率和生产经营能力利用程度等预计的标准成本。这种标准成本可以作为评价实际成本的依据，也可以用来对存货和销货成本计价。

基本标准成本是指一经制定，只要生产的基本条件无重大变化，就不予变动的一种标准成本。所谓生产的基本条件的重大变化是指产品的物理结构变化、重要原材料和劳动力价格的重要变化、生产技术和工艺的根本变化。只有这些条件发生变化，基本标准成本才需要修订。由于市场供求变化导致的售价变化和生产经营能力利用程度变化、由于工作方法改变而引起的效率变化等，不属于生产的基本条件变化，对此不需要修订基本标准成本。由于基本标准成本不按各期实际修订，不宜用来直接评价工作效率和成本控制的有效性。

固定性制造费用差异分析的三因素分析法

固定性制造费用差异的划分除上文提到的两因素分析法外，还有三因素分析法。两因素分析法下，固定性制造费用差异分为固定性制造费用耗费差异和能量差异。三因素分析法下，固定性制造费用差异分为固定性制造费用耗费差异、效率差异和闲置能量差异。三因素分析法是将两因素分析法中的"能量差异"进一步分为两部分：一部分是实际工时未达到标准能量而形成的闲置能量差异；另一部分是实际工时脱离标准工时而形成的效率差异。其计算公式如下：

$$固定制造费用闲置能量差异 = 固定制造费用预算 - 实际工时 \times 固定制造费用标准分配率$$

$$= (生产能量 - 实际工时) \times 固定制造费用标准分配率$$

$$固定制造费用效率差异 = 实际工时 \times 固定制造费用标准分配率 - 实际产量标准工时 \times 固定制造费用标准分配率$$

$$= (实际工时 - 实际产量标准工时) \times 固定制造费用标准分配率$$

预算的种类及其编制方法

预算的种类及其编制方法有多种，如固定预算与弹性预算、增量预算与零基预算、定期预算与滚动预算等。

固定预算，也叫静态预算，是指在编制预算时，只根据预算期内正常的、可实现的某一固定业务量水平作为唯一基础来编制预算的一种方法。由于其编制过于机械呆板、可比性差，因而主要适用于业务量水平较为稳定的企业或非营利组织。弹性预算，也叫变动预算、滑动预算，是指为克服固定预算方法的缺点而设计的，以业务量、成本和利润之间的依存关系为依据，按照预算期可预见的各种业务量水平为基础，编制能够适应多种情况预算的一种方法。由于其预算范围宽、可比性强，因此适用于所有与业务量有关的各种预算，主要用于编制弹性成本费用预算和弹性利润预算。

增量预算方法，又称调整预算方法，是指以基本成本费用水平为基础，结合预算期业务量水平及有关影响成本因素的未来变动情况，通过调整有关原有费用项目而编制预算的一种方法。增量预算方法的有效使用需要一定的前提假设，包括现有的业务活动是企业必需的；原有的各项开支都是合理的；增加费用预算是值得的等。其缺点也相当明显，主要有：受原有费用项目限制，可能导致保护落后；滋长预算中的"平均主义"和"简单化"；不利于企业未来发展。零基预算，又称零底预算，是指在编制成本费用预算时，不考虑以往会计期间所发生的费用项目或费用数额，而是将所有的预算支出均以零为出发点，一切从实际需要与可能出发，逐项审议预算期内各项费用的内容及开支标准是否合理，在综合平衡的基础上编制费用预算的一种方法。相对于增量预算，零基预算的主要优点有，不受现有费用项目和开支水平限制；能够调动各方面降低费用的积极性，有助于企业的发展。但其缺点是工作量大，编制时间较长。

定期预算是指在编制预算时以不变的会计期间（如日历年度）作为预算期的一种预算编制的方法。其优点是能够使预算期间与会计年度相配合，便于考核和评价预算的执行结果；其缺点是远期指导性差、灵活性差和连续性差。滚动预算，又称连续预算或永续预算，是指在编制预算时，将预算期与会计年度脱离，随着预算的执行不断延伸补充预算，逐期向后滚动，使预算期永远保持为一个固定期间的一种预算编制方法。滚动预算按其预算编制和滚动的时间单位不同可分为逐月滚动、逐季滚动和混合滚动 3 种方式。与传统的定期预算方法相比，按滚动预算方法编制的预算具有透明度高、及时性强、连续性好，以及完整性和稳定性突出等优点。

▶ 问答题 Questions

1. Compare variable costs and fixed costs.

2. Define CVP analysis, breakeven point and explain the main approaches to determining the breakeven point.

3. Explain standard costing and the main objective of standard costing.

4. List the usage of variance analysis in management.

5. Explain price and volume variance.

6. Is a favorable variance always an indicator of efficiency in operation?

7. Is there a relationship between direct materials variances and direct labor variances?

8. Match the following causes of variances to the appropriate variance.

Variances	Causes
(a) Favorable labor efficiency	(1) Inexperienced staff in the purchasing department
(b) Adverse sales volume	(2) Materials of input quality than standard
(c) Adverse material price	(3) Unexpected slump in demand
(d) Adverse selling price	(4) Production difficulties
(e) Adverse fixed production overhead volume	(5) Strike
	(6) Poor machine maintenance

9. Match the three pairs of interrelated variances

(a) Adverse selling price

(b) Favorable labor rate

(c) Adverse materials usage

(d) Favorable sales volume

(e) Adverse materials price

(f) Favorable materials usage

(g) Adverse sales volume

10. A company operates a standard costing system. The variance analysis for last month shows a favorable materials price variance and an adverse labor efficiency variance. Which of the following statements are consistent with the variance analysis?

(a) Inferior quality materials were purchased and used.

(b) Superior quality materials were purchased and used.

(c) Lower graded workers were used on production.

(d) Higher graded workers were used on production.

11. List the process of preparing master budget.

12. Classify and describe responsibility centers according to the nature of their activities.

13. List the basic principles of setting target for responsibility centers and their managers.

14. For which of the following is a profit centre manager responsible?

(a) Costs only.

(b) Revenues only.

(c) Costs and revenues.

15. Define Balance Scorecard and describe four perspectives of measuring an organization's performance using BSC.

16. Explain the relationships among four perspectives of BSC.

▶ 练习题 Exercises

Exercises 1

Following is the contribution margin income statement of a single product company:

	Total	Per unit
Sales	$ 1 200 000	$ 80
Less variable expenses	$ 840 000	$ 56
Contribution margin	360 000	$ 24
Less fixed expenses	300 000	
Net operating income	$ 60 000	

Instructions

(1) Calculate break-even point in units and dollars.

(2) What is the contribution margin at break-even point?

(3) Compute the number of units to be sold to earn a profit of $ 36 000.

(4) Compute the margin of safety using original data.

(5) Compute contribution margin ratio. Compute the expected increase in monthly net operating if sales increase by $ 160 000 and fixed expenses do not change.

Exercises 2

A company's budgeted sales for last month were 10 000 units with a standard selling price of $ 20 per unit and a standard contribution of $ 8 per unit. Last month actual sales of 10 500 units at an average selling price of $ 19. 50 per unit were achieved.

Instructions

What were the sales price and sales volume contribution variances for last month?

Exercises 3

A company has a budgeted material cost of $ 125 000 for the production of 25 000 units per month. Each unit is budgeted to use 2 kg of material. The standard cost of material is $ 2. 50 per kg.

Actual materials in the month cost $ 136 000 for 27 000 units and 53 000 kg were purchased and used.

Instructions

What is the material price and usage variances?

Exercises 4

The following information relates to labor costs for the past month:

Budget:

Labor rate	$ 10 per hour
Production time	15 000 hours
Time per unit	3 hours
Production units	5 000 units

Actual:

Wages paid	$ 176 000
Production	5 500 units
Total hours worked	14 000 hours

Instructions

What were the labor rate and efficiency variances?

Exercises 5

A company uses standard costing and the standard variable overhead cost for a product is 6 direct labor hours at $ 10 per hour. Last month when 3 900 units of the product were manufactured, the actual expenditure on variable overheads was $ 235 000 and 24 000 hours were actually worked.

Instructions

What were the variable overhead expenditure and efficiency variances for last month?

Exercises 6

A company operates a standard absorption costing system. The standard fixed production overhead rate is $ 15 per hour.

The following data relate to last month:

Actual hours worked	5 500
Budgeted hours	5 000

Standard hours for actual production　　　4 800

Instructions

What was the fixed production overhead capacity variance?

Exercises 7

A company uses absorption costing for both internal and external reporting purposes as it has a considerable level of fixed production costs.

The following information has been recorded for the past year:

Budgeted fixed production overheads　　　$ 2 500 000

Budgeted (Normal) activity levels:

　　Units　　　　　　　　　　　　62 500 units

　　Labor hours　　　　　　　　　500 000 hours

Actual fixed production overheads　　　$ 2 890 350

Actual levels of activity:

　　Units produced　　　　　　　　70 000 units

　　Labor hours　　　　　　　　　525 000 hours

Instructions

(a) **Calculate the fixed production overhead expenditure and volume variances and briefly explain what each variance shows.**

(b) **Calculate the fixed production overhead efficiency and capacity variances and briefly explain what each variance shows.**

Exercises 8

The following details have been taken from the debtor collection records of W plc:

Invoices paid in the month after sale　　　60%

Invoices paid in the second month after sale　20%

Invoices paid in the third month after sale　50%

Bad debts　　　　　　　　　　　　5%

Customers paying in the month after the sale are allowed a 10% discount.

Invoices for sales are issued on the last day of the month in which the sales are made.

The budgeted credit sales for the final five months of this year are:

Month	August	September	October	November	December
Credit sales	$ 80 000	$ 100 000	$ 120 000	$ 130 000	$ 160 000

Instructions

Calculate the total amount budgeted to be received in December from credit sales.

Exercises 9

A company manufactures and sells one product which requires 8 kg of raw material in its manufacture. The budgeted data relating to the next period are as follows:

	Units
Sales	19 000
Opening inventory of finished goods	4 000
Closing inventory of finished goods	3 000
	Kg
Opening inventory of raw materials	50 000
Closing inventory of raw materials	53 000

Instructions

What is the budgeted raw material purchases for next period (in kg)?

Exercises 10

A company has obtained the following information regarding costs and revenue for the past financial year:

Original budget:

Sales	10 000 units
Production	12 000 units

Standard cost per unit:

	$
Direct materials	5
Direct labor	9
Fixed production overheads	8
	22
Selling price	30

Actual results:

Sales	9 750 units
Revenue	$ 325 000
Production	11 000 units
Material cost	$ 65 000
Labor cost	$ 100 000
Fixed production overheads	$ 95 000

There were no opening inventory.

Instructions

Calculate the variances between the actual and flexed figures for the following:

—sales;

—materials;

—labor; and

—fixed production overhead.

Exercises 11

T is a large pharmaceutical manufacturing company that is implementing a "Kaplan and Norton style" Balanced

Scorecard for its research and development division. The goals and measures for the "customer perspective" and the "financial perspective" have been set.

Instructions

(1) For each of the two perspectives given in the question data, state an appropriate performance measure.

(2) List the other two perspectives in the Balanced Scorecard for T's research and development division, and state for each of the perspectives a relevant goal and performance measure.

International Accounting

国际会计

04

International Accounting Harmonization

国际会计协调

◎ 小案例 Mini Case

Assume you are interested in investing in the telecommunications industry. The four largest telecommunications companies in the world in descending order of revenue size are AT&T (USA), Verizon Communications(USA), Nippon Telegraph and Telephone(JPN) and Deutsche Telekom(DEU). How do you decide which, if any, of these telecommunications companies you should invest in? How do you compare, for example, a U. S. company with a Japanese company?

正文 Text

With the dramatic growth in global trade and the accelerated internationalization of capital markets, financial statements produced in one country are more and more frequently used in other countries. This has brought accounting harmonization to be the forefront issue of international business.

14. 1 Advantages of International Accounting Harmonization

14. 1. 1 Advantages of Harmonization

Accounting is a form of communication. As with all types of communication, though, misunderstandings can arise unless meanings are reasonably clear. **Harmonization** is a process of increasing the compatibility of accounting practices by setting limits on how much they can vary. Accounting harmonization has many dimensions—regional versus global, voluntary versus mandated, piecemeal versus comprehensive, and so forth. What will emerge as the most likely development path for the near future? There are three ways. One way is the use of bilateral agreements. Under this approach, two or more countries agree to recognize each other's national standards on a reciprocal basis. Mutual recognition on a regional level is a second possibility, for instance, among the EU. A third scenario places harmonization at the doorsteps of private, professional groups such as IASB and IFAC. It is generally believed that IFRS issued by IASB has the best potential to provide a common platform on which companies can report and investors can compare financial information.

Harmonization is nowadays often considered an irreversible process, even if some authors consider it an impossible and useless dream. Proponents of international harmonization claim that harmonization has many advantages. It is expected to make financial markets more efficient and to contribute to the establishment of the "rules of the game" in international competition.

Others have argued that financial statement users have difficulty interpreting information produced under nondomestic accounting systems. They claim that harmonization will make it more likely that users will interpret the information correctly, and thus make better decisions based on that information.

14. 1. 2 Prospect of Harmonization

The harmonization debate may never be completely settled. However, national differences in the underlying factors that lead to variation in accounting, disclosure, and auditing practice are narrowing as capital and product markets become more international. Increasing evidence shows that the goal of international harmonization has been so widely accepted that the trend towards international harmonization will continue or accelerate. Harmonization is happening as a natural response to economic forces. Growing numbers of companies are voluntarily adopting International Accounting Standards/International Financial Reporting standards (IASs/IF-RSs). Many countries adopt IASs/IFRSs in their entirety, base their national standards on IASs/IFRSs, or allow the use of IASs/IFRSs. Progress in harmonizing disclosure and auditing has been impressive. But all harmonization efforts require much time and energy. Harmonization is a continuous process.

14. 2 Applicability of International Standards

Accounting harmonization includes the harmonization of (1) accounting standards (which deal with measurement and disclosure); (2) disclosure made by publicly traded companies in connection with securities offerings and stock exchange listings; and (3) auditing standards. Efforts to harmonize accounting standards began even before the creation of the International Accounting Standards Committee(IASC) in 1973. More recently, companies seeking capital outside of their home markets and investors in an attempt to diversify their investments internationally faced increasing problems resulting from national differences in accounting measurement, disclosure, and auditing. In response, harmonization efforts accelerated during the 1990s. International accounting harmonization now is one of the most important issues facing securities regulators, stock exchanges, and those who prepare or use financial statements.

14. 2. 1　Support for International Standards

Most international accounting research studies contain long lists of benefits and costs arising from international accounting standard setting. Among the alleged benefits, these sources mention greater international comparability of financial reports most often. Harmonized standards are free of logical conflicts, and should improve the comparability of financial information from different countries. Financial executives think that a more level playing field will result if international accounting standards are widely used, with reference to items such as cross-border mergers and acquisitions, and securing financing outside the home country. Some economists believe that such standards would improve global business competition, and some international agencies(e. g. UN) advocate international standards as a form of assistance to developing countries. In a more operational sense, international standards may reduce bookkeeping costs and allow more efficient preparation of financial statements. Researchers have identified still other benefits, for example, reconciliation of sometimes adversarial interests between preparers and users of financial statements.

14. 2. 2　Objection to International Standards

Of course, there are also those who object to the very idea of international accounting standards. As early as 1971(before the IASC was formed), some said that international standards setting was too simple a solution for a complex problem. It was claimed that accounting, as a social science, has built-in flexibility and that its ability to adapt to widely different situations is one of its most important values. It was doubted that international standards could be flexible enough to handle differences in national backgrounds, traditions, and economic environments, and some thought that it would be a politically unacceptable challenge to national sovereignty.

Other observers have argued that international accounting standard setting is essentially a tactic of the large international accounting service firms to expand their markets. Multinational accounting firms are indispensable, it is said, to apply international standards in national environments where those standards might seem distant and complex. Also, as international financial institutions and international markets insist on the use of international standards, only large international accounting firms can meet this demand.

Moreover, it has been feared that adoption of international standards may create " standards overload". Corporations must respond to an ever-growing array of national, social, political, and economic pressures and are hard put to comply with additional complex and costly international requirements. A related argument is that national political concerns frequently intrude on accounting standards and that international political influences would compromise accounting standards unacceptably.

14. 2. 3　Application of International Standards

International accounting standards are used as a result of (1) international or political agreement, (2) voluntary (or professionally encouraged) compliance, or (3) decisions by national accounting standard setters. In the 1970s and 1980s attempts had been made to harmonize financial reporting standards across the EU. Owing to mutual political agreement, the EU was able to generate some equality of standards across the Union. Increasing numbers of companies are deciding that the use of IASs/IFRSs is in their interest even if it is not required. Many countries now allow companies to base their financial statements on IASs/IFRSs, and some require it. For example, IFRS may also be used by foreign companies listing on U. S. securities exchanges.

Most international standards efforts in accounting are voluntary in nature. Their acceptance depends on those who use accounting standards. There is no problem when an international standard and a national standard are the same, but when national and international standards differ, national standards usually come first (take primacy). For example, multinational companies may use international accounting standards and also accept and use national standards. When companies adopt more than one set of accounting standards, the result is often that they must issue one set of reports for each set of accounting standards they adopt. This multiple approach to financial reporting by multinational corporations is likely to increase.

14. 3　Major International Organizations Promoting Accounting Harmonization

14. 3. 1　Major Promoters for Harmonization

Several organizations have been involved in financial reporting and related topics and in promoting international accounting harmonization:

- International Accounting Standards Board(IASB) ;
- International Organization of Securities Commissions(IOSCO) ;
- International Federation of Accountants(IFAC) ;
- International Valuation Standards Council (IVSC) ;

- Group of 20 (G20) ;

- European Union(EU)

For many years, many nations have relied on their own standard-setting organizations. The standards issued by these organizations are sometimes principles-based, rules-based, tax-orien-ted or business-based. In other words, they often differ in concept and objective. Starting in 2000, IASB has emerged as one of the primary standard-setting bodies in the world. The IASB is at the center of the global convergence in accounting standards. The IASB is a privately funded non-governmental organization located in London. Its mission is to develop rules and principles for financial reporting that could apply around the world. While acceptance of these rules is not mandatory, it is nevertheless widespread. 144 jurisdictions require IFRS Standards for all or most domestic publicly accountable entities (listed companies and financial institutions) in their cap-ital markets. Although the United States is not committed to adopting IASs/IFRSs, it has accepted to work together with the IASB in order to harmonize U. S. accounting standards(known as Gen-erally Accepted Accounting Principles, GAAP) with IASs/IFRSs. In 2002, the IASB reached an agreement(the Norwalk Agreement) with the Financial Accounting Standards Board(FASB) to undertake a number of short-term and long-term projects that would lead to convergence, as dis-cussed in next chapter.

14. 3. 2　Role of Organizations

IOSCO was established in 1983. Its membership regulates more than 95% of the world's se-curities markets in more than 115 jurisdictions; securities regulators in emerging markets account for 75% of its ordinary membership. There are three categories of members: ordinary, associate and affiliate. In general, the ordinary members (128) are the national securities commissions or similar governmental bodies with significant authority over securities markets in their respective ju-risdictions. IOSCO develops, implements and promotes adherence to internationally recognized standards for securities regulation. It works intensively with the G20 and the Financial Stability Board (FSB) on the global regulatory reform agenda. IOSCO recommends the use of IFRSs to its membership and cooperates in the development and consistent application of IFRSs to promote and facilitate transparency with capital markets.

The International Federation of Accountants(IFAC) was formed in 1977. It is the global or-ganization for the accountancy profession dedicated to serving the public interest by strengthening the profession and contributing to the development of strong international economies. IFAC is com-prised of over 175 members and associates in more than 130 countries and jurisdictions, represen-ting almost 3 million accountants in public practice, education, government service, industry, and commerce. IFAC has established several boards, such as International Auditing and Assurance

Standards Board sets high-quality international standards for auditing, assurance, and quality control that strengthen public confidence in the global profession. International Public Sector Accounting Standards Board develops standards, guidance, and resources for use by public sector entities around the world for preparation of general purpose financial statements. Moreover, International Accounting Education Standards Board establishes standards, in the area of professional accounting education, that prescribe technical competence and professional skills, values, ethics, and attitudes. International Ethics Standards Board for Accountants sets high-quality, internationally appropriate ethics standards for professional accountants, including auditor independence requirements. Member bodies of IFAC are required to use their best endeavors to incorporate IFRSs in their national accounting requirements or to persuade those responsible for developing those requirements that general purpose financial statements should comply with IFRSs, or with local accounting standards that are converged with IFRSs.

The International Valuation Standards Council (IVSC) is an independent, not-for-profit organization that acts as the global standard setter for valuation practice and the valuation profession, serving the public interest. Its core objectives are to develop high quality International Valuation Standards (IVS) which underpin consistency, transparency and confidence in valuations across the world, and encourage the adoption of IVS across the globe, along with professionalism provided by Valuation Professional Organizations. IVSC consists of nearly 100 member organizations from around the world and is supported by numerous sponsors who are leaders in the valuation field. The IVSC commits to provide input to the IASB on proposed amendments to IFRSs and developments in financial reporting that are relevant to fair value.

Group of 20 (G20) is made up of the finance ministers and central bank governors of 19 countries and the European Union. The G20 meets regularly to discuss matters of common interest. As a result of the global financial crisis, the G20 began to explore ways to improve the global financial system, including regulations related to financial reporting and institutions. The G20 has for some time called for the global convergence of accounting standards and has supported the IASB-FASB convergence process. The G20 supports continuing work to achieve convergence to a single set of high quality accounting standards.

The EU, formerly known as the European Community(EC) and its start as the European Common Market, was formed in 1957 by the Treaty of Rome. Its major aims are the free flow of goods, persons, and capital. To encourage capital movement and capital formation, especially to remain competitive against U. S. capital markets, EU leaders believed that a common set of accounting standards for the entire EU was necessary. Although attempts had been made to harmonize financial reporting standards across the EU, these efforts had proved ineffective, allowing too many exceptions. It was clear that creating a new set of common EU accounting standards would prove impossible. The IASB's existing international financial reporting standards were the most sensible choice, both economically and politically. Since January 1, 2005, all companies whose shares are listed on a stock exchange in the EU have to produce their consolidated financial statements according to the standards promulgated by the IASB rather than according to national ones.

The concrete steps of the endorsement process in the EU can be described as follows:

When the IASB issues a new standard, the European Financial Reporting Advisory Group (EFRAG) holds consultations with interest groups. EFRAG delivers its advice to the European Commission whether the standard meets the criteria of endorsement. It also prepares in cooperation with the Commission an effect study about the potential economic effects of the given standard's application in the EU. The Standards Advice Review Group (SARG) issues its opinion whether EFRAG's endorsement advice is well-balanced and objective. Based on the advice of EFRAG and the opinion of SARG, the Commission prepares a draft endorsement Regulation. This Regulation is adopted only after a favorable vote of the Accounting Regulatory Committee (ARC) and favorable opinions of the European Parliament and the Council of the European Union. Following adoption, the Regulation is published in the *Official Journal of the European Union*, at which time it becomes effective.

▶ 核心词汇 Core Words and Expressions

Accounting Regulatory Committee(ARC) 欧盟会计监管委员会

bilateral agreement 双边协议

Code of Ethics for Professional Accountants 注册会计师职业道德规范

comparability 可比性

European Commission 欧盟委员会,又称为欧盟执委会

European Financial Reporting Advisory Group (EFRAG) 欧洲财务报告咨询组

European Union(EU) 欧盟

Financial Accounting Standards Board(FASB) 美国财务会计准则理事会

Financial Stability Board(FSB) 全球金融稳定理事会,成员包括中国在内的所有 G20 成员国

globalization of economies 经济全球化

Group of 20 (G20) 20 国集团

International Accounting Standards Committee (IASC) 国际会计准则委员会,1973 年成立,2001 年被国际会计准则理事会(International Accounting Standards Board,IASB)取代

International Accounting Standards(IASs) 国际会计准则

International Auditing and Assurance Standards Board (IAASB) 国际审计和鉴证准则理事会

International Accounting Education Standards Board (IAESB) 国际会计教育准则理事会

International Ethics Standards Board for Accountants (IESBA) 国际会计师职业道德准则理事会

International Financial Reporting Standards(IFRSs) 国际财务报告准则

International Federation of Accountants(IFAC) 国际会计师联合会

International Organization of Securities Commissions

（IOSCO）　证券委员会国际组织

International Public Sector Accounting Stan-dards Board（IPSASB）　国际公共部门会计准则理事会

International Valuation Standards Council （IVSC）　国际评估准则理事会

Norwalk Agreement　诺沃克协议,IASB 和 FASB

在协议中认为共同努力制定一套统一的高质量、国际性会计准则将更好地服务全球资本市场

mergers and acquisitions　并购

Standards Advice Review Group（SARG）　欧盟准则建议审查小组

stock exchange listing　证券交易所上市

▶ 知识扩展 More Knowledge

国际会计协调（International Accounting Harmonization），又译为国际会计趋同（趋同更多用 convergence），或者会计国际协调。我国于 2006 年发布的新会计准则体系在广泛采纳国际会计准则的同时仍然保留了部分特色，国际会计准则理事会也表示会考虑中国特殊业务的会计问题。由于我国采用的是趋同而不是等同的方式加入国际会计准则体系，因此可以在国际会计准则理事会允许的范围内，根据我国的国情对准则进行修改和补充，以增强准则的适用性。2007 年 12 月 6 日，中国内地与香港会计师公会签署了《内地准则与香港准则等效的联合声明》。2008 年 4 月 22 日，欧盟委员会就欧盟第三国会计准则等效问题发布正式报告。2011 年年底前，欧盟委员会允许中国证券发行者在进入欧洲市场时使用中国会计准则，不需要根据欧盟境内市场采用的国际财务报告准则调整财务报表。自 2011 年来，国际会计准则理事会先后发布并修订了公允价值计量、合并财务报表等一系列准则，发起了国际财务报告准则的新一轮变革。为保持我国会计准则与国际财务报告准则的持续趋同，财政部在 2012 年发布了一系列准则征求意见稿后，于 2014 年正式修订了 5 项、新增了 3 项企业会计准则，发布了一项准则解释，并修改了《企业会计准则——基本准则》中关于公允价值计量的表述。在 2016～2017 年间，财政部又陆续发布了 6 项企业会计准则解释、4 项会计处理规定以及 7 项新增或修订的企业会计准则，涉及终止经营、政府补助、收入、金融工具系列准则等。

证券委员会国际组织（International Organization of Securities Commissions，IOSCO）是一个世界性的证券管理机构。主要宗旨是促进跨国证券的上市和交易，促进国际间的信息交流，建立保护投资者的充分准则。IOSCO 一直致力于国际信息披露和会计准则方面的工作。1995 年，IOSCO 与 IASC 签署协议，委托 IASC 开发研制 40 项国际核心会计准则，以规范跨国发行证券和股票上市公司的财务信息揭示。2000 年 5 月 IOSCO 批准和推荐了 30 份核心准则，建议其成员将核心准则作为跨国上市公司编制报表的基础。

国际会计师联合会（International Federation of Accountants，IFAC）是一个由不同国家职业会计师组织组成的民间机构，一直和 IASC 保持着紧密的关系。IFAC 下设多个专业理事会，其中，国际审计和鉴证准则理事会制定与公布权威性的国际审计准则以协调审计实务，进而促进各国缩小会计实务差异、增进财务信息的可比性。

联合国会计与报告国际准则政府间专家工作组（Intergovernmental Working Group of Experts on International Standards of Accounting and Reporting，ISAR）是目前联合国系统内唯一的一个致力于在全球范围内对各国的会计和报告实务进行协调的政府间组织。ISAR 不是准则制定机构，而是推动会计

国际协调的机构。其目标是提高公司会计和报告的透明度、可靠性和可比性，以及改善发展中国家和经济转型国家中企业公司治理信息披露的问题。同时，ISAR 会议也是个国际性会计论坛。近年来，ISAR 主要侧重于其他组织较少涉及的重要问题，如环境会计、公司治理信息披露等。

经济合作与发展组织会计准则工作组（OECD Working Group）的目的是增强财务信息的国际可比性和促进会计准则的国际协调。工作组基本上每年根据特定题目，邀请有关国家的会计准则制定机构进行非正式会谈，并以"工作纪要"的形式发表会谈结果。同时针对一些重要的专题召开国际会议。OECD 积极地推广国际会计准则和国际审计准则，为跨国公司的行为提出指导性方针或建议，并参与组建地区性职业组织，为会计的国际协调做了很多的工作。

会计准则制定机构国际论坛（International Forum of Accounting Standard Setters，IFASS）是世界会计准则制定小组的下属机构，IFASS 每年召开两次会议，讨论议题涉及近期的 IASB 工作情况、其他会计事项以及有潜力的研究课题。IASB 的成员以观察员或与会者的身份参加 IFASS 的会议。

欧盟（European Union）是区域会计协调的典范。欧盟的早期会计协调主要通过指令的形式对欧盟（前欧共体）各国的会计标准进行协调。迄今发布的指令中与会计和财务报告事项最相关的是：第 4 号指令（关于有限责任公司（包括证券公开发行和不公开发行）的年度财务报表和年度报告，1978 年）；第 7 号指令（公司集团合并财务报表，1983 年）和第 8 号指令（审计师的资格和工作，1984 年）。进入 20 世纪 90 年代后，欧盟开始加速推动成员国会计标准的协调。并在国际会计准则的国际地位不断提升的形势下，最终选择采用国际会计准则进行成员国间的会计协调。

亚洲－大洋洲会计准则制定机构组（Asian-Oceanian Standard-Setters Group，AOSSG）的构想最初由中国在 2008 年 10 月举行的国际财务报告准则亚洲年会上提出。之后，在中国的主导下，联合澳大利亚、韩国、日本、马来西亚、新加坡、新西兰等国会计准则制定机构，共同倡议成立 AOSSG。2009 年 11 月 4 日至 5 日，AOSSG 第一次全体会议在吉隆坡举行。AOSSG 旨在讨论和分享国际财务报告准则的运用，以推动国际财务报告准则在本地区的一致应用，并更加有效地参与国际财务报告准则的制定工作。

泛非会计师联合会（Pan-African Federation of Accountants，PAFA）于 2011 年 5 月 5 日在达喀尔宣布成立。该组织由来自非洲 35 个国家的 37 个职业会计组织组成，秘书处设在南非特许会计师协会。由于非洲国家的经济持续增长，会计职业对公司治理、公共部门财务报告的作用变得越来越重要。PAFA 将加速非洲会计职业的发展，提升非洲会计职业组织在国际舞台的声音。

▶ 问答题 Questions

1. Briefly describe accounting harmonization.

2. What is meant by mutual recognition? Is mutual recognition a feasible solution to the issue of allowing foreign companies to register on the stock exchanges of other countries?

3. What are the advantages and disadvantages of financial statements prepared according to international standards?

4. As the world economy becomes more integrated, one question facing financial analysts is whether financial ratios can be compared across national boundaries. For example, at one time the average P/E ratio for Japanese companies was around 60, while the average for U. S. companies was between 15 and 20. This dra-

matic variation was a result of differences in two national economies and in their accounting methods. In addition to differences in accounting methods, what other challenges are faced by financial analysts in comparing the financial ratios of U. S. companies to those of a Japanese, German or British company?

5. How does the IFAC promote international accounting harmonization?

6. Nestle S. A. is a very large company headquartered in a very small country (Switzerland). It has operations in more than 50 different countries around the world. Much of the company's international expansion has been through the acquisition of local (i. e. foreign) companies. What major problems does worldwide accounting diversity cause for a company like Nestle?

7. Some say that IFRS are now GAAP in the European Union. How is this statement true and how is it false?

International Accounting Standards Board

国际会计准则理事会

◎ 小案例 Mini Case

Mr. Li plans to practice accounting in China with Chinese companies using Chinese accounting standards and regulations. Accordingly, he sees no reason to know anything about the International Accounting Standards Board or cross-national differences in accounting practices. Is there any rationale in his view? What might you say to him to get him to reconsider his position?

正文 Text

In an attempt to harmonize conflicting standards, the International Accounting Standards Committee (IASC) was formed in 1973 by professional accounting organizations in nine countries to develop worldwide accounting standards. This body now represents more than 142 accountancy bodies from 103 countries. The early standards of the IASC were primarily catalogs of the diverse accounting practices then used worldwide. The IASC was often blamed in that its standards included too many alternative accounting treatments and were not rigorous enough. In 2001 the reorganization made IASC into an umbrella organization under which the International Accounting Standards Board (IASB) carries out standard-setting work.

15. 1　Organization of International Accounting Standards Board

In 1999 the Board of the IASC approved a report Recommendations on Shaping IASC for the Future which recommended that a new structure for the IASC was required to reflect the IASC's increased importance. On February 6, 2001, the International Financial Reporting Standards

Foundation (IFRS Foundation) was also incorporated as a tax-exempt organization in Delaware. The IFRS Foundation has a three-tier governance structure, based on an independent standard-setting Board of experts (International Accounting Standards Board), governed and overseen by Trustees from around the world (IFRS Foundation Trustees) who in turn are accountable to a monitoring board of public authorities (IFRS Foundation Monitoring Board). The IFRS Advisory Council provides advice and counsel to the Trustees and the Board. The IFRS Interpretations Committee is the interpretative body of the International Accounting Standards Board. The Interpretations Committee works with the Board in supporting the application of IFRS Standards.

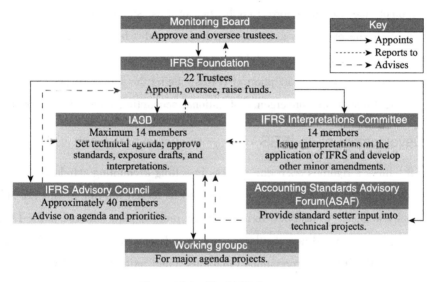

Figure 15-1   The IASB Structure

The 22 trustees of IFRS Foundation are responsible for governance issues and ensuring that each body is properly funded. The trustees act by simple majority vote except for amendments to the IFRS Foundation Constitution, which require a three-fourths majority. The IASB consists of 14 members. All Board members should be appointed for a first term of five years and then for a second term, which would normally be three years, but with the flexibility to extend that for up to five years, capped at 10 years. The IASB is solely responsible for issuing new International Accounting Standards. The IASB has announced that its new standards will be called International Financial Reporting Standards (IFRSs), but the existing standards will continue to be called International Accounting Standards (IASs). In general, the term "IFRSs" refers both to the existing IASs issued by the former IASC and to the IFRSs from the IASB. The IFRS Interpretations Committee issues rapid guidance on accounting matters where divergent interpretations of IFRSs have arisen. The IFRS Advisory Council provides a forum for a range of experts from different countries and different business sectors to offer advice to the IASB when drawing up new standards.

15. 1. 1　Objectives of the IFRS Foundation/IASB

Under the IFRS Foundation Constitution, the IFRS Foundation/IASB's objectives are:

(a) to develop, in the public interest, a single set of high quality, understandable, enforceable and globally accepted financial reporting standards based upon clearly articulated principles. These standards should require high quality, transparent and comparable information in financial statements and other financial reporting to help investors, other participants in the world's capital markets and other users of financial information make economic decisions;

(b) to promote the use and rigorous application of those standards;

(c) in fulfilling the objectives associated with (a) and (b), to take account of, as appropriate, the needs of a range of sizes and types of entities in diverse economic settings;

(d) to promote and facilitate adoption of IFRSs, being the standards and interpretations issued by the IASB, through the convergence of national accounting standards and IFRSs.

15. 1. 2　Development of an IFRS

The IASB follows a rigorous open due process in setting accounting standards. All meeting of the IASB and of the IFRS Interpretations Committee and its formal working groups are held in public and are usually webcast. In overview terms, the due process steps followed in the IASB's standard-level projects, i. e. proposed new standards, and amendments to existing standards and interpretations developed by the IFRS Interpretations Committee (and ratified by the IASB), are:

- research programme
- developing a proposal for publication
- redeliberations and finalization
- post-implementation reviews

Research programme involves the analysis of possible financial reporting problems by collecting evidence on the nature and extent of the perceived shortcoming and assessing potential ways to improve financial reporting or to remedy a deficiency. Also includes the consideration of broader financial reporting issues, such as how financial reporting is evolving, to encourage international debate on financial reporting matters. A discussion paper, request for information or research paper may be released, which are designed to elicit comments from interested parties. At this stage, the above publication of a discussion document requires a simple majority of IASB members by way of ballot.

Once the IASB has formally decided to add a project to its agenda (requiring a simple majority vote at a public IASB meeting), it proceeds to the development of an exposure draft. The exposure draft is issued (requiring the approval of 9 out of 13 Board members or more, or 8 out of 12 or fewer members) for public consultation and the IASB may also undertake additional outreach activities such as meetings, discussion forums and roundtable meetings.

After the publication of an exposure draft, the IASB proceed to consider feedback from the consultative process (with comment period of normally 120 days). In some cases, the IASB may decide to re-expose proposals before proceeding to a finalized pronouncement. Once deliberations have been finalized, the IASB's technical staff will prepare the final standard for balloting and voting on by the Board (requiring the approval of 9 out of 13 Board members or more, or 8 out of 12 or fewer members).

The IASB must conduct a post-implementation review of each new standard or major amendment, usually after they have been applied for around two years. This means the post-implementation review process will commence around 2. 5-3 years after the effective date of the pronouncement, but may be deferred in some cases.

15. 1. 3　Use and Application of IFRSs

Neither the IASB nor the accountancy profession has the power to enforce compliance with IFRSs. There are two primary methods used by countries to incorporate IFRS into their financial reporting requirements for listed companies: (a) full adoption of IFRS as issued by the IASB, without any intervening review or approval by a local body and (b) adoption of IFRS after some form of national or multinational review and approval process. The EU follows the second method with individual IFRS going through a multistep process of review as explored in Chapter 14.

Most countries of economic importance require or permit domestic listed companies to use IFRS in preparing their consolidated financial statements. The most important exceptions are China and U. S. , the two largest economies in the world. In 2006, China adopted a completely new set of Chinese Accounting Standards that is based on IFRS. More details about U. S. standpoint to IFRS will be covered in section 4 of the chapter.

15. 2　Conceptual Framework for Financial Reoprting

As well as developing its accounting standards, the IASB has adopted an important document setting out the concepts underlying the preparation and presentation of financial statements for external users—*The Framework for the Preparation and Presentation of Financial Statements*. The Framework was originally developed by the IASC in July 1989. As much of the early international work on developing a conceptual framework was carried out in the US, the IASC largely used US achievements (a series of Statements of Financial Accounting Concepts) to develop its own *Framework*. Then, the UK "Statement of Principles" was largely based on the IASC *Frame-*

work. Since there is so much common agreement on the concepts underpinning financial accounting, it is hoped that standards based on these concepts can be agreed throughout the world. In 2004, the IASB and the US FASB decided to review and develop an improved conceptual framework for IFRSs and US GAAP. In September 2010, the Boards announced the completion of the first phase of their joint project. This first phase of the conceptual framework deals with the objective and qualitative characteristics of financial reporting, as discussed in Part 1. However, in September 2012, the IASB decided to reactivate the Conceptual Framework project as the IASB-only comprehensive project.

15. 2. 1 Purpose of the Framework

The *Framework* is, in effect, the conceptual framework upon which all IASs and IFRSs are based and hence which determines how financial statements are prepared and the information they contain. The purpose of the Framework is to:

- assist the IASB in the development of future IFRSs and in its review of existing IASs;
- assist the IASB in promoting harmonization of regulations, accounting standards and procedures relating to the presentation of financial statements by providing a basis for reducing the number of alternative accounting treatments permitted by IASs;
- assist national standard-setting bodies in developing national standards;
- assist preparers of financial statements in applying IFRSs and in dealing with topics that have yet to form the subject of an IFRS;
- assist auditors in forming an opinion as to whether financial statements conform with IFRSs;
- assist users of financial statements in interpreting the information contained in financial statements prepared in conformity with IFRSs;
- provide those who are interested in the work of IASB with information about its approach to the formulation of IFRSs.

The *Framework* is not an IFRS and so does not overrule any individual IFRS. In the (rare) cases of conflict between an IAS or IFRS and the *Framework*, the IAS or IFRS will prevail. These cases will diminish over time as the *Framework* will be used as a guide in the production of future IFRSs. The *Framework* itself will be revised occasionally depending on the experience of the IASB in using it.

In March 2018, the IASB published its revised Conceptual Framework. Included are revised definitions of an asset and a liability as well as new guidance on measurement and derecognition, presentation and disclosure. The new Conceptual Framework does not constitute a substantial revision of the document as was originally intended when the project was first taken up in 2004. Instead the IASB focused on topics that were not yet covered or that showed obvious shortcomings that needed to be dealt with.

15. 2. 2 Scope of the Framework

The 2018 Conceptual Framework is structured into an introductory explanation on the status and purpose of the Conceptual Framework, eight chapters and a glossary:

- the objective of general purpose financial reporting;
- qualitative characteristics of useful financial information;
- financial statements and the reporting entity;
- the elements of financial statements;
- recognition and derecognition;
- measurement;
- presentation and disclosure;
- concepts of capital and capital maintenance.

As several topics have been dealt with in Part 1, we are only concerned with the last issue below.

15. 2. 3 Concepts of Capital and Capital Maintenance

Definitions of profit may refer to the need to maintain the capital of the enterprise. In fact there are two main concepts of capital maintenance, i. e. financial capital maintenance and physical capital maintenance. Under the concept of financial capital maintenance, a profit is earned only if the financial or money amount of the net assets at the end of a period exceeds the financial or money amount of net assets at the beginning of the period. Under the concept of physical capital maintenance, a profit is earned only if the physical productive capacity of the business at the end of the period exceeds the physical productive capacity at the beginning of the period. The physical capital maintenance concept requires the adoption of the current cost basis of measurement. The content in this chapter was taken over from 1989 Conceptual Framework and the IASB might consider revising the description and discussion of capital maintenance in the future if it considers such a revision necessary.

15. 3 Core Standards by International Accounting Standards Committee

15. 3. 1 Agreement between IOSCO and IASC/IFRS Foundation

The IASB (and the former IASC) has been striving to develop accounting standards that will be accepted by securities regulators around the world. As part of that effort, the IASC adopted a work plan to produce a comprehensive core set of high-quality standards. In July 1995, the IOSCO Technical Committee stated its agreement with the work plan. Completion of comprehensive core standards that are acceptable to the Technical Committee will allow the Technical Committee to recommend endorsement of IAS for cross-border capital raising and listing purposes in all global markets.

In September 2013, IOSCO and the IFRS Foundation announced agreement on a set of protocols to improve consistency in the implementation of IFRS. The Statement of Protocols for Cooperation on International Financial Reporting Standards reiterates the current relationship between the two organizations and identifies new areas for mutually supportive work.

15. 3. 2　Completion of Core Standards

The Core Standards were completed with the approval of IAS 39 (Financial Instruments: Recognition and Measurement) in December 1998. IOSCO's review of the Core Standards began in 1999 and in 2000 it endorsed the use of IASC Standards for cross-border offerings and listings. IOSCO recommended that its members permit incoming multinational issuers to use the IASC Standards to bring great benefits in the form of cost savings for preparers, auditors and users of financial statements and clearer, less confusing communication about financial matters. A list of Core Standards is as Table 15-1.

Table 15-1　IOSCO Core Standards and Corresponding IFRS (including IAS)

Core Standards (40 items) as set forth by IOSCO in 1993		Current IFRS (last revision)
General	Disclosure of accounting policies	IAS1 (2007)
	Changes in accounting policies	IAS8 (2003)
	Information disclosed in financial statements	IAS1 (2007)
Income statement	Revenue recognition	IFRS15 (2014)
	Construction contracts	IFRS15 (2014)
	Production and purchase costs	IAS2 (2005)
	Depreciation	IAS16 (2003)
	Impairment	IAS36 (2004)
	Taxes	IAS12 (1996)
	Extraordinary items	IAS8 (2003)
	Government grants	IAS20 (1983)
Income statement	Retirement benefits	IAS26 (1987)
	Other employee benefits	IAS19 (2011)
	Research and development	IAS38 (2004)
	Interest	IAS23 (2007)
	Hedging	IFRS9 (2014)
Statement of financial position	Property, plant and equipment	IAS16 (2003)
	Leases	IAS17 (2003)
	Inventories	IAS2 (2005)
	Deferred taxes	IAS12 (1996)
	Foreign currency	IAS21 (2003)

(continued)

Core Standards (40 items) as set forth by IOSCO in 1993		Current IFRS (last revision)
Statement of financial position	Investments	IFRS9 (2014) and IAS40 (2003)
	Financial instruments/ off balance sheet items	IAS32 (2003) and IFRS7 (2005)
	Joint ventures	IAS28 (2011)
	Contingencies	IAS37 (1998)
	Events occurring after the balance sheet date	IAS10 (2003)
	Current assets and current liabilities	IAS1 (2007)
	Business combinations (including goodwill)	IFRS3 (2008)
	Intangibles other than R&D and goodwill	IAS38 (2004)
Statement of cash flow		IAS7 (1992)
Other standards	Consolidated financial statements	IFRS10 (2011)
	Subsidiary in hyperinflationary economies	IAS21 (2003) and IAS29 (1989)
	Associates and equity financing	IAS28 (2011)
	Segment reporting	IFRS8 (2006)
	Interim reporting	IAS34 (1998)
	Earnings per share	IAS33 (2003)
	Related party disclosures	IAS24 (2009)
	Discontinuing operations	IFRS5 (2004)
	Fundamental errors	IAS8 (2003)
	Changes in estimates	IAS8 (2003)

15. 4 IFRSs and US GAAP

15. 4. 1 Working towards a single set of global standards

The Securities and Exchange Commission (SEC) requires those companies that list their shares on a US stock exchange to report their financial information in accordance with US GAAP. The objective is to protect American investors from misunderstanding financial information prepared according to foreign standards. But as capital became more mobile internationally, such policies became increasingly unsustainable. In November 2007, the SEC voted to allow foreign issuers to submit financial statements prepared using IFRSs as issued by the IASB without having to include a reconciliation to the IFRS figures to US GAAP. In November 2008, the SEC issued a proposed rule for the potential use of IFRS by U. S. public companies. This so-called IFRS Roadmap sets forth several milestones that, if achieved, could lead to the required use of IFRS by U. S. issuers. The roadmap indicated 2014 as the first year of IFRS adoption, but a subsequent SEC Release in February 2010 pushed that date back to "approximately 2015 or 2016".

For the past several years, the IASB and FASB have been working together to achieve convergence of IFRSs and US GAAP. In 2002, as part of the Norwalk Agreement, the Boards issued a Memorandum of Understanding (MOU) formalizing their commitment to making their existing financial reporting standards fully compatible as soon as practicable, and coordinating their future work programmes to ensure that, once achieved, compatibility is maintained.

15. 4. 2　Memorandum of Understanding (2008)

On September 11, 2008, an updated MOU was published, which sets out priorities and milestones to be achieved on major joint projects by 2011. The Boards have acknowledged that, although considerable progress has been achieved on a number of designated projects, achievements on other projects have been limited for various reasons, including differences in views over issues of agenda size and project scope, differences in views over the most appropriate approach, and differences in views about whether and how similar issues in active projects should be resolved consistently. As a result, the scopes and objectives of many of the projects have been or are expected to be revised. In updating the MOU, the Boards noted that the major joint projects will take account of the ongoing work to improve and converge their respective Conceptual Frameworks. Also, the Boards will consider staggering effective dates of standards to ensure an orderly transition to new standards. Consistent with its current practice, the IASB will consider permitting early adoption of its Standards. In June 2010, the IASB and FASB modified their convergence strategy. The IASB issued a modified work plan that prioritizes certain projects such as financial instruments, revenue recognition and leases, etc.

Through these projects, some covering major components of the financial statements, the Boards intend to improve financial reporting information for investors while also aligning US and international accounting standards. These projects are a significant move toward achieving a common accounting framework, a necessary step in the globalization of business and investment.

As of January 2013, the IASB-FASB convergence process had resulted in changes made to U. S. GAAP, IFRS, or both in the following areas:

- Business combinations
- Consolidated financial statements
- Share-based payment
- Fair value measurement
- Accounting changes
- Borrowing costs
- Post-employment benefits
- Nonmonetary asset exchanges, etc.

However, the switch to IFRS would be a complex, multi-year process that would involve significant changes to the U. S. financial reporting system, including changes in auditing standards, licensing requirements and how accountants are educated. In July 2012, the SEC staff issued a report that summarized analysis on the possible use of IFRS by U. S. companies, but it did not include conclusions or recommendation for action by the SEC and did not provide insight into the nature or timetable for next steps. As of September 2016, more than 500 foreign private issuers with a market capitalization in excess of US \$ 7 trillion file with the SEC financial statements prepared on the basis of IFRS Standards. Meanwhile the SEC does not permit its domestic issuers to use IFRS Standards in preparing their financial statements; rather, it requires them to use US GAAP.

▶ 核心词汇 Core Words and Expressions

Accounting Standards Advisory Forum （ASAF）
　会计准则咨询论坛

conceptual framework　概念框架

convergence　趋同

Discussion Paper　讨论稿

due process　充分程序，也称应循程序

Exposure Draft　征求意见稿

financial capital maintenance　财务资本保全

hedge　套期保值

hyperinflationary economies　恶性通货膨胀经济

IFRS Foundation　国际财务报告准则基金会

IFRS Foundation Constitution　国际财务报告准则基金会章程

IFRS Interpretations Committee　国际财务报告准则解释委员会

IOSCO Technical Committee　IOSCO 技术委员会

off-balance sheet items　资产负债表外项目

physical capital maintenance　实物资本保全

Standards Advisory Council （SAC）　准则咨询委员会

IFRS Advisory Council　国际财务报告准则咨询委员会

securities regulator　证券监管者

Statement of Principles　（英国）原则公告

Statements of Financial Accounting Concepts　（美国）财务会计概念公告

trustee　受托人

▶ 知识扩展 More Knowledge

国际会计准则理事会的主要准则

IAS 1 （International Accounting Standard 1—Presentation of financial statements）　国际会计准则第 1 号——财务报表列报

IAS 7 （International Accounting Standard 7—Statement of cash flows）　国际会计准则第 7 号——现金流量表

IAS 8 （International Accounting Standard 8—Accounting policies, changes in accounting estimate and errors）　国际会计准则第 8 号——会计政策、会计估计变更和差错

IAS 16 （International Accounting Standard 16—Property, plant and equipment）　国际会计准则第 16 号——不动产、厂场和设备

IAS 19 （International Accounting Standard 19—Employee benefits）　国际会计准则第 19 号——雇员福利

IAS 20 （International Accounting Standard 20—Accounting for government grants and disclosure of government assistance）　国际会计准则第 20 号——政府补助会计和政府援助的披露

IAS 21（International Accounting Standard 21—The effects of changes in foreign exchange rates）　国际会计准则第 21 号——外汇汇率变动的影响

IAS 23（International Accounting Standard 23—Borrowing costs）　国际会计准则第 23 号——借款费用

IAS 24（International Accounting Standard 24—Related party disclosure）　国际会计准则第 24 号——关联方披露

IAS 28（International Accounting Standard 28—Investments in associates and joint ventures）　国际会计准则第 28 号——在联营企业和合营企业中的投资

IAS 32（International Accounting Standard 32—Financial instruments：presentation）　国际会计准则第 32 号——金融工具：列报

IAS 36（International Accounting Standard 36—Impairment of assets）　国际会计准则第 36 号——资产减值

IAS 37（International Accounting Standard 37—Provisions，contingent liabilities and contingent assets）国际会计准则第 37 号——准备、或有负债和或有资产

IAS 38（International Accounting Standard 38—Intangible assets）　国际会计准则第 38 号——无形资产

IAS 40（International Accounting Standard 40—Investment property）　国际会计准则第 40 号——投资性房地产

IAS 41（International Accounting Standard 41—Agriculture）　国际会计准则第 41 号——农业

IFRS 2（International Financial Reporting Standard 2—Share-based payment）　国际财务报告准则第 2 号——股份支付

IFRS 3（International Financial Reporting Standard 3—Business combination）　国际财务报告准则第 3 号——企业合并

IFRS 9（International Financial Reporting Standard 9—Financial instruments）　国际财务报告准则第 9 号——金融工具

IFRS 10（International Financial Reporting Standard 10—Consolidated financial statements）　国际财务报告准则第 10 号——合并财务报表

IFRS 11（International Financial Reporting Standard 11—Joint arrangements）　国际财务报告准则第 11 号——合营安排

IFRS 13（International Financial Reporting Standard 13—Fair value measurement）　国际财务报告准则第 13 号——公允价值计量

IFRS 15（International Financial Reporting Standard 15—Revenue from Contracts with Customers）　国际财务报告准则第 15 号——与客户之间的合同产生的收入

IFRS 16（International Financial Reporting Standard 16—Leases）　国际财务报告准则第 16 号——租赁

为实现"趋同"目标，IASB 继续寻求与各主要国家的准则制定机构建立良好的合作关系，特别

是与美、英、加、澳、德、法、日 7 个发达国家的准则制定机构建立了战略性合作伙伴关系，并在准则制定和修订方面与它们开展了实质性的合作，以便及时发现和解决准则的差异。

　　IASB 全球会计准则的提出，迅速得到很多国家和重要组织的认可，并取得国际资本市场强有力的支持。IOSCO、IFAC、世界银行、国际货币基金组织、OECD、八国集团、巴塞尔银行监管委员会、国际审计和鉴证准则理事会、ISAR 等相继发表声明，认可和支持全球会计准则的建设，支持 IASB 作为全球会计准则的制定主体所做的努力。据 IASB 网站在 2017 年 12 月对全球 93 家证券交易所的统计，世界上大多数证券交易所都承认和支持上市公司以 IASs/IFRSs 为基础编制财务报告。截至 2018 年 4 月 25 日，IASB 已完成 166 个国家或地区的 IFRS 使用情况调研，全球已有 144 个国家或地区采用了国际会计准则或与之实现了趋同。IASB 的努力得到了巨大的回报，以 IASs/IFRSs 为主体的会计标准体系正在赢得全球会计准则的地位。全球会计准则趋同是当今会计国际协调的现实选择，是大势所趋。

▶ 问答题　Questions

1. Why are differing national accounting standards converging to a common global standard?

2. Historically, some countries such as the U. S. refused to allow foreign securities complying with IASC standards to trade in their domestic stock exchanges. What is the rationale behind the refusal to IASC standards? Explain from one country's perspective, such as the U. S.

3. Describe the structure of the IASB.

4. Summarize the due process by the IASB to establish standards.

5. As a Chinese accountant, do you see any reason to know anything about the International Accounting Standards Board or cross-national differences in accounting practices?

6. What have the IASB and FASB agreed to do in the Norwalk Agreement?

7. How is the process of convergence with IASB standards as followed by the FASB different from the adoption of IFRS as occurred in European Union?

Special Accounting Treatments in Multinational Corporations

跨国公司的特殊业务会计处理

◎ **小案例** Mini Case

As the chief financial officer for a large Chinese company, which owns a French subsidiary, you are responsible for preparing the consolidated financial statements. What procedures would you take in consolidating related financial statements?

正文 Text

16. 1　Foreign Currency Transactions and Translations

An entity may carry on foreign activities in two ways. It may have transactions in foreign currencies or it may have foreign operations. In addition, an entity may present its financial statements in a foreign currency. To determine foreign currency, the functional currency must first be determined. Defined in IAS 21 functional currency is the currency of the primary economic environment in which the entity operates. In most instances, the functional currency is the currency in which most of the entity's transactions are denominated, e. g. local or domestic currency. Therefore, foreign currency is the currency other than the functional currency of the entity.

16. 1. 1　Foreign Currency Transactions

Foreign currency transactions occur whenever an enterprise purchases or sells goods or services for which settlement is made in a foreign currency or when it borrows or lends foreign currency. A foreign currency transaction should be recorded on initial recognition in the functional currency, by applying to the foreign currency amount the spot exchange rate between the functional currency and the foreign currency at the date of transaction. Then at each reporting date foreign currency monetary items (settled in a fixed or determinable number of units of currency) should be translated using the closing rate. Concurrently, exchange differences will arise and should be immediately recognized in profit or loss as well as on the settlement of monetary items.

Assume on November 1 20 × 1 Washing Company purchased inventory from Franc Company and the invoice was denominated in francs with a purchase price of 50 000 francs. At the time of purchase, the exchange rate was 5 francs per US $. Washing would make the journal entry:

November 1 20 × 1

Inventory	$ 10 000	
Accounts payable (franc)		$ 10 000

If the terms call for payment of the liability on February 1 20 × 2, the spot rate for that day is 4.7 francs per US $. Washing would make the journal entry:

February 1 20 × 2

Accounts payable (franc)	$ 10 000	
Exchange loss	638	
Cash		$ 10 638

Or suppose Washing's accounting period ends on December 31 and the exchange rate on December 31 20 × 1 is 4.8 francs per US $. Washing would make the journal entry:

December 31 20 × 1

Exchange loss	$ 417	
Accounts payable (franc)		$ 417

Then on February 1 20 × 2 Washing would make the journal entry:

February 1 20 × 2

Accounts payable (franc)	$ 10 417	
Exchange loss	221	
Cash		$ 10 638

16.1.2 Foreign Currency Translations

It is necessary whenever a company with operations in more than one country prepares consolidated financial statements that combine financial statements denominated in one national currency with statements denominated in another (i.e. the parent country's) currency. Many of its problems stem from the fact that foreign exchange rates are seldom fixed. Foreign currency translation is the process of expressing amounts dominated or measured in one currency in terms of another currency by use of the exchange rate between the two currencies. Translation is not the same as conversion, which is the physical exchange of one currency for another. Translation is simply a change in monetary expression. No physical exchange occurs and no accountable transaction takes place as it does in conversion.

Companies operating internationally use a variety of methods to express, in terms of their domestic currency, the assets, liabilities, revenues and expenses that are stated in a foreign currency. These translation methods can be classified into two types: those that use a single translation rate to restate foreign balances to their presentation currency equivalents and those that use multiple rates. The single rate method, long popular in Europe, applies a single exchange rate, the current or closing rate, to all foreign currency assets and liabilities. Multiple rate method combines the current and historical exchange rates in the translation process. Amongthe category are current-noncurrent method, monetary-nonmonetary method and temporal method.

The current (single) rate method of translation is straightforward translation from one currency to another. There is neither change in the nature of the accounts (only their particular form of expression is changed) nor change in the initial relationships (i. e. financial ratios) in the foreign currency statements, as all account balances are simply multiplied by a constant. IAS 21 applies the current rate method in the requirements of translation, stating:

- Assets and liabilities for each statement of financial position presented (including comparatives) shall be translated at the closing rate at the date of that statement. Share capital and pre-acquisition retained earnings are translated at the historical rate, i. e. the rate when the investing company acquired its interest.

- Income and expenses for each income statement (including comparatives) shall be translated at exchange rates at the dates of the transactions. For practical reasons, a rate that approximates the exchange rates at the dates of the transactions, for example an average rate for the period, is often used to translate income and expenses items.

- All resulting exchange differences shall be recognized as a separate component of equity. These exchange differences are not recognized in profit or loss because the changes in exchange rates have little or no direct effect on the present and future cash flows from operations.

Assume A Company (£) purchased B Company (US $) on January 1 20 ×2 for $ 50 000. On the date, the exchange rate for $ 1 was £ 0. 25, so the acquisition price was equivalent to £ 12 500. On December 31 20 × 2, the following trial balance for B is available. The current rate is £ 0. 28, and the average rate for the year was £ 0. 27. Dividends were declared and paid when the exchange rate was £ 0. 275 (see Table 16-1).

Table 16-1

	US $		US $
Cash	10 000	Trade payables	50 000
Trade receivables	35 000	Long-term debt	80 000
Inventory	65 000	Share capital	30 000
Equipment	90 000	Retained earnings	20 000
Cost of sales	60 000	Sales	120 000
Expenses	30 000		
Dividends	10 000		
Total debits	300 000	Total credits	300 000

B's financial statements are required to translate into £ for consolidation with A's financial statements. The translation process is as Table 16-2:

Table 16-2

December 31 20 ×2	Trial balance in US $	Exchange rate	Trial balance in £
Cash	10 000	£ 0. 28	2 800
Trade receivables	35 000	£ 0. 28	9 800
Inventory	65 000	£ 0. 28	18 200
Equipment	90 000	£ 0. 28	25 200
Cost of sales	60 000	£ 0. 27	16 200
Expenses	30 000	£ 0. 27	8 100
Dividends	10 000	£ 0. 275	2 750
	300 000		83 050
Trade payables	50 000	£ 0. 28	14 000
Long-term debt	80 000	£ 0. 28	22 400
Share capital	30 000	£ 0. 25	7 500
Retained earnings	20 000	£ 0. 25	5 000
Sales	120 000	£ 0. 27	32 400
Exchange difference			1 750
	300 000		83 050

In this example, B requires an additional credit of £ 1 750 to balance the Sterling pound trial balance. This exchange difference can be recognized in equity on consolidated financial statements.

16. 2 Business Combination and Consolidated Financial Statements

16. 2. 1 Business Combination

A business combination is the bringing together of separate entities or businesses into one open reporting entity. The usual example of a business combination is when a parent company has acquired a controlling interest in a subsidiary and consolidated financial statements are being prepared.

IFRS 3 requires that all business combinations within its scope must be accounted for using the acquisition method (also called the purchase method). In the past another method called the uniting of interests method (also called the pooling of interests method or merger accounting) was used to prepare consolidated financial statements in certain circumstances. The situation has now been simplified since IFRS3 states that the acquisition method must be used in all circumstances.

16. 2. 2　Goodwill

An acquirer must be identified for every business combination. The acquirer is the combining enterprise that obtains control over the other combining enterprises. Goodwill must be calculated at the acquisition date, being the difference between the fair value of the consideration transferred (i. e. the fair value of shares issued and cash paid) and the aggregate of the fair value of the separable net assets acquired. Separable net assets are those assets (and liabilities) which can be identifiedand sold off separately without necessarily disposing of the business as a whole. They include identifiable intangible assets such as patents, licenses and trademarks.

It is necessary to draw a distinction between purchased and non-purchased (or inherent) goodwill. Goodwill exists in any successful business. However, if the business has never changed hands, this goodwill will not be recognized in the financial statements because no event has occurred to identify its value. It is not capable of being measured reliably, failing to satisfy the recognition criteria in the Framework. This is non-purchased goodwill and is not recognized. Purchased goodwill is recognized within the financial statements because at a specific point in time, the fact of purchase has established a figure of value for the business as a whole which can be compared with the fair value of the individual net assets acquired. Of course, a business which has acquired another and thus purchased goodwill may then build up inherent goodwill of its own, but only the former will be reflected in the financial statements.

IFRS 3 requires that goodwill acquired on the purchase of a subsidiary should be recognized as an asset but should not be amortized. Instead it must be tested for impairment annually or more frequently if events or circumstances indicate that it might be impaired following the rule of IAS 36.

A Ltd pays $ 100 000 cash to acquire 100% of B Ltd, whose identifiable net assets at the date of acquisition have an aggregate fair value of $ 80 000. Cost of goodwill = $ 100 000 − $ 80 000 = $ 20 000. The goodwill will be presented as an intangible noncurrent asset of $ 20 000 on the consolidated statement of financial position and subjected to annual impairment tests.

16. 2. 3　Negative Goodwill

There will be cases where the fair value of the separable net assets exceeds the fair value of the business as a whole. This difference is called negative goodwill. IFRS 3 has changed the previous treatment of negative goodwill. It is first necessary to review the fair values placed on identifiable assets and liabilities to ensure that they have been properly stated. After this review has been carried out, it is possible that some negative goodwill will still remain. It should be recognized immediately as a profit in the consolidated income statement.

16. 2. 4　Consolidated Financial Statements

Although every company is a separate entity from the legal point of view, from the economic point of view several companies may not be separate at all. In particular when one company owns enough shares in another company to have a majority of votes at that company's annual general meeting, the degree of control enables the first company (the parent) to manage the trading activities and future plans of the second company (a subsidiary) as if it were merely a department of the first company. The best way of showing the results of a group is to imagine that all the transactions of the group had been carried out by a single equivalent company and to prepare a statement of financial position, income statement and statement of cashflows for that company. IFRS 10 requires a parent company to produce consolidated financial statements. Each company in a group prepares its accounting records and annual financial statements in the usual way. From the individual companies' financial statements, the parent company prepares consolidated financial statements for the group.

16. 2. 5　Entity Concept and Proprietary Concept

Consolidated financial statements are prepared by replacing the cost of investments with the individual assets and liabilities underlying that investment. If the subsidiary is only partly owned (non-controlling interests exist), this does not affect the amount of assets and liabilities of the subsidiary which are consolidated, but results in the need to show the non-controlling shareholders' interests in those net assets. The entity concept focuses on the existence of the group as an economic unit rather than looking at it only through the eyes of the dominant shareholder group. It concentrates on the resources controlled by the entity. The usual method of consolidation under this concept is acquisition accounting or purchase method. IFRS 3 requires all business combinations to be consolidated under entity concept.

The proprietary concept is different from the entity concept only where there are non-controlling interests. There are two main variants:
- The parent company concept, which in terms of the mechanics of consolidation is similar to the entity concept except that non-controlling interests are shown as liabilities rather than as part of a group equity.

- The proportional consolidation method is where only the group share of individual assets and liabilities is included in the relevant group totals. Thus non-controlling shareholders' interest in the net assets is not shown.

16. 2. 6 Consolidation of Statement of Financial Position

The summarized draft statements of financial position of the companies in a group at December 31 20 ×4 were as Table 16-3.

Table 16-3

	P	S
Sundry assets	$ 105 000	$ 34 400
Investment in S at cost	27 000	—
Total assets	132 000	34 400
Ordinary share capital ($ 1 shares)	100 000	20 000
Retained earnings	22 000	6 500
Payables	10 000	7 900
Total equity and liabilities	132 000	34 400

P acquired 16 000 ordinary shares (80% partly owned) in S for $ 27 000 on January 1 20 ×4, when S had accumulated profit of $ 6 000. Property which was not depreciated was estimated by the directors of P to be under-valued by $ 5 000 on January 1 20 ×4. No adjustment has been made in the books of S. Prepare the consolidated statement of financial position at December 31 20 ×4.

Solution

The consolidated statement of financial position will differ from the parent's statement of financial position in that investment in subsidiary will be replaced by the underlying net assets which the investment represents. If acquisition takes place earlier than current reporting date, when looking at the revenue reserves of subsidiary at the year end, a distinction must be made between those reserves of subsidiary which existed at the date of acquisition by the parent (pre-acquisition reserves) and the increase in the reserves of subsidiary which arose after acquisition (post-acquisition reserves). Only assets and liabilities of subsidiary existing at the date of acquisition can be recognized in calculating goodwill. If the parent acquires less than 100% shares of subsidiary, non-controlling interests must be recorded and presented immediately after the subtotal capital and reserves. Under no circumstances will any share capital of any subsidiary ever be included in the figure of share capital on consolidated statement of financial position. Moreover appropriate fraction of the fair value adjustment must be allocated to non-controlling interests.

Fair value of net assets of S at acquisition = $ (20 000 + 6 000 + 5 000) = $ 31 000

Table　16-4

Consideration transferred	$ 27 000
Less share of net assets at acquisition （at fair value）	
80% × $ 31 000	(24 800)
Goodwill on consolidation	2 200

Table　16-5

Consolidated reserves	
P	$ 22 000
S　80% × （6 500 – 6 000）	400
	22 400
Non-controlling interests	
Net assets of S at the reporting date ＝ 20% × $ （20 000 + 6 500 + 5 000） ＝ $ 6 300	

Table 16-6　Consolidated statement of financial position at December 31 20 ×4

Goodwill		$ 2 200
Sundry assets	105 000 + 34 400 + 5 000	144 400
Total assets		146 600
Share capital		100 000
Retained earnings		22 400
Non-controlling interests		6 300
Total equity		128 700
Payables	10 000 + 7 900	17 900
Total equity and liabilities		146 600

The individual statements of financial position of the parent and subsidiary companies are likely to include inter-company items, i. e. amounts owing between the group companies. In addition, where goods have been sold by one group company to another at a profit and some of these goods are still in the purchaser's inventory at the reporting date, the profit included in these goods is unrealized from the point view of the group as a whole. All of these items make consolidation complicated and should be eliminated properly to show the group financial position correctly.

16. 2. 7　Income Statement Consolidation

Consolidated income statement has three sections:

- Section A, to show the whole of sales revenue, cost of sales, gross profit, taxation and profit or loss after tax;
- Section B, to show deduction for non-controlling interests' share of profits of subsidiaries not wholly owned by group;
- Section C, to show dividends, retained profits or transfers to reserves. Alternatively, Section C may be included in the *Statement of Changes in Equity.*

P acquired, several years ago, 75% of share capital of S. Their results for the year ended

November 30 20 ×4 were as Table 16-7 and Table 16-8.

Table　16-7

	P	S
Sales revenue	$ 8 400 000	$ 2 000 000
Cost of sales and expenses	7 550 000	1 780 000
Profit before tax	850 000	220 000
Income taxes	400 000	100 000
Profit after tax	450 000	120 000

Non-controlling interests in the profit are shown after group tax charge, amounting to:

$$25\% \times \$ 120\ 000 = \$ 30\ 000$$

Table 16-8　Consolidated income statement for year ended November 30 20 ×4

Sales revenue	8 400 000 + 2 000 000	$ 10 400 000
Cost of sales and expenses	7 550 000 + 1 780 000	9 330 000
Group profit before tax		1 070 000
Income taxes	400 000 + 100 000	500 000
Profit after tax		570 000
Non-controlling interests		30 000
Group net profit for the period		540 000

As with consolidated statement of financial position, there are such items as intra-group transactions influencing income statement consolidation. In consolidating income statements a rather more complicated adjustment is required on the treatment of unrealized profits on transactions.

▶ 核心词汇 Core Words and Expressions

acquisition method（purchase method）　购买法

annual general meeting　股东大会

closing rate　期末汇率

comparative　可比数据

consideration　对价

conversion　兑换

current rate method　现行汇率法

current-noncurrent method　区分流动和非流动性项目法

entity concept　实体理论

exchange difference　汇兑差额，折算差额

functional currency　功能货币

non-controlling interest　非控制权益（合并财务状况表内），非控制收益（合并利润表内）

monetary-nonmonetary method　区分货币和非货币性项目法

multiple rate method　多种汇率法

negative goodwill　负商誉

parent company concept　母公司理论

proportional consolidation method　比例合并法

proprietary concept　业主理论

single rate method　单一汇率法

spot exchange rate　即期汇率

temporal method　时态法

uniting of interests method（pooling of interests method or merger accounting）　权益集合法

▶ 知识扩展 More Knowledge

外币财务报表折算方法——时态法

无论在历史成本计量还是在现行成本计量模式下，现金总是按照资产负债表日持有的金额计量，应收款和应付款则是按资产负债表日可望在未来收回或偿付的货币金额计量，因此，货币性的资产和负债都按现行汇率折算；对于用历史成本计量的非货币性资产和负债，应按交易确认时的历史汇率折算，用现行成本计量的非货币性的资产和负债，应按现行汇率折算；对于所有者权益，国外主体的实收资本总是按股份发行日的历史汇率进行折算，留存收益则为轧算的平衡数字；利润表项目除折旧费用及无形资产摊销费用应按相关的固定资产和无形资产的历史汇率折算，其他项目通常用平均汇率予以折算。外币报表折算过程中所形成的折算损益，均计入当年已折算的净收益。故时态法的实质是：保留国外主体在其单独资产负债表上的资产和负债项目的计价基础，折算时相应选用不同的汇率。

合并范围判断——控制

控制是指投资方拥有对被投资方的权力，通过参与被投资方的相关活动而享有可变回报，并且有能力运用对被投资方的权力影响其回报金额。相关活动是指对被投资方的回报产生重大影响的活动。被投资方的相关活动应当根据具体情况进行判断，通常包括商品或劳务的销售和购买、金融资产的管理、资产的购买和处置、研究与开发活动以及融资活动等。投资方享有现时权利使其目前有能力主导被投资方的相关活动，而不论其是否实际行使该权利，视为投资方拥有对被投资方的权力。两个或两个以上投资方分别享有能够单方面主导被投资方不同相关活动的现时权利的，能够主导对被投资方回报产生最重大影响的活动的一方拥有对被投资方的权力。

投资方在判断是否拥有对被投资方的权力时，应当仅考虑与被投资方相关的实质性权利，包括自身所享有的实质性权利以及其他方所享有的实质性权利。实质性权利是指持有人在对相关活动进行决策时有实际能力行使的可执行权利。仅享有保护性权利的投资方不拥有对被投资方的权力。保护性权利是指仅为了保护权利持有人利益却没有赋予持有人对相关活动决策权的一项权利。

除非有确凿证据表明其不能主导被投资方相关活动，下列情况表明投资方对被投资方拥有权力：

- 投资方持有被投资方半数以上的表决权的。
- 投资方持有被投资方半数或以下的表决权，但通过与其他表决权持有人之间的协议能够控制半数以上表决权的。

投资方持有被投资方半数或以下的表决权，但综合考虑下列事实和情况后，判断投资方持有的表决权足以使其目前有能力主导被投资方相关活动的，视为投资方对被投资方拥有权力：

- 投资方持有的表决权相对于其他投资方持有的表决权份额的大小，以及其他投资方持有表决权的分散程度。
- 投资方和其他投资方持有的被投资方的潜在表决权，如可转换公司债券、可执行认股权证等。
- 其他合同安排产生的权利。
- 被投资方以往的表决权行使情况等其他相关事实和情况。

▶ 问答题 Questions

1. A foreign subsidiary's functional currency determines whether its financial statements should be translated. Identify the primary factor in determining a subsidiary's functional currency.

2. When financial statements are translated, what is the difference between the resulting debits and credits called? Where is this difference disclosed on the statement of financial position?

3. What are the two major issues related to the translation of foreign currency financial statements?

4. What is a business combination?

5. What is the accounting valuation basis for consolidating assets and liabilities in a business combination?

6. How should a parent company consolidate its subsidiary's revenues and expenses?

7. Under what conditions may goodwill be reported as an asset? River Company engages in a widespread advertising campaign on behalf of new products, charging above-normal expenditures to goodwill. Do you approve of this practice? Why or why not?

8. How is the proprietary concept different from the entity concept? Which concept is accepted by the IASB?

9. Why should consolidated financial statements be prepared for companies in the group?

▶ 练习题 Exercises

Exercise 1

Root Company, a U.S. computer supplies firm, sold 2 400 computer hard drives to a Canada firm, Locker Inc., on December 28, 20×2. Locker Inc. agreed to pay 148 Canadian dollars per hard drive. Payment was received by Root Company on January 10, 20×3.

U.S. dollar value of 1 unit of Canadian dollar:

As of Date of Sale	As of Balance Sheet Date	As of Date of Receipt
$0.910	$0.935	$0.905

Instructions

Prepare journal entries necessary for Root Company to record above transaction for the following: (1) date of the original transaction, (2) balance sheet date and (3) date of receipt of cash.

Exercise 2

On December 31, 20×2, the following trial balance for Metals Inc., a Japanese company is available.

	Japanese yen		Japanese yen
Cash	¥ 6 000 000	Trade payables	¥ 24 000 000
Trade receivables	18 500 000	Long-term debt	12 000 000
Inventory	21 250 000	Share capital	20 000 000
Equipment	27 700 000	Retained earnings	15 950 000
Cost of sales	36 000 000	Sales	58 000 000
Expenses	15 500 000		
Dividends	5 000 000		

Total debits	¥ 129 950 000	Total credits	¥ 129 950 000

On the date, the exchange rate was \$ 0. 007, and the average rate for the year was \$ 0. 0065. Dividends were declared and paid when the exchange rate was \$ 0. 0067. The exchange rate on January 1, 20 × 1 when the company was purchased was \$ 0. 0055. The computed retained earnings balance from the previous year's translated financial statements was \$ 105 000.

Instructions

Prepare a translated trial balance in \$ for Metals Inc. using the information provided.

Exercise 3

Carry Inc. is considering purchasing Proper Company, which has the following assets and liabilities.

	Cost	Fair market value
Trade receivables	\$ 240 000	\$ 220 000
Inventory	240 000	250 000
Prepaid insurance	10 000	10 000
Buildings and equipment (net)	70 000	200 000
Trade payables	(160 000)	(160 000)
Net assets	\$ 400 000	\$ 520 000

Instructions

Make the journal entry necessary for Carry Inc. to record the purchase if the purchase price is \$ 630 000 cash.

Exercise 4

The summarized draft statements of financial position of the companies in a group at December 31, 20 × 0 were:

Statements of financial position at December 31, 20 × 0

	P	S
	\$ 000	\$ 000
Non-current assets	50	40
Investment in S at cost	70	
Current assets	30	40
Ordinary share capital (\$ 1 shares)	100	50
Retained earnings	30	20
Current liabilities	20	10

P acquired 40 000 \$ 1 shares in S on June 30, 20 × 0 for \$ 70 000 when retained earnings of S amounted to \$ 15 000. Moreover, for all the assets and liabilities, the book value equaled fair value.

Instructions

Prepare the consolidated statement of financial position at December 31, 20 × 0.

Exercise 5

Pack Co. acquired, several years ago, 80% of share capital of Seat Inc. Their results for the year ended November 30, 20 × 2 were as follows:

	Pack Co.	Seat Inc.
Sales revenue	$ 2 400 000	$ 800 000
Cost of sales and expenses	2 160 000	720 000
Profit before tax	240 000	80 000
Income taxes	100 000	35 000
Profit after tax	140 000	45 000

Instructions

Prepare the consolidated income statement for the year ended November 30, 20 × 2. Ignore goodwill.

第五部分
Part 5

Audit

审 计

05

Audit Framework

审计框架

◎ 小案例 Mini Case

Accountants in public practice earn much of their revenue from the provision of external audit services. Companies pay substantial fees for the services of external auditors. However, the work of external auditors does not appear to improve companies' profitability so it is not immediately apparent what the benefit of an external audit is. Why is financial statements audit compulsory? Are the benefits derived from the work of external auditors?

正文 Text

17. 1 Agency and Nature of Audit

17. 1. 1 Need for Auditing

Modern auditing has developed since the concept of a company as a separate legal entity came into existence in the late nineteenth century. This led to the separation of ownership (shareholders) from control (directors) and a consequent need to safeguard the interests of the owners, who in all but the smallest of business (where shareholders and directors were one and the same) were not involved in the day-to-day decisions made by the management.

The need for an audit centers on the requirement of the users of the accounts, the stakeholders. The financial statements account annually to the shareholders for the stewardship of the directors and the management. There are also many other outside parties who use the financial statements as a basis for making decision regarding a company. Bankers, trade and loan creditors as well as potential investors and employees all have an interest in the state of the company's financial affairs. The independent audit requirement fulfils the need to ensure that those financial statements are objective, free from bias and manipulation and relevant to the needs of the users.

17. 1. 2 The Nature of Audit

According to IAS 200, the purpose of an audit is to enhance the degree of confidence of intended users in the financial statements. This is achieved by the expression of an opinion by the auditor on whether the financial statements are prepared, in all material respects, in accordance with an applicable financial reporting framework. In the case of most general purpose frameworks, that opinion is on whether the financial statements are presented fairly, in all material respects, or give a true and fair view in accordance with the framework. The financial reporting framework may be a fair presentation framework or a compliance framework.

The term "fair presentation framework" is used to refer to a financial reporting framework that requires compliance with the requirements of the framework and:

(1) Acknowledges explicitly or implicitly that, to achieve fair presentation of the financial statements, it may be necessary for management to provide disclosures beyond those specifically required by the framework; or (2) Acknowledges explicitly that it may be necessary for management to depart from a requirement of the framework to achieve fair presentation of the financial statements. Such departures are expected to be necessary only in extremely rare circumstances.

The term "compliance framework" is used to refer to a financial reporting framework that requires compliance with the requirements of the framework, but does not contain the acknowledgements in (1) or (2) above.

The financial statements subject to audit are those of the entity, prepared by management of the entity with oversight from those charged with governance. The term "financial statements" ordinarily refers to a complete set of financial statements as determined by the requirements of the applicable financial reporting framework, but can also refer to a single financial statement. Financial statements is a structured representation of historical financial information, including related notes, intended to communicate an entity's economic resources or obligations at a point in time or the changes therein for a period of time in accordance with a financial reporting framework. The related notes ordinarily comprise a summary of significant accounting policies and other explanatory information. What is included in the audited financial statements, and what is excluded, is determined largely by national legislation and accounting standards.

Note that auditors do not certify the financial statements or guarantee that the financial statements are correct; they only give a reasonable assurance that the information audited is free of material misstatement.

17.1.3 Agency Theory and Auditing

Modern organization theory views an organization as being comprised of various interest groups. The relationships between the various interested parties in the firm are often described in terms of **agency theory**. Agency relationships occur when one party, the **principal**, employs another party, the **agent**, to perform a task on their behalf. For example, directors can be seen as the agents of shareholders, employees as the agents of directors and auditors as agents of shareholders.

Principals need to recognize that although they are employing the agents, agents will have interests of their own to protect and thus may not carry out fully the requirements of the principals, which is agency relationship conflict. Auditors have a potential conflict of interest in carrying out their function to the shareholders and also remaining on good terms with the directors.

Despite having recognized the conflicts of interest that may arise, agency theory predicts that matters can be organized so that, by behaving rationally, the agent will not act against the interests of the principal. If this is true, the principal effect of agency theory on auditing is to conclude that statutory regulation is unnecessary. The management of large companies will pay high fees for extensive and sophisticated audits as they have the greatest need to convince shareholders of the management's honesty. In contrast a small company where the management and shareholders are largely the same group will not pay high fees for an audit. It can be argued that in the latter situation this is a reasonable result as the shareholders have no great need for an audit. However this conclusion does not necessarily satisfy other users of the accounting information such as lenders and tax authorities.

17.1.4 Advantages of an Audit

The needs for an audit arise primarily when the ownership and management of an enterprise are separated. There are, however, certain inherent advantages in having financial statements audited even where no statutory requirement exists for such an audit.

- Disputes between management may be more easily settled. For instance, a partnership which has complicated profit-sharing arrangements may require an independent examination of those accounts to ensure as far as possible an accurate assessment and division of those profits.
- Major changes in ownership may be facilitated if past accounts contain an unmodified audit report, for instance, where two sole traders merge their business to form a new partnership.
- Application to third parties for finance may be enhanced by audited accounts. However,

do remember that a bank, for instance, is likely to be far more concerned about the future of the business and the available security than the past historical cost accounts, audited or otherwise.

- The audit is likely to involve an in-depth examination of the business and so may enable the auditor to give constructive advice to management on improving the efficiency of the business.

17. 1. 5　Disadvantages of an Audit

These are basically twofold:

- The audit fee! Clearly the services of an auditor must be paid for. It is for this reason that few partnerships and even fewer sole traders are likely to have their accounts audited, unless such an audit is required by the local statute. The accountant's role as the preparer of financial statements, as a tax adviser and general financial adviser, becomes much more important to such concerns.

- The audit involves the client's staff and management in giving time providing information to the auditor. A professional auditor should therefore plan his audit carefully to minimize the disruption which his work will cause.

17. 1. 6　Stages of an Audit

Auditing is essentially a practical task and no audit will be identical to any other. It is however possible to identify a number of stages.

Planning—Staffing, timing, the overall audit strategy and the audit procedures to be employed are the key decisions made at this stage of the audit.

Understanding the entity is inseparable from the planning process in order to be able to assess the risks of material misstatement.

Interim audit—It is carried out during the period of review. Work tends to focus on risk assessment and on documenting and testing internal controls. Some substantive procedures can also be carried out but these are limited.

Final audit—It is taken place after the year end. It focuses on the audit of the financial statements and concludes with which the auditor issuing a report.

Reporting—It is the final stage when the auditor expresses an opinion on the financial statements.

The figure 17-1 shows the process of Auditing. In the stage of planning, the auditor will make a preliminary evaluation of the enterprise's internal controls.

(1) If the controls are likely to lead to a "true and fair" set of financial statements the audi-

tor will test those controls.

(2) If they appear weak he will not "rely" on the internal controls but carry out extensive testing of the transactions and balances which appear in the financial statements.

(3) If the controls are operating correctly the auditor can reduce the extensive testing described above and adopt a "reliance approach".

(4) If not he will be forced into a "substantive approach".

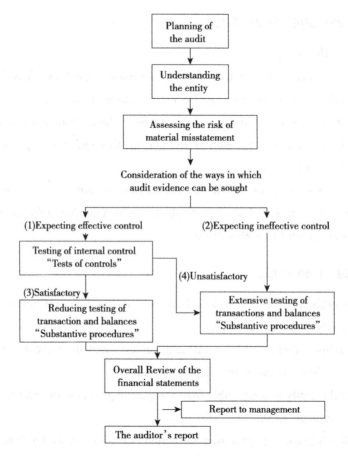

Figure 17-1 the Stages of an audit

Finally the auditor will review the financial statements as a whole and formulate his audit opinion.

The approach above is called a **risk-based approach** to auditing. In this approach, auditors analyze the risks associated with the client's business, transactions and systems which could lead to misstatements in the financial statements, and direct their testing to risky areas.

17. 2 Professional Ethics and Codes of Conduct

Over the years, the ethical requirements for auditors have increased significantly, as the auditing and reporting requirements for companies have been extended. IFAC has its own ethical guide, called the *IESBA's Code of Ethic for Professional Accountants* (the *Code*), which establishes ethical requirements for professional accountants and provides a conceptual framework for all professional accountants to ensure compliance with the five fundamental principles of professional ethics. These principles are integrity, objectivity, professional competence and due care, confidentiality, and professional behavior. Under the framework, all professional accountants are required to identify threats to these fundamental principles and, if there are threats, apply safeguards to ensure that the principles are not compromised.

17. 2. 1　Introduction

A distinguishing mark of the accountancy profession is its acceptance of the responsibility to act in the public interest. Therefore, a professional accountant's responsibility is not exclusively to satisfy the needs of an individual client or employing organization. In acting in the public interest, a professional accountant shall comply with this Code. If a professional accountant is prohibited from complying with certain parts of this Code by law or regulation, the professional accountant shall comply with all other parts of this Code.

17. 2. 2　Fundamental Principles

There are five fundamental principles of ethics for professional accountants:

- *Integrity*　to be straightforward and honest in all professional and business relationships. Integrity also implies fair dealing and truthfulness.
- *Objectivity*　not to compromise professional or business judgments because of bias, conflict of interest or undue influence of others.
- *Professional Competence and Due Care*　to:
  - Attain and maintain professional knowledge and skill at the level required to ensure that a client or employing organization receives competent professional service, based on current technical and professional standards and relevant legislation; and
  - Act diligently and in accordance with applicable technical and professional standards.
- *Confidentiality*　to respect the confidentiality of information acquired as a result of professional and business relationships.
- *Professional Behavior*　to comply with relevant laws and regulations and avoid any conduct that the professional accountant knows or should know might discredit the profession.

It is impossible to define every situation that creates threats to compliance with the fundamental principles and specify the appropriate action. Therefore, this Code establishes a conceptual framework that requires a professional accountant to identify, evaluate, and address threats to compliance with the fundamental principles. Threats to compliance with the fundamental principles might be created by a broad range of facts and circumstances. It is not possible to define every situation that creates threats. In addition, the nature of engagements and work assignments might differ and, consequently, different types of threats might be created, such as self-interest threat, self-review threat, advocacy threat, familiarity threat and intimidation threat.

A professional accountant who identifies a breach of any other provision of the Code shall evaluate the significance of the breach and its impact on the accountant's ability to comply with the fundamental principles. The accountant shall also take whatever actions might be available, as soon as possible, to address the consequences of the breach satisfactorily; and determine whether to report the breach to the relevant parties.

17. 2. 3 Confidentiality in Practice

Confidentiality serves the public interest because it facilitates the free flow of information from the professional accountant's client or employing organization to the accountant in the knowledge that the information will not be disclosed to a third party. A professional accountant shall remain alert to the principle of confidentiality, including when making disclosures or sharing information within the firm or network and seeking guidance from third parties.

A professional accountant shall comply with the principle of confidentiality, which requires an accountant to respect the confidentiality of information acquired as a result of professional and business relationships. An accountant shall:

- Be alert to the possibility of inadvertent disclosure, including in a social environment, and particularly to a close business associate or an immediate or a close family member;
- Maintain confidentiality of information within the firm or employing organization;
- Maintain confidentiality of information disclosed by a prospective client or employing organization;
- Not disclose confidential information acquired as a result of professional and business relationships outside the firm or employing organization without proper and specific authority, unless there is a legal or professional duty or right to disclose;
- Not use confidential information acquired as a result of professional and business relationships for the personal advantage of the accountant or for the advantage of a third party;
- Not use or disclose any confidential information, either acquired or received as a result of a professional or business relationship, after that relationship has ended; and
- Take reasonable steps to ensure that personnel under the accountant's control, and individuals from whom advice and assistance are obtained, respect the accountant's duty of confi-

dentiality.

The following are circumstances where professional accountants are or may be required to disclose confidential information or when such disclosure may be appropriate:

- Disclosure is permitted by law and is authorized by the client or the employer;
- Disclosure is required by law, for example:
  - (i) Production of documents or other provision of evidence in the course of legal proceedings; or
  - (ii) Disclosure to the appropriate public authorities of infringements of the law that come to light; and
- There is a professional duty or right to disclose when not prohibited by law:
  - (i) To comply with the quality review of a member body or professional body;
  - (ii) To respond to an inquiry or investigation by a member body or regulatory body;
  - (iii) To protect the professional interests of a professional accountant in legal proceedings; or
  - (iv) To comply with technical and professional standards, including ethics requirements.

In deciding whether to disclose confidential information, professional accountants should consider the following points:

- Whether the interests of all parties, including third parties whose interests may be affected, could be harmed if the client or employing organization consents to the disclosure of information by the professional accountant;
- Whether all the relevant information is known and substantiated, to the extent practicable. Factors affecting the decision to disclose include unsubstantiated facts, incomplete information and unsubstantiated conclusions.
- The proposed type of communication, and to whom it is addressed.
- Whether the parties to whom the communication is addressed are appropriate recipients.

A professional accountant shall continue to comply with the principle of confidentiality even after the end of the relationship between the accountant and a client or employing organization. When changing employment or acquiring a new client, the accountant is entitled to use prior experience but shall not use or disclose any confidential information acquired or received as a result of a professional or business relationship.

17. 2. 4　Integrity, Objectivity and Independence

Integrity requires the professional accountant to be straightforward and honest. For example, the accountant complies with the principle of integrity by being straightforward and honest when raising concerns about a position taken by a client; and pursuing inquiries about inconsistent information and seeking further audit evidence to address concerns about statements that might be materially false or misleading in order to make informed decisions about the appropriate course of action in the circumstances. In doing so, the accountant demonstrates the critical assessment of audit evidence that contributes to the exercise of professional skepticism.

Objectivity requires the professional accountant not to compromise professional or business judgment because of bias, conflict of interest or the undue influence of others. For example, the accountant complies with the principle of objectivity by recognizing circumstances or relationships such as familiarity with the client, that might compromise the accountant's professional or business judgment; and considering the impact of such circumstances and relationships on the accountant's judgment when evaluating the sufficiency and appropriateness of audit evidence related to a matter material to the client's financial statements. In doing so, the accountant behaves in a manner that contributes to the exercise of professional skepticism.

In some ways a conflict of interest creates threats to compliance with the principle of objectivity and might create threats to compliance with the other fundamental principles. Such threats might be created when a professional accountant undertakes a professional activity related to a particular matter for two or more parties whose interests with respect to that matter are in conflict; or the interest of a professional accountant with respect to a particular matter and the interests of a party for whom the accountant undertakes a professional activity related to that matter are in conflict. But objectivity is a state of mind, so in certain roles the preservation of objectivity has to be shown by the maintenance of independence from those influences which could impair objectivity.

Independence enhances the auditor's ability to act with integrity, to be objective and to maintain an attitude of professional skepticism. A professional accountant in public practice who provides an audit service is required to be independent of the audit client. Independence of mind and in appearance is necessary to enable the professional accountant in public practice to express a conclusion, and be seen to express a conclusion, without bias, conflict of interest or undue influence of others.

- **Independence of mind** is the state of mind that permits the expression of a conclusion without being affected by influences that compromise professional judgment, thereby allowing an individual to act with integrity, and exercise objectivity and professional skepticism.

- **Independence in appearance** is the avoidance of facts and circumstances that are so significant that a reasonable and informed third party would be likely to conclude, that a firm's, or an audit team member's, integrity, objectivity or professional skepticism has been compromised.

The conceptual framework approach shall be applied by professional accountants to:

（a）Identify threats to independence；

（b）Evaluate the significance of the threats identified；and

（c）Apply safeguards，when necessary，to eliminate the threats or reduce them to an acceptable level.

When the professional accountant determines that appropriate safeguards are not available or cannot be applied to eliminate the threats or reduce them to an acceptable level，the professional accountant shall eliminate the circumstance or relationship creating the threats or decline or terminate the audit engagement.

▶ 核心词汇 Core Words and Expressions

agency theory　代理理论

agent　受托人

assurance　鉴证业务

confidence　信任

confidentiality　保密

credibility　可信性

independence in appearance　形式上的独立性

independence of mind　实质上的独立性

independence　独立性

integrity　真实

objectivity　客观

principal　委托人

professional behavior　职业行为

professional competence and due care　职业能力和适当关注

professionalism　职业精神

quality of services　服务质量

substantive procedures　实质性测试

tests of controls　符合性测试

true and fair　真实和公允

▶ 知识扩展 More Knowledge

国际审计准则制定机构的变迁

国际会计师联合会（IFAC）是会计职业团体的全球性组织，成立于 1977 年，总部位于纽约。国际会计师联合会现有超过 150 个职业会计师团体会员，代表着世界上 124 个国家或地区的 250 万名注册会计师。国际会计师联合会下属 7 个委员会。其中，国际审计及鉴证准则委员会（IAASB）负责颁布国际审计准则。2002 年以前，该委员会被叫作国际审计实务委员会（IAPC）。2002 年 IFAC 决定提高该委员会的地位，将其命名为国际审计及鉴证准则委员会。

IAASB 是一个独立的准则制定机构，通过制定高质量的审计、质量控制、复核及其他鉴证业务和相关服务准则，以及方便国际和各国审计准则的整合，进而提高全球审计实务的质量和一致性，并加强公众对全球审计和鉴证职业团体的信任。

IAASB 主要制定和颁布的准则有：审计人员在财务信息审计过程中应用的国际审计准则（ISAs）、国际鉴证业务准则（ISAEs）、国际质量控制准则（ISQCs）、国际复核业务准则（ISREs）和国际相关服务准则（ISRSs），另外，IAASB 还发布国际审计实务说明书（IAPSs）为执行审计准则和改进审计实务提供实务指南。IAASB 发布公告的结构如图 17-2 所示。

图 17-2 国际审计与鉴证准则委员会发布公告结构图

▶ 问答题 Questions

1. Give a definition of an audit, and explain the signification of the terms therein.

2. State the advantages of having an external audit.

3. List the stages of an audit.

4. Identify the five fundamental principles in the IFAC Code of Ethic for Professional Accountants.

5. Under what circumstances can an auditor disclose confidential client information to a third party?

6. Define independence in audit and the relationship between independence and the professional ethical principles.

Collecting Audit Evidence

收集审计证据

◎ 小案例 Mini Case

Your firm has recently been appointed as the external auditor to EWheels, a private "dot. com" company that operates an internet auction service for the sale of used vehicles. You are planning the audit of the financial statements. What kind of audit approach could be used? What audit procedures should be performed? How would you audit EWheels' financial statements?

正文 Text

Audit evidence is the information used by the auditor in arriving at the conclusions on which the auditor's opinion is based. Audit evidence includes both information contained in the accounting records underlying the financial statements and other information. Auditors obtain audit evidence by one or more of the following procedures: inspection of tangible assets, inspection of documentation or records, observation, inquiry, confirmation, recalculation, reperformance and analytical procedures. Evidence will normally be sought from a variety of different sources as evidence is persuasive rather than conclusive and auditors seek reasonable, not absolute assurance.

The auditor obtains audit evidence to draw reasonable conclusions on which to base the audit opinion by performing audit procedures to:

a. Risk assessment procedures

b. Tests of controls, and

c. Substantive procedures.

The auditor must always perform risk assessment procedures to provide a satisfactory assessment of risks. Tests of controls are necessary to test the controls to support the risk assessment, and also when substantive procedures alone do not provide sufficient appropriate audit evidence. Substantive procedures must always be carried out for material classes of transactions, account balances and disclosures.

18. 1　Risk-Based Audit

Risk-based audit is primarily (but not exclusively) used by external auditors to identify the high risk areas of a client's business and hence focus the audit effort. Consequently this is used for short-term planning on a particular audit after the decision has been made to accept the assignment.

Auditors usually follow a risk-based approach to auditing as required by ISAs. This is in contrast to a **procedural approach** which is not in accordance with ISAs. In a procedural approach, the auditor would perform a set of standard tests regardless of the client and its business. The risk of the auditor providing an incorrect opinion on the truth and fairness of the financial statements might be higher if a procedural approach was adopted.

18. 1. 1　Audit Risk

Audit risk is the risk that the auditor expresses an inappropriate audit opinion when the financial statements are materially misstated. Audit risk is a function of the risk of material misstatement and the risk that the auditor will not detect such misstatement (**detection risk**).

The risk of material misstatement is the risk that the financial statements are materially misstated prior to audit. This consists of two components: **inherent risk** and **control risk**. Inherent risk is the susceptibility of an assertion to a misstatement that could be material, either individually or when aggregated with other misstatements assuming that there were no related internal controls. Control risk is the risk that a misstatement that could occur in an assertion and that could be material, either individually or when aggregated with other misstatements, will not be prevented or detected and corrected on a timely basis by the entity's internal control.

Detection risk is the risk that the auditor's procedures will not detect a misstatement that exists in an assertion that could be material, either individually or when aggregated with other misstatements.

Therefore these two risks multiplied together give total audit risk. Thus:

Audit Risk (AR) = Risk of Material Misstatement × Detection Risk (DR)

Audit risk can be set at any level. The auditor should plan and perform the audit to reduce audit risk to an acceptably low level that is consistent with the objectives of an audit.

In practice, auditors "set" audit risk at 4% to 6% and tailor their audit procedures accordingly. Broadly, the lower risk level required, the greater the audit work required. Inherent risk is assessed at both the financial statement (entity) level, and at the level of individual balances and transactions. Then, when tests of control are complete, auditors could review their preliminary assessment of control risk. If control risk and inherent risk are high then detection risk will be low. The lower the level of detection risk acceptable, the greater the level of testing required.

An audit should be planned so that the greatest amount of audit work focuses on the areas with the highest-risk factors. The auditor performs audit procedures to assess the risk of material misstatement and seeks to limit detection risk by performing further audit procedures based on that assessment. The audit process involves the exercise of professional judgment in designing the audit approach, through focusing on what can go wrong at the assertion level (see ISA 500, *Audit Evidence*) and performing audit procedures in response to the assessed risks in order to obtain sufficient appropriate audit evidence.

18. 1. 2　Materiality

Materiality for the financial statements as a whole and performance materiality must be calculated at the planning stages of all audits. The calculation or estimation of materiality should be based on experience and judgment. Materiality for the financial statements as a whole must be reviewed throughout the audit and revised if necessary.

ISA 320 provides guidance to auditors in this area and states the objective of the auditor is to apply the concept of materiality appropriately in planning and performing the audit.

ISA 320 does not define materiality (in relation to the financial statements as a whole) but notes that whilst it may be discussed in different terms by different financial reporting frameworks the following are generally the case:

- Misstatements, including omissions, are considered to be material if they, individually or in the aggregate, could reasonably be expected to influence the economic decisions of users taken on the basis of the financial statements;
- Judgments about materiality are made in light of surrounding circumstances, and are affected by the size or nature of a misstatement, or a combination of both; and
- Judgments about matters that are material to users of the financial statements are based on a consideration of the common financial information needs of users as a group.

The practical implication of this is that the auditor must be concerned with identifying "material" errors, omissions and misstatements. Both the amount (quantity) and nature (quality) of misstatements need to be considered.

The auditor has to set his or her own materiality levels, which will always be a matter of judgement and will depend on the level of audit risk. The higher the anticipated risk, the lower the value of materiality will be.

The materiality level will impact on the auditor's decisions relating to:

- How many items to examine
- Which items to examine
- Whether to use sampling techniques
- What levels of misstatement is likely to result in a modified audit opinion.

The concept of materiality is applied by the auditor both in planning and performing the audit, and in evaluating the effect of identified misstatements on the audit and of uncorrected misstatements, if any, on the financial statements and in forming the opinion in the auditor's report.

1. Materiality when Planning the Audit

In planning the audit, the auditor makes judgments about the size of misstatements that will be considered material. These judgments provide a basis for:

- Determining the nature, timing and extent of risk assessment procedures;
- Identifying and assessing the risks of material misstatement; and
- Determining the nature, timing and extent of further audit procedures.

The auditor must establish materiality for the financial statements as a whole and must set performance materiality levels.

Determining materiality for the financial statements as a whole involves the exercise of professional judgment. Generally, a percentage is applied to a chosen benchmark as a starting point for determining materiality for the financial statements as a whole. Factors that may affect the identification of an appropriate benchmark include the following:

- The elements of the financial statements;
- Whether there are items on which the attention of the users tends to be focused;
- The nature of the entity, the industry and economic environment in which the entity operates;
- The entity's ownership structure and the way it is financed; and
- The relative volatility of the benchmark.

The following benchmarks and percentages may be appropriate in the calculation of materiality for the financial statements as a whole, depending on the circumstances of the entity.

Value	%
Profit before tax	5
Gross profit	0.5 ~ 1
Revenue	0.5 ~ 1
Total assets	1 ~ 2
Net assets	2 ~ 5
Profit after tax	5 ~ 10

The auditor shall determine performance materiality for purposes of assessing the risks of material misstatement and determining the nature, timing and extent of further audit procedures. **Performance materiality** is the amount or amounts set by the auditor at less than materiality for the financial statements as a whole to reduce to an appropriately low level the probability that the aggregate of uncorrected and undetected misstatements exceeds materiality for the financial statements as a whole. If applicable, performance materiality also refers to the amount or amounts set by the auditor at less than the materiality level or levels for particular classes of transactions, account balances or disclosures. This means a lower threshold is applied during testing. The risk of misstatements which could add up to a material misstatement is therefore reduced.

Materiality also has qualitative aspects. Some misstatements may fall under specified benchmarks, but are still considered material overall due to their qualitative effects. Factors may cause misstatements of quantitatively small amounts to be material and could reasonably be expected to influence the economic decisions of users taken on the basis of the financial statements include the following:

- Whether law, regulation or the applicable financial reporting framework affect users' expectations regarding the measurement or disclosure of certain items (for example, related party transactions, and the remuneration of management and those charged with governance).
- The key disclosures in relation to the industry in which the entity operates (for example, research and development costs for a pharmaceutical company).
- Whether attention is focused on a particular aspect of the entity's business that is separately disclosed in the financial statements (for example, a newly acquired business).

2. Revision as the Audit Progresses

The auditor shall revise materiality for the financial statements as a whole (and, if applicable, the materiality level or levels for particular classes of transactions, account balances or disclosures) in the event of becoming aware of information during the audit that would have caused the auditor to have determined a different amount (or amounts) initially.

If the auditor concludes that a lower materiality for the financial statements as a whole (and, if applicable, materiality level or levels for particular classes of transactions, account balances or disclosures) than that initially determined is appropriate, the auditor shall determine whether it is necessary to revise performance materiality, and whether the nature, timing and extent of the further audit procedures remain appropriate.

Materiality and audit risk are considered throughout the audit, in particular, when:

- Identifying and assessing the risks of material misstatement;
- Determining the nature, timing and extent of further audit procedures; and

- Evaluating the effect of uncorrected misstatements, if any, on the financial statements and in forming the opinion in the auditor's report.

18. 2　Internal Control Systems

To external auditors, the principal reason why internal control interests the auditor is that the reliance on internal control will reduce the amount of substantive testing required. If the auditor is satisfied that the internal control system is functioning, there is therefore a reduce risk of error in the accounting records. By recording the accounting system and checking its operation by tests of control, the auditor can reduce the number of substantive procedures needed to be carried out. The total amount of work is reduced as a result.

Another reason is that the auditor usually has an additional responsibility under legislation to form an opinion as to whether proper accounting records have been kept. This also implies the operation of a sound system of internal control.

18. 2. 1　Definition of Internal Control System

ISA 315 defines **internal control** as the process designed and effected by those charged with governance, management and other personnel to provide reasonable assurance about the achievement of the entity's objectives with regard to reliability of financial reporting, effectiveness and efficiency of operations and compliance with applicable laws and regulations.

Internal control consists of **control environment**, the **entity's risk assessment process**, **information system and communication**, **control activities** and **monitoring of controls** according to COSO Report: *Internal control—integrated Framework* (1994).

In obtaining an understanding of internal control, the auditor must understand the design of the internal control and the implementation of that control.

At an early stage in their work, auditors have to decide the extent to which they wish to place reliance on the internal controls of the enterprise. As the audit proceeds, that decision will be kept under review and, depending on the results of the examination, the auditor may decide to place more or less reliance on these controls.

Control activities are the policies and procedures that help ensure that management directives are carried out. Control activities, whether within IT or manual systems, have various objectives and are applied at various organizational and functional levels. Control activities include these activities designed to prevent or to detect and correct errors. Control activities can take a number of forms: **authorization**, **performance reviews**, **information processing**, **physical controls**, **segregation of duties** and so on.

18. 2. 2　Types of Internal Control

There are a number of types of internal control that any auditor should consider.

Preventative

These are controls that prevent risks occurring. For example, authorization controls should prevent fraudulent or erroneous transactions taking place. Other preventative controls include segregation of duties, recruiting and training the right staff and having an effective control culture.

Detective

These are controls that detect if any problems have occurred. They are designed to pick up errors that have not been prevented. These could be exception types of reports that reveal that controls have been circumvented. For example, large amounts were paid without being authorized. Other examples could include reconciliations, supervision and internal checks.

Corrective

Corrective controls are ones that address any problems that have occurred. Where problems are identified, the controls ensure that they are properly rectified. Examples of corrective controls include follow-up procedures and management action.

Clearly the most powerful type of control is preventative. It is more effective to have a control that stops problems occurring rather than to detect or correct them once they have occurred.

18. 2. 3　Specific Control Activities

These include:

- reporting, reviewing and approving reconciliations;
- checking the arithmetical accuracy of the records;
- maintaining and reviewing control accounts and trail balances;
- approval and control of document;
- comparing internal data with external sources of information;
- comparing the results of cash, security and inventory counts with the accounting records;
- limiting direct physical access to assets and records an important general principle with respect to assets and records is that of segregation. In particular there should be a division of responsibilities for:
  - authorizing or initiating the transactions;
  - the physical custody and control of assets involved;
  - recording the transactions.
- comparing and analyzing the financial results with budgeted amounts.

Because the assessment of the risk of material misstatement takes account of internal control, the extent of substantive procedures may need to be increased when the results from tests of controls are unsatisfactory.

18. 3　Understanding the Entity and Its Environment

ISA 315 states that the objective of the auditor is to identify and assess the risks of material misstatement, whether due to fraud or error, at the financial statement and assertion levels, through understanding the entity and its environment, including the entity's internal control, thereby providing a basis for designing and implementing responses to the assessed risks of material misstatement.

Obtaining an understanding of the entity and its environment could enable the auditor to identify and assess the risks of material misstatement in the financial statements, to design and perform audit procedures and to provide a frame of reference for exercising audit judgment, for example, when setting audit materiality.

The auditor shall obtain an understanding of the entity and its environment including the following:

- Relevant industry, regulatory, and other external factors including the applicable financial reporting framework;
- The nature of the entity, including operations, ownership and governance, investments, structures and financing;
- The entity's selection and application of accounting policies;
- The entity's objectives and strategies, and those related business risks that may result in risks of material misstatement;
- The measurement and review of the entity's financial performance;
- The entity's internal control.

18. 4　Assessing the Risks of Material Misstatement

Risk assessment procedures are the audit procedures performed to obtain an understanding of the entity and its environment, including the entity's internal control, to identify and assess the risks of material misstatement, whether due to fraud or error, at the financial statement and assertion levels.

For this purpose, the auditor shall:

- Identify risks throughout the process of obtaining an understanding of the entity and its environment;

- Assess the identified risks, and evaluate whether they relate more pervasively to the financial statements as a whole and potentially affect many assertions;
- Relate the identified risks to what can go wrong at the assertion level, taking account of relevant controls that the auditor intends to test; and
- Consider the likelihood of misstatement, including the possibility of multiple misstatements, and whether the potential misstatement is of a magnitude that could result in a material misstatement.

The risk assessment procedures shall include the following:

- Inquiries of management, and of others within the entity who in the auditor's judgment may have information that is likely to assist in identifying risks of material misstatement due to fraud or error;
- Analytical procedures;
- Observation and inspection;
- Prior period knowledge;
- Client acceptance or continuance process;
- Discussion by the audit team of the susceptibility of the financial statements to material misstatement;
- Information from other engagements undertaken for the entity.

As part of the risk assessment as described above, the auditor shall determine whether any of the risks are significant risks. A **significant risk** is an identified and assessed risk of material misstatement that, in the auditor's judgment, requires special audit consideration.

In exercising judgment as to which risks are significant risks, the auditor shall consider at least the following:

- Whether the risk is a risk of fraud;
- Whether the risk is related to recent significant economic, accounting or other developments and, therefore, requires specific attention;
- The complexity of transactions;
- Whether the risk involves significant transactions with related parties;
- The degree of subjectivity in the measurement of financial information related to the risk, especially those measurements involving a wide range of measurement uncertainty; and
- Whether the risk involves significant transactions that are outside the normal course of business for the entity, or that otherwise appear to be unusual.

If the auditor has determined that a significant risk exists, the auditor shall obtain an understanding of the entity's controls, including control activities, relevant to that risk.

18.5　Responding to the Risk Assessment

The auditor shall design and implement overall responses to address the assessed risks of material misstatement at the financial statement level. Overall responses include such issues as emphasizing to the team the importance of professional skepticism, allocating more staff, using experts or providing more supervision.

The auditor shall design and perform further audit procedures whose nature, timing and extent are based on and are responsive to the assessed risks of material misstatement at the assertion level. "Nature" refers to the purpose and the types of test that is carried out, which include tests of controls and substantive tests. In designing the further audit procedures to be performed, the auditor shall:

- Consider the reasons for the assessment given to the risk of material misstatement at the assertion level for each class of transactions, account balance, and disclosure, including:
  - The likelihood of material misstatement due to the particular characteristics of the relevant class of transactions, account balance, or disclosure (that is, the inherent risk); and
  - Whether the risk assessment takes account of relevant controls (that is, the control risk), thereby requiring the auditor to obtain audit evidence to determine whether the controls are operating effectively (that is, the auditor intends to rely on the operating effectiveness of controls in determining the nature, timing and extent of substantive procedures); and
- Obtain more persuasive audit evidence the higher the auditor's assessment of risk.

On the one hand, the auditor shall design and perform tests of controls to obtain sufficient appropriate audit evidence as to the operating effectiveness of relevant controls if:

- The auditor's assessment of risks of material misstatement at the assertion level includes an expectation that the controls are operating effectively (that is, the auditor intends to rely on the operating effectiveness of controls in determining the nature, timing and extent of substantive procedures); or
- Substantive procedures alone cannot provide sufficient appropriate audit evidence at the assertion level.

On the other hand, the auditor shall design and perform substantive procedures for each material class of transactions, account balance, and disclosure irrespective of the assessed risks of material misstatement and consider whether external confirmation procedures are to be performed as substantive audit procedures.

In addition, the auditor's substantive procedures shall include the following audit procedures related to the financial statement closing process:

- Agreeing or reconciling the financial statements with the underlying accounting records; and

- Examining material journal entries and other adjustments made during the course of preparing the financial statements.

18. 6　Tests of Controls and Substantive Procedures

18. 6. 1　Tests of Controls

The key to thinking about internal control is to imagine what might go wrong if controls are badly designed or missing. Controls usually require some time and effort and may involve some cost, so it is unlikely that control procedures will ever exist without some good reason.

Remember that **control objectives** for all systems are in outline as follows:

That only authorized transactions are promptly recorded at the correct amount in the accordance accounts in the proper accounting period, that access to assets is only in accordance with proper authorization and that recorded assets are compared with existing assets.

Detailed **control procedures** are often similar across sales, purchases and other areas and include:

- **sequential numbering** of documents with subsequent checking of the sequence for completeness;

- the maintenance of **batch control** and other **control totals** at the input stage with subsequent checking to output for completeness and accuracy;

- the maintenance of **control accounts** which are checked to ensure that they reconcile to the ledgers;

- **authorization**, evidenced by the signature of responsible officials for the raising, input and distribution of documents.

Tests of controls are audit procedures designed to evaluate the operating effectiveness of controls in preventing, or detecting and correcting, material misstatements at the assertion level. Test of control can be taken by reperformance, enquiry, inspection and observation.

In designing and performing tests of controls, the greater the reliance the auditor places on the effectiveness of a control, the auditor shall obtain more persuasive audit evidence.

Testing the operating effectiveness of controls is different from obtaining an understanding of and evaluating the design and implementation of controls although the same types of audit procedures are used. Therefore, in designing and performing tests of controls, the auditor shall:

- Perform other audit procedures in combination with inquiry to obtain audit evidence about the operating effectiveness of the controls, including:
  - How the controls were applied at relevant times during the period under audit;
  - The consistency with which they were applied; and
  - By whom or by what means they were applied.
- Determine whether the controls to be tested depend upon other controls (indirect controls), and, if so, whether it is necessary to obtain audit evidence supporting the effective operation of those indirect controls.

When considering timing in relation to tests of controls, the purpose of the test will be important. For example, if the company carries out a year-end inventory count, controls over the inventory count can only be tested at the year-end. Other controls will operate all year round, and the auditor may need to test that those controls have been effective throughout the period.

If the auditor plans to use audit evidence from a previous audit about the operating effectiveness of specific controls, the auditor shall establish the continuing relevance of that evidence by obtaining audit evidence about whether significant changes in those controls have occurred subsequent to the previous audit and test the controls if they have changed. But if the auditor plans to rely on controls over a risk the auditor has determined to be a significant risk, the auditor shall test those controls in the current period.

Control objectives and control procedures are the responsibility of the client. Tests of control are the responsibility of the auditor.

18. 6. 2　Substantive Procedures

Substantive procedures are audit procedures design to detect material misstatements at the assertion level; they include:

- Tests of details (of classes of transactions, account balances; and disclosures);
- Substantive analytical procedures.

Substantive analytical procedures are generally more applicable to large volumes of transactions that tend to be predictable over time. Tests of detail may be appropriate to gain information about account balances and to matters which have been identified as significant risks.

Assertions are the representations by management, explicit or otherwise, that are embodied in the financial statements, as used by the auditor to consider the different types of potential misstatements that may occur. Assertions used by the auditor in considering the different types of potential misstatements that may occur may fall into the following categories:

- Assertions about classes of transactions and events, and related disclosures, for the period under audit:

- Occurrence—transactions and events that have been recorded or disclosed, have occurred, and such transactions and events pertain to the entity.
- Completeness—all transactions and events that should have been recorded have been recorded, and all related disclosures that should have been included in the financial statements have been included.
- Accuracy—amounts and other data relating to recorded transactions and events have been recorded appropriately, and related disclosures have been appropriately measured and described.
- Cutoff—transactions and events have been recorded in the correct accounting period.
- Classification—transactions and events have been recorded in the proper accounts.
- Presentation—transactions and events are appropriately aggregated or disaggregated and clearly described, and related disclosures are relevant and understandable in the context of the requirements of the applicable financial reporting framework.
- Assertions about account balances, and related disclosures, at the period end:
  - Existence—assets, liabilities, and equity interests exist.
  - Rights and obligations—the entity holds or controls the rights to assets, and liabilities are the obligations of the entity.
  - Completeness—all assets, liabilities and equity interests that should have been recorded have been recorded, and all related disclosures that should have been included in the financial statements have been included.
  - Accuracy, valuation and allocation—assets, liabilities, and equity interests have been included in the financial statements at appropriate amounts and any resulting valuation or allocation adjustments have been appropriately recorded, and related disclosures have been appropriately measured and described.
  - Classification—assets, liabilities and equity interests have been recorded in the proper accounts.
  - Presentation—assets, liabilities and equity interests are appropriately aggregated or disaggregated and clearly described, and related disclosures are relevant and understandable in the context of the requirements of the applicable financial reporting framework.

In substantive procedures, auditors could use the following model for drawing up an audit plan:
- Agree opening balances with previous year's working papers;
- Review general ledger for unusual records;
- Agree client schedules to/from accounting records to ensure completeness;
- Carry out analytical review;
- Test transactions in detail;

- Test balances in detail;
- Review presentation and disclosure in accounts.

Note that the occurrence assertion relates to transactions. The equivalent assertion for an asset or liability balance is existence.

Two of the most important assertion tests are for completeness and existence. These are tests going in the "opposite direction" to each other. In practice, auditors test debit balances for existence and credit balances for completeness. Tests of debits work away from the financial statements and tests of credits work towards them, which is **directional testing**.

The best test of the existence of an asset is to check its physical existence if it is tangible and the entity's document to title if it is not.

18. 7　Sufficient Appropriate Audit Evidence

ISA 500 Audit evidence requires auditors to "design and perform audit procedures that are appropriate in the circumstance for the purpose of obtaining sufficient appropriate audit evidence". Sufficiency is the measure of the quantity of audit evidence. Appropriateness is the measure of the quality of audit evidence; that is, its relevance and its reliability in providing support for the conclusions on which the auditor's opinion is based. They are interrelated and apply to both tests of controls and substantive procedures.

The quantity of audit evidence required is affected by the level of risk in the area being audited. It is also affected by the quality of evidence obtained. However, obtaining a high quantity of poor quality evidence will not cancel out its poor quality.

The ISA requires that the auditor shall consider the relevance and reliability of the information to be used as audit evidence when designing and performing audit procedures.

Relevance deals with the logical connection with the purpose of the audit procedure and the assertion under consideration. The relevance of information may be affected by the direction of testing.

Reliability is influenced by the source and nature of the information, including the controls over its preparation and maintenance. The following generalization may help in assessing the reliability of audit evidence.

- The reliability of audit evidence is increased when it is obtained from independent sources outside the entity.
- The reliability of audit evidence that is generated internally is increased when the related controls, including those over its preparation and maintenance, imposed by the entity are effective.

- Audit evidence obtained directly by the auditor (for example, observation of the application of a control) is more reliable than audit evidence obtained indirectly or by inference (for example, inquiry about the application of a control).

- Audit evidence in documentary form, whether paper, electronic, or other medium, is more reliable than evidence obtained orally.

- Audit evidence provided by original documents is more reliable than audit evidence provided by photocopies or facsimiles, or documents that have been filmed, digitized or otherwise transformed into electronic form, the reliability of which may depend on the controls over their preparation and maintenance.

When using information produced by the entity, the auditor shall evaluate whether the information is sufficiently reliable for the auditor's purposes, including, as necessary in the circumstances, obtaining audit evidence about the accuracy and completeness of the information; and evaluating whether the information is sufficiently precise and detailed for the auditor's purposes.

If audit evidence obtained from one source is inconsistent with that obtained from another; or the auditor has doubts over the reliability of information to be used as audit evidence, the auditor shall determine what modifications or additions to audit procedures are necessary to resolve the matter, and shall consider the effect of the matter, if any, on other aspects of the audit.

18. 8　Revenue System

Using revenue system as an example, this part explains enterprises' control objectives and control procedures and auditor's tests of controls and substantive procedures over it.

1. Control Objectives

For many businesses, sales are made on credit and thus the sales cycle includes control objectives for receivables. These control objectives include the following:

- Sales are made in accordance with company objectives, with agreements in place with all customers.

- Customers' orders should be authorized, controlled and recorded in order to execute them promptly and determine any allowance required for losses arising from unfulfilled commitments.

- Goods shipped and work completed should be controlled to ensure that invoices are issued and revenue recorded for all sales.

- Goods returned and claims by customers should be controlled in order to determine the liability for goods returned and claims received but not entered in the accounting records.

- Invoices and credits should be appropriately checked as being accurate and authorized before being entered in the accounting records.

- Validated receivables transactions, and only these transactions, should be accurately entered in the accounting records.
- There should be procedures to ensure that sales invoices are subsequently paid and that doubtful amounts are identified in order to determine any allowances required.

2. Control Procedures over Sales and Receivables

There are a large number of controls that may be required in the sales cycle due to the importance of this area in any business and the possible opportunities that exist for diverting sales away from the business and other persons benefiting.

Order

- The orders should be checked against the customer's account; this should be evidenced by initiating. Any new customer should be referred to the credit control department before the order is accepted.
- Existing customers should be allocated a credit limit and it should be ascertained whether this limit is to be exceeded if the new order is accepted. If so, the matter should be referred to the credit limit.
- All orders received should be recorded on pre-numbered sales order documents.
- All orders should be authorized before any goods are dispatched.
- The sales order should be used to produce a dispatch note for the goods outwards department. No goods may be dispatched without a dispatch note.

Dispatch

- Dispatch notes should be pre-numbered and a register should be kept of them to relate to sales invoices and orders.
- Goods dispatch notes should be authorized as goods leave and be checked periodically to ensure they are complete and that all have been invoiced.

Invoicing and credit notes

- Sales invoices should be authorized by a responsible official and referenced to the original authorized order and dispatch note.
- All invoices and credit notes should be entered in sales day book records, the accounts receivable ledger, and accounts receivable control accounts. Batch totals should be maintained for this purpose.
- Sales invoices and credit notes should be checked for prices, casts and calculations by a person other than the one preparing them.
- All invoices and credit notes should be serially pre-numbered and regular sequence checks should be carried out.

- Credit notes should be authorized by someone unconnected with dispatch or accounts receivable ledger functions.
- Copies of cancelled invoices should be retained.
- Any invoice cancellation should lead to a cancellation of the appropriate dispatch note.
- Cancelled and free of charge invoices should be signed by a responsible official.
- Each invoice should distinguish between different types of sales and any sales taxes. Any coding of invoices should be periodically checked independently.

Returns

- Any goods returned by the customers should be checked for obvious damage and, when accepted, a document should be raised.
- All goods returned should be used to prepare appropriate credit notes.

Receivables

- A receivables ledger control account should be prepared regularly and checked to individual sales ledger balances by an individual official.
- Receivables ledger personnel should be independent of dispatch and cash receipt functions.
- Statements should be sent regularly to customers.
- Formal procedures should exist for following-up overdue debts which should be highlighted either by the preparation of an aged list of balances or in the preparation of statements to customers.
- Letters should be sent to customers for collection of overdue debts.

Bad Debts

- The authority to write off a bad debt should be given in writing and adjustments made to the accounts receivable ledger.
- The use of court action or the writing-off of a bad debt should be authorized by an official independent of the cash receipt functions.

3. Tests of controls

Tests of controls should be designed to check that the control procedures are being applied and that objectives are being achieved. Tests may be appropriate under the following broad headings:

- Carry out sequence test checks on invoices, credit notes, dispatch notes and orders to ensure that all items are included and that there are no omission or duplications.
- Check the authorization for the:
  - acceptance of the order (the creditworthiness check);
  - dispatch of goods;
  - raising of the invoice or credit note;

- pricing and discounts;
- write-off of bad debts.
- Check both that the relevant signature exists and that the control has been applied.
- Seek evidence of checking of the arithmetical accuracy of
  - invoices;
  - credit notes;
  - sales taxes.
- Check dispatch notes and goods returned notes to ensure that they are referenced to invoices and credit notes and vice versa.
- Check that control account reconciliations have been performed and reviewed. Reperform the control by checking the reconciliation to source documentation.
- Ensure that batch total controls have been applied by seeking signatures and tracing batches from input to output.

In all cases, tests should be performed on a sample basis. The auditor should investigate errors and consider the need for further testing to obtain comfort on the proper application of the control procedures.

4. Substantive Procedures

(1) Accounting records

- Check additions and cross-cast of the sales day book and sales returns day book.
- Check the posting of individual invoices to the general ledger and the control account.
- Check entries in the sales day book and sales returns day book back to original invoices, credit notes and dispatch notes, and vice versa.

(2) Invoices and credit notes

- Obtain a sample of potential sales.
- Check the preparation of associated sales invoices, ensuring that quantities and descriptions are correctly stated.
- Compare invoiced prices with authorized, up-to-date price lists, quotations and correspondence.
- Check calculations and additions of invoices and credit notes.
- Ensure that invoices are posted to the appropriate account in the nominal ledger. This may involve tracing payments through the computerized accounting records.
- Scrutinize credit notes for large or unusual items.

(3) General

Where returns or allowances affect the calculations of commissions, ensure that adjustments have been made properly.

（4） Control accounts

Test the year end control account reconciliation, checking back to source documentation to ensure that any reconciling items are dealt with properly.

（5） Analytical procedures

Analytical procedures include comparisons of sales fluctuations, especially before and after the year end. Auditors should be care of cut-off problems.

（6） Disclosure

Ensure that sales revenue must be disclosed according to IASs or a national accounting standards. According to IASs, sales revenue must be disclosed by class of business and geographical market.

The tests of controls and substantive procedures noted above sometimes appear to be very similar and one test can serve both as a test of controls and as a substantive procedure. But this does not mean that tests of controls and substantive procedures are interchangeable. It is vital that you understand the conceptual difference between the two types of tests.

▶ 核心词汇 Core Words and Expressions

assertion   认定

accuracy   精确性

analytical procedure   分析性程序

audit evidence   审计证据

audit risk   审计风险

authorization   授权

batch control   批控制

classification   分类

completeness   完整性

control activities   控制活动

control environment   控制环境

control objective   控制目标

control procedure   控制过程

control risk   控制风险

corrective control   更正控制

detection risk   检查风险

detective control   检查控制

directional testing   方向测试

existence   存在性

financial statement assertions   财务报表认定

information system and communication   信息与沟通

information processing   信息处理

inherent risk   固有风险

internal control system   内部控制系统

materiality   重要性水平

misstatement   错报

monitoring of control   内部控制监管

occurrence   发生性

performance reviews   业绩复核

physical controls   实物控制

preventative control   预防控制

rights and obligations   权利与义务

Entity's risk assessment process   企业风险评估流程

risk of material misstatement   重大错报风险

risk-based audit   风险基础审计

segregation of duties   职责分工

sequential numbering   顺序编号

significant risk   重大风险

subsequent events　期后事项	total control　总数控制
substantive procedures　实质性程序	understandability　可理解性
test of controls　控制测试	valuation　估值

▶ 知识扩展 More Knowledge

财务报表审计完成阶段

审计完成阶段是财务报表审计的最后阶段。注册会计师在汇总审计测试结果的基础上，进行更加综合性的审计工作，如评价审计中的重大发现，评价审计过程中发现的错报，关注期后事项对财务报表的影响，复核审计工作底稿和财务报表，等等。在此基础上，评价审计结果，在与客户沟通以后，获取管理者声明，确定应出具的审计报告意见类型，进而编制并致送审计报告，终结审计工作。

期后事项

期后事项是指财务报表日至审计报告日之间发生的事项，以及注册会计师在审计报告日后知悉的事实。审计报告的日期向财务报表使用者表明，注册会计师已考虑其知悉的、截至审计报告日发生的事项和交易的影响。

期后事项通常分为以下两类：（1）财务报表日后调整事项，是指对财务报表日已经存在的情况提供证据的事项，或对财务报告日已经存在的情况提供了新的或进一步证据的事项。这类事项影响财务报表金额，需提请被审计单位管理层调整财务报表及与之相关的披露信息。（2）财务报表日后非调整事项，是指对财务报表日后发生的情况提供证据的事项。此类事项虽不影响财务报表金额，但可能影响对财务报告的正确理解，需提请被审计单位管理层在财务报表附注中进行适当披露。

首先，对于财务报表日至审计报告日之间发生的事项，注册会计师应当设计和实施审计程序，获取充分、适当的审计证据，以确定所有在财务报表日至审计报告日之间发生的、需要在财务报表中调整或披露的事项均已得到识别。但是，注册会计师并不需要对之前已实施审计程序并已得出满意结论的事项执行追加的审计程序。对于这一时段的期后事项，注册会计师负有主动识别的义务，应当设计专门的审计程序来识别这些期后事项，并根据这此事项的性质判断其对财务报表的影响，进而确定是进行调整还是披露。

其次，在审计报告日后，注册会计师没有义务针对财务报表实施任何审计程序。但在审计报告日后至财务报表报出日前发现的期后事项，注册会计师的识别比较困难，因而无法承担主动识别责任，但管理层有责任将发现的可能影响财务报表的事实告知注册会计师，注册会计师也可能从媒体报道、举报信或证券监管部门告知等途径获影响财务报表的期后事项。在审计报告日后至财务报表报出日前，如果知悉了某事实，且若在审计报告日知悉可能导致修改审计报告，注册会计师应当与管理层和治理层（如适用）讨论该事项；确定财务报表是否需要修改；如果需要修改，询问管理层将如何在财务报表中处理该事项。

如果管理层修改财务报表，注册会计师应当根据具体情况对有关修改实施必要的审计程序；除下段所述的特定情况外，应将用以识别期后事项的审计程序延伸至新的审计报告日，并针对修改后的财务报表出具新的审计报告。新的审计报告日不应早于修改后的财务报表被批准的日期。

在有关法律法规或适用的财务报告编制基础未禁止的情况下，如果管理层对财务报表的修改仅限于反映导致修改的期后事项的影响，被审计单位的董事会、管理层或类似机构也仅对有关修改进行批准，注册会计师可以仅针对有关修改将审计程序延伸至新的审计报告日（以下简称特定情况）。在审计报告中，注册会计师可以选用下列处理方式之一：

（一）修改审计报告，针对财务报表修改部分增加补充报告日期，从而表明注册会计师对期后事项实施的审计程序仅限于财务报表相关附注所述的修改。

（二）出具新的或经修改的审计报告，在强调事项段或其他事项段中说明注册会计师对期后事项实施的审计程序仅限于财务报表相关附注所述的修改。

最后，在财务报表报出后，注册会计师没有义务针对财务报表实施任何审计程序，但不排除注册会计师通过媒体等其他途径获悉可能对财务报表产生重大影响的期后事项的可能性。在财务报表报出后，如果知悉了某事实，且若在审计报告日知悉可能导致修改审计报告，注册会计师应当与管理层和治理层（如适用）讨论该事项；确定财务报表是否需要修改；如果需要修改，询问管理层将如何在财务报表中处理该事项。但对此类事项有较严格的限制：（1）这类期后事项应当是在审计报告日已经存在的事实。（2）该事实如果被注册会计师在审计报告日前获知，可能影响审计报告。只有同时满足这两个条件，注册会计师才需要采取行动。

如果管理层修改了财务报表，注册会计师应当根据具体情况对有关修改实施必要的审计程序；复核管理层采取的措施能否确保所有收到原财务报表和审计报告的人士了解这一情况；延伸实施审计程序，并针对修改后的财务报表出具新的审计报告；在特定情况下，修改审计报告或提供新的审计报告。同时，注册会计师应当在新的或经修改的审计报告中增加强调事项段或其他事项段，提醒财务报表使用者关注财务报表附注中有关修改原财务报表的详细原因和注册会计师提供的原审计报告。

▶ 问答题 Questions

1. Explain audit risk and the content of audit risk.

2. What do you understand by the concept of materiality in relation to an audit?

3. What are the main objectives of a system of internal control and list the three categories of internal control that any auditor should consider.

4. Name seven of the typical internal control procedures.

5 ISA 315 Understanding the Entity and its Environment and Assessing the Risks of Material Misstatement states 'the auditor should perform risk assessment procedures to obtain an understanding of the entity and its environment, including its internal control.'

Instructions

（a）**Explain the purpose of risk assessment procedures.**

（b）**Outline the sources of audit evidence the auditor can use as part of risk assessment procedures.**

6. Discuss the differences between tests of controls and substantive procedures.

7. What would the auditor do if the results of a test of control were unsatisfactory?

▶ 练习题 Exercises

Exercise 1

Two company, Tom and Jenny, are summarised below:

Type of risk	Tom	Jenny
Inherent	Retail supermarket	Insurance brokers
Control	Extensive computer systems and large internal audit department	No formal controls, claims paid with little review by senior staff

Tom has a business that provides goods for which demand is steady and with a good internal control system. Jenny is subject very much to market forces and bad weather, etc. , with little formal internal controls.

Instructions

If the total audit risk required is the same for each company, which one will have the lower detection risk and hence require increased audit testing?

Exercise 2

Sticky Bar Chocolates employs 50 salesmen each with a defined geographical area to cover. Each salesman is supplied with a new car, changed every three years. At the end of each week, each salesman submits a claim on a preprinted form for expenses with supporting vouchers. Expenditure is on petrol, repairs and servicing of the car, hotels, lunches and entertaining. Each claim is scrutinized by Mr. Tim who is deputy chief accountant. He verifies that the claims are supported by vouchers. He clears any inconsistencies with the salesmen concerned and makes out cheques for signature by two directors of the company. The total amount paid out by the company in the year to 30 December 20 × 8 was $ 300 000. the company made a profit in that year of $ 1. 5 million.

Instructions

(a) **Discuss the shortcomings of this system and suggest ways of improving the system.**

(b) **Describe tests of control and list the tests of control that the auditor would perform on this system.**

(c) **Describe substantive procedures and tabulate the substantive procedures that the auditor would perform on the item "salesmen expenses".**

(d) **During the audit, the auditor discovered that the salesman in one area was submitting false claims for entertaining customers. What further action should the auditor take?**

Exercise 3

You are the audit manager for Parker, a limited liability company which sells books, CDs, DVDs and similar items via two divisions: mail order and on-line ordering on the internet. Parker is a new audit client. You are commencing the planning of the audit for the year-ended 31 May 2015. An initial meeting with the directors has provided the information below.

The company's turnover is in excess of $ 85 million with net profits of $ 4 million. All profits are currently earned in the mail order division, although the internet division is expected to return a small net profit next year. Turnover is growing at the rate of 20% p. a. Net profit has remained almost the same for the last four years.

In the next year, the directors plan to expand the range of goods sold through the internet division to include toys, garden furniture and fashion clothes. The directors believe that when one product has been sold on the internet, then any other product can be as well.

The accounting system to record sales by the mail order division is relatively old. It relies on extensive manual input to transfer orders received in the post onto Parker's computer systems. Recently errors have been known to occur, in the input of orders, and in the invoicing of goods following despatch. The directors maintain that the accounting system produces materially correct figures and they cannot waste time in identifying relatively minor errors. The company accountant, who is not qualified and was appointed because he is a personal friend of the directors, agrees with this view.

The directors estimate that their expansion plans will require a bank loan of approximately $ 30 million, partly to finance the enhanced website but also to provide working capital to increase inventory levels. A meeting with the bank has been scheduled for three months after the year end. The directors expect an unmodified auditor's report to be signed prior to this time.

Instructions

Identify and describe THE MATTERS that give rise to audit risks associated with Parker.

External Auditor's Report
对外审计报告

◎ 小案例 Mini Case

You, a partner of an accountant firm, are currently engaged in reviewing the working papers of several audit assignments recently carried out by your audit practice. Each of the audit assignments is nearing completion, but certain matters have recently come to light. List what kinds of matters may affect your audit opinion on each of the assignments. How many audit opinions exist? What is the meaning of each audit opinion?

正文 Text

The objectives of the auditor are:

- To form an opinion on the financial statements based on an evaluation of the conclusions drawn from the audit evidence obtained; and
- To express clearly that opinion through a written report.

In order to form the opinion, the auditor shall conclude as to whether the auditor has obtained reasonable assurance about whether the financial statements as a whole are free from material misstatement, whether due to fraud or error. The auditor's conclusion shall take into account:

- The auditor's conclusion, in accordance with ISA 330, whether sufficient appropriate audit evidence has been obtained;
- The auditor's conclusion, in accordance with ISA 450, whether uncorrected misstatements are material, individually or in aggregate;
- The auditor shall evaluate whether the financial statements are prepared, in all material respects, in accordance with the requirements of the applicable financial reporting framework. This evaluation shall include consideration of the qualitative aspects of the entity's

accounting practices, including indicators of possible bias in management's judgments.

- The financial statements appropriately disclose the significant accounting policies selected and applied. In making this evaluation, the auditor shall consider the relevance of the accounting policies to the entity, and whether they have been presented in an understandable manner;

- The accounting policies selected and applied are consistent with the applicable financial reporting framework and are appropriate;

- The accounting estimates made by management are reasonable;

- The information presented in the financial statements is relevant, reliable, comparable, and understandable. In making this evaluation, the auditor shall consider whether:

  - The information that should have been included has been included, and whether such information is appropriately classified, aggregated or disaggregated, and characterized.

  - The overall presentation of the financial statements has been undermined by including information that is not relevant or that obscures a proper understanding of the matters disclosed.

- The financial statements provide adequate disclosures to enable the intended users to understand the effect of material transactions and events on the information conveyed in the financial statements; and

- The terminology used in the financial statements, including the title of each financial statement, is appropriate.

- When the financial statements are prepared in accordance with a fair presentation framework, the auditor's evaluation as to whether the financial statements achieve fair presentation shall include consideration of:

  - The overall presentation, structure and content of the financial statements; and

  - Whether the financial statements represent the underlying transactions and events in a manner that achieves fair presentation.

- The auditor shall evaluate whether the financial statements adequately refer to or describe the applicable financial reporting framework.

The auditor's report shall be in writing, which is usually the channel of communication between the auditor and the shareholders of the company whose financial statements have been subject to audit.

19. 1 Types of Audit Opinions and Auditor's Report

19. 1. 1 Unmodified Audit Opinion

The large majority of audit reports are unmodified reports. An **unmodified opinion** is the opinion expressed by the auditor when the auditor concludes that the financial statements are prepared, in all material respects, in accordance with the applicable financial reporting framework.

If financial statements prepared in accordance with the requirements of a fair presentation framework do not achieve fair presentation, the auditor shall discuss the matter with management and, depending on the requirements of the applicable financial reporting framework and how the matter is resolved, shall determine whether it is necessary to modify the opinion in the auditor's report in accordance with ISA 705.

When the financial statements are prepared in accordance with a compliance framework, the auditor is not required to evaluate whether the financial statements achieve fair presentation. However, if in extremely rare circumstances the auditor concludes that such financial statements are misleading, the auditor shall discuss the matter with management and, depending on how it is resolved, shall determine whether, and how, to communicate it in the auditor's report.

Emphasis of matter paragraphs and other matter paragraphs can be included in the auditor's report under certain circumstances. Their use does not modify the auditor's opinion on the financial statements although the report is modified.

An **emphasis of matter paragraph** is a paragraph included in the auditor's report that refers to a matter appropriately presented or disclosed in the financial statements that, in the auditor's judgment, is of such importance that it is fundamental to users' understanding of the financial statements. ISA 706 calls on the auditor to exercise judgment in deciding where to place the emphasis of matter paragraph in the auditor's report. Where there is a Key Audit Matters section, the emphasis of matter paragraph can come either before or after the KAMs, depending on how significant the matters discussed is. But an emphasis of matter paragraph is not used when the issue has been covered as a Key audit matter. The paragraph must contain a clear reference to the matter being emphasized and to where relevant disclosures that fully describe it can be found in the financial statements. The paragraph must state that the auditor's opinion is not modified in respect of the matter emphasized. In addition, the paragraph must clearly state that the audit opinion is not modified.

An **other matter paragraph** is a paragraph included in the auditor's report that refers to a matter other than those presented or disclosed in the financial statements that, in the auditor's judgment, is relevant to users' understanding of the audit, the auditor's responsibilities or the auditor's report. The content of the other matter paragraph must reflect clearly that the other matter is not required to be presented and disclosed in the financial statements, and does not include information that the auditor is prohibited from providing by law and regulations or other standards, or information that is required to be provided by management.

19. 1. 2　Modified Audit Opinion

If the auditor concludes that, based on the audit evidence obtained, the financial statements as a whole are not free from material misstatement; or is unable to obtain sufficient appropriate audit evidence to conclude that the financial statements as a whole are free from material misstatement, the auditor shall modify the opinion in the auditor's report in accordance with ISA 705.

There are three types of modified opinion: a qualified opinion, an adverse opinion, and a disclaimer of opinion. The type of modification issued depends on the following:

- The nature of the matter giving rise to the modification, that is, whether the financial statements are materially misstated or, in the case of an inability to obtain sufficient appropriate audit evidence, may be materially misstated; and
- The auditor's judgment about the pervasiveness of the effects or possible effects of the matter on the financial statements.

Table 19-1 illustrates how the auditor's judgment about the nature of the matter giving rise to the modification, and the pervasiveness of its effects or possible effects on the financial statements, affects the type of opinion to be expressed.

Table 19-1　Summary of modifications and impact on the auditor's report

Nature of Matter Giving Rise to the Modification	Auditor's Judgment about the Pervasiveness of the Effects or Possible Effects on the Financial Statements	
	Material but not pervasive	Material and Pervasive
Financial statements are materially misstated	Qualified opinion	Adverse opinion
Auditor unable to obtain sufficient appropriate audit evidence	Qualified opinion	Disclaimer of opinion

Pervasiveness is a term used, in the context of misstatements, to describe the effects on the financial statements of misstatements or the possible effects on the financial statements of misstatements, if any, that are undetected due to an inability to obtain sufficient appropriate audit evidence. Pervasive effects on the financial statements are those that, in the auditor's judgment:

(a) Are not confined to specific elements, accounts or items of the financial statements;

(b) If so confined, represent or could represent a substantial proportion of the financial statements; or

(c) In relation to disclosures, are fundamental to users' understanding of the financial statements.

According to ISA 450, a **misstatement** is a difference between the amount, classification, presentation, or disclosure of a reported financial statement item and the amount, classification, presentation, or disclosure that is required for the item to be in accordance with the applicable financial reporting framework. Accordingly, a **material misstatement** of the financial statements may arise in relation to:

- The appropriateness of the selected accounting policies;
- The application of the selected accounting policies; or
- The appropriateness or adequacy of disclosures in the financial statements.

The auditor's inability to obtain sufficient appropriate audit evidence (also referred to as a limitation on the scope of the audit) may arise from:

- Circumstances beyond the control of the entity;
- Circumstances relating to the nature or timing of the auditor's work; or
- Limitations imposed by management.

Types of external audit opinions are shown as Figure 19-1.

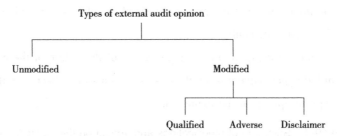

Figure 19-1   the types of audit opinions

19. 2   Format and Content of External Auditor's Report

To convey information in a succinct form, the audit report has become an extremely formalized group of phrases, each of which has special significance. Any deviation from the standard format is regarded by accountants as being significant and may provide important extra information.

19. 2. 1   Unmodified Auditor's Report

The standard unmodified report is as follows, with tutorial discussion given in italics.

INDEPENDENT AUDITOR'S REPORT

To the Shareholders of ABC Company [or Other Appropriate Addressee]

Report on the Audit of the Financial Statements

Opinion

We have audited the financial statements of ABC Company (the Company), which comprise the statement of financial position as at December 31, 20 × 1, and the statement of comprehensive income, statement of changes in equity and statement of cash flows for the year then ended, and notes to the financial statements, including a summary of significant accounting policies.

In our opinion, the accompanying financial statements present fairly, in all material respects, (or *give a true and fair view of*) the financial position of the Company as at December 31, 20×1, and (*of*) its financial performance and its cash flows for the year then ended in accordance with International Financial Reporting Standards (IFRSs).

Basis for Opinion

We conducted our audit in accordance with International Standards on Auditing (ISAs). Our responsibilities under those standards are further described in the *Auditor's Responsibilities for the Audit of the Financial Statements* section of our report. We are independent of the Company in accordance with the International Ethics Standards Board for Accountants' *Code of Ethics for Professional Accountants (IESBA Code)* together with the ethical requirements that are relevant to our audit of the financial statements in [*jurisdiction*], and we have fulfilled our other ethical responsibilities in accordance with these requirements and the IESBA Code. We believe that the audit evidence we have obtained is sufficient and appropriate to provide a basis for our opinion.

Key Audit Matters

Key audit matters are those matters that, in our professional judgment, were of most significance in our audit of the financial statements of the current period. These matters were addressed in the context of our audit of the financial statements as a whole, and in forming our opinion thereon, and we do not provide a separate opinion on these matters.

[*Description of each key audit matter in accordance with ISA 701, which applies to audits of the financial statements of listed entities.*]

Other Information

Management is responsible for the other information. The other information comprises the information included in the *X report*, but does not include in the financial statements and our auditor's report thereon.

Our opinion on the financial statements does not cover the other information and we do not express any form of assurance conclusion thereon.

In connection with our audit of the financial statements, our responsibility is to read the other information and, in doing so, consider whether the other information is materially inconsistent with the financial statements or our knowledge obtained in the audit or otherwise appears to be materially misstated. If, based on the work we have performed, we conclude that there is a material misstatement of this other information, we are required to report that fact. We have nothing to report in this regard.

Responsibilities of Management and Those Charged with Governance for the Financial Statements

Management is responsible for the preparation and fair presentation of the financial statements in accordance with IFRSs, and for such internal control as management determines is necessary to enable the preparation of financial statements that are free from material misstatement, whether due to fraud or error.

In preparing the financial statements, management is responsible for assessing the Company's ability to continue as a going concern, disclosing, as applicable, matters related to going concern and using the going concern basis of accounting unless management either intends to liquidate the Company or to cease operations, or has no realistic alternative but to do so.

Those charged with governance are responsible for overseeing the Company's financial reporting process.

Auditor's Responsibilities for the Audit of the Financial Statements

Our objectives are to obtain reasonable assurance about whether the financial statements as a whole are free from material misstatement, whether due to fraud or error, and to issue an auditor's report that includes our opinion. Reasonable assurance is a high level of assurance, but is not a guarantee that an audit conducted in accordance with ISAs will always detect a material misstatement when it exists. Misstatements can arise from fraud or error and are considered material if, individually or in the aggregate, they could reasonably be expected to influence the economic decisions of users taken on the basis of these financial statements.

As part of an audit in accordance with ISAs, we exercise professional judgement and maintain professional skepticism throughout the audit. We also:

- Identify and assess the risks of material misstatement of the financial statements, whether due to fraud or error, design and perform audit procedures responsive to those risks, and obtain audit evidence that is sufficient and appropriate to provide a basis for our opinion. The risk of not detecting a material misstatement resulting from fraud is higher than for one resulting from error, as fraud may involve collusion, forgery, misrepresentations, or the override of internal control.

- Obtain an understanding of internal control relevant to the audit in order to design audit procedures that are appropriate in the circumstances, but not for the purpose of expressing an opinion on the effectiveness of the Company's internal control.

- Evaluate the appropriateness of accounting policies used and the reasonableness of accounting estimates and related disclosures made by management.

- Conclude on the appropriateness of management's use of the going concern basis of accounting and, based on the audit evidence obtained, whether a material uncertainty exists related to events or conditions that may cast significant doubt on the Company's ability to continue as a going concern. If we conclude that a material uncertainty exists, we are required to draw attention in our auditor's report to the related disclosures in the financial statements or, if such disclosures are inadequate, to modify our opinion. Our conclusions are based on the audit evidence obtained up to the date of our auditor's report. However, future events or conditions may cause the Company to cease to continue as a going concern.

- Evaluate the overall presentation, structure and content of the financial statements, including the disclosures, and whether the financial statements represent the underlying transactions and events in a manner that achieves fair presentation.

We communicate with those charged with governance regarding, among other matters, the planned scope and timing of the audit and significant audit findings, including any significant deficiencies in internal control that we identify during our audit.

We also provide those charged with governance with a statement that we have complied with relevant ethical requirements regarding independence, and to communicate with them allrelationships and other matters that may reasonably be thought to bear on our independence, and where applicable, related safeguards.

From the matters communicated with those charged with governance, we determine those matters that were of most significance in the audit of the financial statements IASB of the current period and are therefore the key audit matters. We describe these matters in our auditor's report unless law or regulation precludes public disclosure about the matter or when, in extremely rare circumstances, we determine that a matter should not be communicated in our report because the adverse consequences of doing so would reasonably be expected to outweigh the public interest benefits of such communication.

Report on Other Legal and Regulatory Requirements

[*The form and content of this section of the auditor's report would vary depending on the nature of the auditor's other reporting responsibilities prescribed by local law, regulation or national auditing standards. The matters addressed by other law, regulation or national auditing standards (referred to as "other reporting responsibilities") shall be addressed within this section unless the other reporting responsibilities address the same topics as those presented under the reporting responsibilities required by the ISAs as part of the Report on the Audit of the Financial Statements section. The reporting of other reporting responsibilities that address the same topics as those required by the ISAs may be combined (i. e. , included in the Report on the Audit of the Financial Statements section under the appropriate subheadings) provided that the wording in the auditor's report clearly differentiates the other reporting responsibilities from the reporting that is*) *required by the ISAs where such a difference exists.*]

The engagement partner on the audit resulting in this independent auditor's report is [*name*].

[*Signature in the name of the audit firm, the personal name of the auditor, or both, as appropriate for the particular jurisdiction*]

[*Auditor Address*]

[*Date*]

Preparing a formal auditor's report

To prepare a formal auditor's report the following elements need to be considered.

Title

The auditor's report shall have a title that clearly indicates that it is the report of an independent auditor. This signifies that the auditor has met all the ethical requirements concerning independence and therefore distinguishes the auditor's report from other reports.

Addressee

The auditor's report shall be addressed as appropriate, based on the circumstances of the engagement, which is likely to be the shareholders or those charged with governance.

Auditor's Opinion paragraph

The first section of the auditor's report shall include the auditor's opinion, and shall have the heading "Opinion." The Opinion section of the auditor's report shall identify the entity whose financial statements have been audited, state that the financial statements have been audited, identify the title of each statement comprising the financial statements, refer to the notes, including the summary of significant accounting policies; and specify the date of, or period covered by, each financial statement comprising the financial statements.

When expressing an unmodified opinion on financial statements prepared in accordance with a fair presentation framework, the auditor's opinion shall, unless otherwise required by law or regulation, use one of the following phrases, which are regarded as being equivalent:

(a) In our opinion, the accompanying financial statements present fairly, in all material respects, [...] in accordance with [the applicable financial reporting framework]; or

(b) In our opinion, the accompanying financial statements give a true and fair view of [...] in accordance with [the applicable financial reporting framework].

Basis for Opinion

The auditor's report shall include a section, directly following the Opinion section, with the heading "Basis for Opinion", that:

(a) States that the audit was conducted in accordance with International Standards on Auditing;

(b) Refers to the section of the auditor's report that describes the auditor's responsibilities under the ISAs;

(c) Includes a statement that the auditor is independent of the entity in accordance with the relevant ethical requirements relating to the audit, and has fulfilled the auditor's other ethical responsibilities in accordance with these requirements. The statement shall identify the jurisdiction of origin of the relevant ethical requirements or refer to the International Ethics Standards Board for Accountants' Code of Ethics for Professional Accountants (IESBA Code); and

(d) States whether the auditor believes that the audit evidence the auditor has obtained is sufficient and appropriate to provide a basis for the auditor's opinion.

Going Concern

Where applicable, the auditor shall report in accordance with ISA 570. Where the auditor considers a material uncertainty related to going concern exists, this should be described in a separate section headed "Material uncertainty related to going concern".

Key Audit Matters

For the audit of listed entities, or when the auditor is otherwise required by law or regulation or decides to communicate key audit matters in the auditor's report, the auditor shall communicate key audit matters in the auditor's report with a "Key audit matter" section. This section describes the matters that, in the auditor's professional judgment, are most significant to the audit.

Key audit matters (KAMs) are those matters that, in the auditor's professional judgment, were of most significance in the audit of the financial statements of the current period. Key audit matters are selected from matters communicated with those charged with governance.

The purpose of communicating key audit matters is to enhance the communicative value of the auditor's report by providing greater transparency about the audit that was performed. Communicating key audit matters provides additional information to intended users of the financial statements ("intended users") to assist them in understanding those matters that, in the auditor's professional judgment, were of most significance in the audit of the financial statements of the current period. Communicating key audit matters may also assist intended users in understanding the entity and areas of significant management judgment in the audited financial statements.

KAMs are part of every listed company auditor's report, and can be included by other auditors if needs. The auditor shall determine, from the matters communicated with those charged with governance, those matters that required significant auditor attention in performing the audit. Then the auditor shall describe each key audit matter, using an appropriate subheading, in a separate section of the auditor's report under the heading "Key Audit Matters," unless that law or regulation precludes public disclosure about the matter; or that the adverse consequences of doing so would reasonably be expected to outweigh the public interest benefits of such communication in extremely rare circumstances.

The introductory language in this section of the auditor's report shall state that:

- Key audit matters are those matters that, in the auditor's professional judgment, were of most significance in the audit of the financial statements [of the current period]; and
- These matters were addressed in the context of the audit of the financial statements as a whole, and in forming the auditor's opinion thereon, and the auditor does not provide a separate opinion on these matters.

Then the section should describe each key audit matter with a reference to the related disclosure (s), if any, in the financial statements and shall address:

- Why the matter was considered to be one of most significance in the audit and therefore determined to be a key audit matter; and
- How the matter was addressed in the audit.

If a modified opinion is expressed, the matter that gives rise to the modified opinion will be described in the "Basis for modified opinion" paragraph, so it must not be included as a KAM.

Other Information

For the audit of listed entities or any other entity where the auditor has obtained other information, an "Other information" section should be included in the auditor's report. This section should include:

- A statement that management is responsible for the other information;
- An identification of the other information, if any, obtained by the auditor prior to the date of the auditor's report and other information of a listed entity, if any, expected to be obtained after the date of the auditor's report.
- A statement that the auditor's opinion does not cover the other information and, accordingly, that the auditor does not express (or will not express) an audit opinion or any form of assurance conclusion thereon;
- A description of the auditor's responsibilities relating to reading, considering and reporting on other information; and
- When other information has been obtained prior to the date of the auditor's report, either a statement that the auditor has nothing to report; or a description of any uncorrected material misstatement of the other information.

The objectives of the auditor, having read the other information, are:

- To consider whether there is a material inconsistency between the other information and the financial statements;
- To consider whether there is a material inconsistency between the other information and the

auditor's knowledge obtained in the audit;

- To respond appropriately when the auditor identifies that such material inconsistencies appear to exist, or when the auditor otherwise becomes aware that other information appears to be materially misstated; and

- To report in accordance with ISA 720.

Responsibilities for the Financial Statements

The auditor's report shall include a section with a heading "Responsibilities of Management for the Financial Statements." The auditor's report shall use the term that is appropriate in the context of the legal framework in the particular jurisdiction and need not refer specifically to "management". In some jurisdictions, the appropriate reference may be to those charged with governance.

This section of the auditor's report shall describe management's responsibility for:

- Preparing the financial statements in accordance with the applicable financial reporting framework, and for such internal control as management determines is necessary to enable the preparation of financial statements that are free from material misstatement, whether due to fraud or error; and

- Assessing the entity's ability to continue as a going concern and whether the use of the going concern basis of accounting is appropriate as well as disclosing, if applicable, matters relating to going concern. The explanation of management's responsibility for this assessment shall include a description of when the use of the going concern basis of accounting is appropriate.

This section of the auditor's report shall also identify those responsible for the oversight of the financial reporting process, when those responsible for such oversight are different from those who fulfill the responsibilities described above.

Reference shall be made to "the preparation and fair presentation of these financial statements" (or "the presentation of financial statements that give a true and fair view") where the financial statements are prepared in accordance with a fair presentation framework.

Auditor's Responsibilities for the Audit of the Financial Statements

The auditor's report shall include a section with the heading "Auditor's Responsibilities for the Audit of the Financial Statements." This section of the auditor's report shall state that:

- The objectives of the auditor are to obtain reasonable assurance about whether the financial statements as a whole are free from material misstatement, whether due to fraud or error; and issue an auditor's report that includes the auditor's opinion.

- Reasonable assurance is a high level of assurance, but is not a guarantee that an audit conducted in accordance with ISAs will always detect a material misstatement when it exists; and

- Misstatements can arise from fraud or error, and either describe that they are considered material if, individually or in the aggregate, they could reasonably be expected to influence the economic decisions of users taken on the basis of these financial statements; or provide a definition or description of materiality in accordance with the applicable financial reporting framework.

The section shall further:

- State that, as part of an audit in accordance with ISAs, the auditor exercises professional judgmentand maintains professional skepticism throughout the audit; and

- Describe an audit by stating that the auditor's responsibilities are:

  - To identify and assess the risks of material misstatement of the financial statements, whether due to fraud or error; to design and perform audit procedures responsive to those risks; and to obtain audit evidence that is sufficient and appropriate to provide a basis for the auditor's opinion. The risk of not detecting a material misstatement resulting from fraud is higher than for one resulting from error, as fraud may involve collusion, forgery, intentional omissions, misrepresentations, or the override of internal control.

  - To obtain an understanding of internal control relevant to the audit in order to design audit procedures that are appropriate in the circumstances, but not for the purpose of expressing an opinion on the effectiveness of the entity's internal control. In circumstances when the auditor also has a responsibility to express an opinion on the effectiveness of internal control in conjunction with the audit of the financial statements, the auditor shall omit the phrase that the auditor's consideration of internal control is not for the purpose of expressing an opinion on the effectiveness of the entity's internal control.

  - To evaluate the appropriateness of accounting policies used and the reasonableness of accounting estimates and related disclosures made by management.

  - To conclude on the appropriateness of management's use of the going concern basis of accounting and, based on the audit evidence obtained, whether a material uncertainty exists related to events or conditions that may cast significant doubt on the entity's ability to continue as a going concern. If the auditor concludes that a material uncertainty exists, the auditor is required to draw attention in the auditor's report to the related disclosures in the financial statements or, if such disclosures are inadequate, to modify the opinion. The auditor's conclusions are based on the audit evidence obtained up to the date of the auditor's report. However, future events or conditions may cause an entity to cease to continue as a going concern.

  - When the financial statements are prepared in accordance with a fair presentation framework, to evaluate the overall presentation, structure and content of the financial statements, including the disclosures, and whether the financial statements represent the underlying transactions and events in a manner that achieves fair presentation.

Other Reporting Responsibilities

If the auditor is required by law to report on any other matters, this must be done in an additional paragraph titled *Report on Other Legal and Regulatory Requirements* or otherwise as appropriate.

Name of the Engagement Partner

The name of the engagement partner shall be included in the auditor's report on financial statements of listed entities unless, in rare circumstances, such disclosure is reasonably expected to lead to a significant personal security threat.

Auditor's Signature

The report must contain the auditor's signature, whether this is the auditor's own name or the audit firm's name or both.

Auditor's Address

The location where the auditor practices must be included.

Date of the Report

The auditor's report shall be dated no earlier than the date on which the auditor has obtained sufficient appropriate audit evidence on which to base the auditor's opinion on the financial statements, including evidence that all the statements and disclosures that comprise the financial statements have been prepared; and that those with the recognized authority have asserted that they have taken responsibility for those financial statements.

19. 2. 2 Modified Opinions in Auditor's Reports

The auditor shall modify the opinion in the auditor's report when:

- The auditor concludes that, based on the audit evidence obtained, the financial statements as a whole are not free from material misstatement; or
- The auditor is unable to obtain sufficient appropriate audit evidence to conclude that the financial statements as a whole are free from material misstatement.

When the auditor modifies the opinion on the financial statements, the auditor shall, include a paragraph in the auditor's report that provides a description of the matter giving rise to the modification. The auditor shall place this paragraph immediately after the opinion paragraph in the auditor's report and use the heading *Basis for Qualified Opinion*, *Basis for Adverse Opinion*, or *Basis for Disclaimer of Opinion*, as appropriate.

Qualified Opinions

The auditor shall express a qualified opinion when:

- The auditor, having obtained sufficient appropriate audit evidence, concludes that misstatements, individually or in the aggregate, are material, but not pervasive, to the financial statements; or
- The auditor is unable to obtain sufficient appropriate audit evidence on which to base the opinion, but the auditor concludes that the possible effects on the financial statements of undetected misstatements, if any, could be material but not pervasive.

Example 19-1: An auditor's report containing a qualified opinion due to a material misstatement of the financial statements.

Qualified Opinion

We have audited the financial statements of ABC Company (the Company), which comprise the statement of financial position as at December 31, 20 ×1, and the statement of comprehensive income, statement of changes in equity and statement of cash flows for the year then ended, and notes to the financial statements, including a summary of significant accounting policies.

In our opinion, except for the effects of the matter described in the *Basis for Qualified Opinion* section of our report, the accompanying financial statements present fairly, in all material respects, (or *give a true and fair view of*) the financial position of the Company as at December 31, 20 ×1, and (*of*) its financial performance and its cash flows for the year then ended in accordance with International Financial Reporting Standards (IFRSs).

Basis for Qualified Opinion

The Company's inventories are carried in the statement of financial position at × × ×. Management has not stated the inventories at the lower of cost and net realizable value but has stated them solely at cost, which constitutes a departure from IFRSs. The Company's records indicate that, had management stated the inventories at the lower of cost and net realizable value, an amount of × × × would have been required to write the inventories down to their net realizable value. Accordingly, cost of sales would have been increased by × × ×, and income tax, net income and shareholders' equity would have been reduced by × × ×, × × × and × × ×, respectively.

We conducted our audit in accordance with International Standards on Auditing (ISAs). Our responsibilities under those standards are further described in the Auditor's Responsibilities for the Audit of the Financial Statements section of our report. We are independent of the Company in accordance with the ethical requirements that are relevant to our audit of the financial statements in [jurisdiction], and we have fulfilled our other ethical responsibilities in accordance with these requirements. We believe that the audit evidence we have obtained is sufficient and appropriate to provide a basis for our qualified opinion.

Example 19-2: An auditor's report containing a qualified opinion due to the auditor's inability to obtain sufficient appropriate audit evidence regarding a foreign associate.

Qualified Opinion

We have audited the consolidated financial statements of ABC Company and its subsidiaries (the Group), which comprise the consolidated statement of financial position as at December 31, 20×1, and the consolidated statement of comprehensive income, consolidated statement of changes in equity and consolidated statement of cash flows for the year then ended, and notes to the consolidated financial statements, including a summary of significant accounting policies. In our opinion, except for the possible effects of the matter described in the *Basis for Qualified Opinion* section of our report, the accompanying consolidated financial statements present fairly, in all material respects, (or *give a true and fair view of*) the financial position of the Group as at December 31, 20×1, and (*of*) its consolidated financial performance and its consolidated cash flows for the year then ended in accordance with International Financial Reporting Standards (IFRSs).

Basis for Qualified Opinion

The Group's investment in XYZ Company, a foreign associate acquired during the year and accounted for by the equity method, is carried at ×× × on the consolidated statement of financial position as at December 31, 20×1, and ABC's share of XYZ's net income of × × × is included in ABC's income for the year then ended. We were unable to obtain sufficient appropriate audit evidence about the carrying amount of ABC's investment in XYZ as at December 31, 20×1 and ABC's share of XYZ's net income for the year because we were denied access to the financial information, management, and the auditors of XYZ. Consequently, we were unable to determine whether any adjustments to these amounts were necessary.

We conducted our audit in accordance with International Standards on Auditing (ISAs). Our responsibilities under those standards are further described in the Auditor's Responsibilities for the Audit of the Consolidated Financial Statements section of our report. We are independent of the Group in accordance with the ethical requirements that are relevant to our audit of the consolidated financial statements in [jurisdiction], and we have fulfilled our other ethical responsibilities in accordance with these requirements. We believe that the audit evidence we have obtained is sufficient and appropriate to provide a basis for our qualified opinion.

Adverse Opinions

The auditor shall express an adverse opinion when the auditor, having obtained sufficient appropriate audit evidence, concludes that misstatements, individually or in the aggregate, are both material and pervasive to the financial statements.

Example 19-3: An auditor's report containing an adverse opinion due to a material misstatement of the consolidated financial statements.

Adverse Opinion

　　We have audited the consolidated financial statements of ABC Company and its subsidiaries (the Group), which comprise the consolidated statement of financial position as at December 31, 20 ×1, and the consolidated statement of comprehensive income, consolidated statement of changes in equity and consolidated statement of cash flows for the year then ended, and notes to the consolidated financial statements, including a summary of significant accounting policies. In our opinion, because of the significance of the matter discussed in the *Basis for Adverse Opinion* section of our report, the accompanying consolidated financial statements do not present fairly (or *do not give a true and fair view of*) the consolidated financial position of the Group as at December 31, 20 ×1, and (*of*) its consolidated financial performance and its consolidated cash flows for the year then ended in accordance with International Financial Reporting Standards (IFRSs).

Basis for Adverse Opinion

　　As explained in Note X, the Group has not consolidated subsidiary XYZ Company that the Group acquired during 20 ×1 because it has not yet been able to determine the fair values of certain of the subsidiary's material assets and liabilities at the acquisition date. This investment is therefore accounted for on a cost basis. Under IFRSs, the Company should have consolidated this subsidiary and accounted for the acquisition based on provisional amounts. Had XYZ Company been consolidated, many elements in the accompanying consolidated financial statements would have been materially affected. The effects on the consolidated financial statements of the failure to consolidate have not been determined.

　　We conducted our audit in accordance with International Standards on Auditing (ISAs). Our responsibilities under those standards are further described in the Auditor's Responsibilities for the Audit of the Consolidated Financial Statements section of our report. We are independent of the Group in accordance with the ethical requirements that are relevant to our audit of the consolidated financial statements in [jurisdiction], and we have fulfilled our other ethical responsibilities in accordance with these requirements. We believe that the audit evidence we have obtained is sufficient and appropriate to provide a basis for our adverse opinion.

Disclaimers of Opinion

　　The auditor shall disclaim an opinion when the auditor is unable to obtain sufficient appropriate audit evidence on which to base the opinion, and the auditor concludes that the possible effects on the financial statements of undetected misstatements, if any, could be both material and pervasive.

　　The auditor shall disclaim an opinion when, in extremely rare circumstances involving multiple uncertainties, the auditor concludes that, notwithstanding having obtained sufficient appropriate audit evidence regarding each of the individual uncertainties, it is not possible to form an opinion on the financial statements due to the potential interaction of the uncertainties and their possible cumulative effect on the financial statements.

Example 19-4: An auditor's report containing a disclaimer of opinion due to the auditor's inability to obtain sufficient appropriate audit evidence about a single element of the consolidated financial statements.

Disclaimer of Opinion

We were engaged to audit the consolidated financial statements of ABC Company and its subsidiaries (the Group), which comprise the consolidated statement of financial position as at December 31, 20 × 1, and the consolidated statement of comprehensive income, consolidated statement of changes in equity and consolidated statement of cash flows for the year then ended, and notes to the consolidated financial statements, including a summary of significant accounting policies.

We do not express an opinion on the accompanying consolidated financial statements of the Group. Because of the significance of the matter described in the *Basis for Disclaimer of Opinion* section of our report, we have not been able to obtain sufficient appropriate audit evidence to provide a basis for an audit opinion on these consolidated financial statements.

Basis for Disclaimer of Opinion

The Group's investment in its joint venture XYZ Company is carried at × × × on the Group's consolidated statement of financial position, which represents over 90% of the Group's net assets as at December 31, 20 × 1. We were not allowed access to the management and the auditors of XYZ Company, including XYZ Company's auditors' audit documentation. As a result, we were unable to determine whether any adjustments were necessary in respect of the Group's proportional share of XYZ Company's assets that it controls jointly, its proportional share of XYZ Company's liabilities for which it is jointly responsible, its proportional share of XYZ's income and expenses for the year, and the elements making up the consolidated statement of changes in equity and the consolidated cash flow statement.

Example 19-5: An auditor's report containing a disclaimer of opinion due to the auditor's inability to obtain sufficient appropriate audit evidence about multiple elements of the financial statements.

Disclaimer of Opinion

We were engaged to audit the financial statements of ABC Company (the Company), which comprise the statement of financial position as at December 31, 20 × 1, and the statement of comprehensive income, statement of changes in equity and statement of cash flows for the year then ended, and notes to the financial statements, including a summary of significant accounting policies.

We do not express an opinion on the accompanying financial statements of the Company. Because of the significance of the matters described in the *Basis for Disclaimer of Opinion* section of our report, we have not been able to obtain sufficient appropriate audit evidence to provide a basis for an audit opinion on these financial statements.

Basis for Disclaimer of Opinion

We were not appointed as auditors of the Company until after December 31, 20 ×1 and thus did not observe the counting of physical inventories at the beginning and end of the year. We were unable to satisfy ourselves by alternative means concerning the inventory quantities held at December 31, 20 ×0 and 20 ×1, which are stated in the statements of financial position at × × × and × × ×, respectively. In addition, the introduction of a new computerized accounts receivable system in September 20 ×1 resulted in numerous errors in accounts receivable. As of the date of our report, management was still in the process of rectifying the system deficiencies and correcting the errors. We were unable to confirm or verify by alternative means accounts receivable included in the statement of financial position at a total amount of × × × as at December 31, 20 ×1. As a result of these matters, we were unable to determine whether any adjustments might have been found necessary in respect of recorded or unrecorded inventories and accounts receivable, and the elements making up the statement of comprehensive income, statement of changes in equity and statement of cash flows.

▶ 核心词汇 Core Words and Expressions

adverse opinion　反对意见

board of directors　董事会

disclaimer of opinion　无法发表意见

emphasis of matter　重要事项说明、强调事项

modified auditor's report　非无保留意见审计报告

opinion paragraph　意见段

other matter paragraph　其他事项段

pervasiveness　牵扯性，广泛性

qualified auditor's report　保留意见审计报告

scope paragraph　范围段

shareholder　股东

unmodified auditor's report　无保留意见审计报告

unmodified opinion　无保留意见

▶ 知识扩展 More Knowledge

2016 年我国审计准则修订的主要内容

2016 年中国注册会计师协会颁布了 12 项审计准则，此次修订充分体现了准则的国际趋同。其中《中国注册会计师审计准则第 1504 号——在审计报告中沟通关键审计事项》为新制定准则，《中国注册会计师审计准则第 1501 号——对财务报表形成审计意见和出具审计报告》《中国注册会计师审计

准则第 1502 号——在审计报告中发表非无保留意见》《中国注册会计师审计准则第 1503 号——在审计报告中增加强调事项段和其他事项段》《中国注册会计师审计准则第 1151 号——与治理层的沟通》《中国注册会计师审计准则第 1324 号——持续经营》和《中国注册会计师审计准则第 1521 号——注册会计师对其他信息的责任》6 项准则做出实质性修改，还有《中国注册会计师审计准则第 1111 号——就审计业务约定条款达成一致意见》《中国注册会计师审计准则第 1131 号——审计工作底稿》《中国注册会计师审计准则第 1301 号——审计证据》《中国注册会计师审计准则第 1332 号——期后事项》《中国注册会计师审计准则第 1341 号——书面声明》5 项是为保持审计准则休系的内在一致性而做出相应文字调整。

《中国注册会计师审计准则第 1501 号——对财务报表形成审计意见和出具审计报告》不再以"标准审计报告""非标准审计报告"表述报告类型，并改变了传统审计报告的行文顺序为先表述审计意见、形成审计意见的基础和关键审计事项，之后才是责任段。其次，新颁布的《中国注册会计师审计准则第 1504 号——在审计报告中沟通关键审计事项》要求注册会计师在上市实体审计报告中增加关键审计事项部分，披露审计工作中的重点难点等审计项目的个性化信息，并规范了关键审计事项的恰当表述。而其他实质性修订主要是明确与关键审计事项的关系，以及强化审计人员对持续经营及其他信息等的责任界限。

▶ 问答题　Questions

1. Distinguish between an unmodified and a modified audit report.

2. List and explain the basic elements of an auditor's report.

3. Draw a table that summarizes the different modified opinions that can arise in the auditor's report.

▶ 练习题　Exercises

Exercise

You are the audit manager in charge of the audit of MSV Co for the year ended 28 February 20 × 5. MSV Co is based in a seaside town and hires motor boats and yachts to individuals for amounts of time between one day and one week. The majority of receipts are in cash, with a few customers paying by debit card. Consequently, there are no trade receivables on the balance sheet. The main non-current assets are the motor boats and yachts. The company is run by four directors who are also the major shareholders. Total income for the year was about $10 million.

The following issues have been identified during the audit:

Issue 1

Audit tests on sales indicate a weakness in the internal control system, with a potential understatement of income in the region of $500 000. The weakness occurred because sales invoices are not sequentially numbered, allowing one of the directors to remove cash sales prior to recording in the sales day book. This was identified during analytical procedures of sales, when the audit senior noted that on the days when this director was working, sales were always lower than on the days when the director was not working.

Issue 2

During testing of non-current assets, one yacht was found to be located at the property of one of the directors. This yacht has not been hired out during the year and enquiries indicate that the director makes personal use of it. The yacht is included in the non-current assets balance in the financial statements.

Instructions

For each of the issues above, Assuming that you have performed all the audit procedures that you can but the issues are still unresolved, explain the potential effect (if any) on the audit report.

参考文献

［1］德勤. 国际财务报告准则第 15 号——与客户之间的合同产生的收入［J］. 会计聚焦, 2014（5）.

［2］IASB, International Financial Reporting Standard 15: Revenue from Contracts with Customers, 2014, 5

［3］Abbas Ali Mirza, Graham J Holt, Magnus Orrell. Practical Implementation Guide and Workbook (Wiley Regulatory Reporting)［M］. 3rd ed. New Jersey: John Wiley & Sons, Inc., 2011.

［4］ACCA. Auditing and Internal Review (INT'L)［M］. London: FTC Foulks Lynch, 2011.

［5］BPP Learning Media. Audit and Assurance INT'L［M］. 武汉: 华中科技大学出版社, 2012.

［6］Charles T Horngren, Gary L Sundem, Dave Burgstahler, etc. Introduction to Management Accounting［M］. 15th ed. New Jersey: Prentice Hall, 2011.

［7］Charles T Horngren, Srikant M Datar, Madhav Rajan. Cost Accounting: A Managerial Emphasis［M］. 14th ed. New Jersey: Prentice Hall, 2012.

［8］Christopher W Nobes, Robert H Parker. Comparative International Accounting［M］. 9th ed. New Jersey: Prentice Hall, 2007.

［9］Colin Drury. Cost and Management Accounting［M］. Boston: Thomson Learning, 2006.

［10］Donald E Kieso, Jerry J Weygandt, Terry D Warfield. Intermediate Accounting［M］. 12th ed. 北京: 机械工业出版社, 2007.

［11］Fred Skousen, Earl K Stice, James D Stice. Intermediate Accounting［M］. 16th ed. Boston: South-Western College Publishing, Thomson Learning, 2007.

［12］Frederick D S, Choi, Gary K Meek. International Accounting［M］. 7th ed. New Jersey: Prentice Hall, 2010.

［13］International Federation of Accountants, Handbook of International Quality Control, Auditing, Review, Other Assurance and Related Services Pronouncements, New York, 2014.

［14］Joe B Hoyle, Thomas F Schaefer, Timothy S Doupnik. Advanced Accounting［M］. 10th ed. New York: McGraw-Hill Irwin, 2011.

［15］John J Wild, Kermit D Larson, Barbara Chiappetta. Fundamental Accounting Principles: Media-enhanced Edition ［M］. 18th ed. New York: McGaw-Hill College, 2007.

［16］Keith Alfredson, Ken Leo, Ruth Picker, etc. Appling International Financial Reporting Standards ［M］. New Jersey: John Wiley & Sons Australia, Ltd. , 2007.

［17］Krishna G Palepu, Paul M Healy, Victor L Bernard. Business Analysis & valuation: Using Financial Statements ［M］. 4th ed. Boston: South-Western College Publishing, Thomson Learning, 2007.

［18］International Auditing and Assurance Standards Board, 2016, Handbook of International Quality Control, Auditing, Review, Other Assurance, and Related Services Pronouncements, 2016 – 2017 Edition, Volume I, http://www. iaasb. org/.

［19］IASB, 2018, Conceptual Framework for Financial Reporting, IFRS Foundation.